Writers of the Caribbean Diaspora
shifting homelands, travelling identities

Writers of the Caribbean Diaspora

shifting homelands, travelling identities

Edited by
Jasbir Jain
Supriya Agarwal

STERLING PUBLISHERS PRIVATE LIMITED

STERLING PUBLISHERS PRIVATE LIMITED
A-59, Okhla Industrial Area, Phase-II,
New Delhi-110020.
Tel: 26387070, 26386209; Fax: 91-11-26383788
E-mail: sterlingpublishers@airtelmail.in
ghai@nde.vsnl.net.in
www.sterlingpublishers.com

Writers of the Caribbean Diaspora:
Shifting Homelands, Travelling Identities
© 2008, Authors
ISBN 978-81-207-3610-8

All rights are reserved. No part of this publication may be reproduced, stored in a retrieval system or transmitted, in any form or by any means, mechanical, photocopying, recording or otherwise, without prior written permission of the original publisher.

Printed and Published by Sterling Publishers Pvt. Ltd., New Delhi- 110 020.

For
Frank Birbalsingh

Contents

Introduction		1
1.	Shaping the Environment: Sugar Plantation or Life After CYRIL DABYDEEN	11
2.	Teaching West Indian Literature in Britain DAVID DABYDEEN	26
3.	Inventions of Auto-Narratives in Braithwaite and Phillips JASBIR JAIN	44
4.	Images of the Caribbean in the Early Works of Jean Rhys MANVEEN BRAR	55
5.	Between Two Cultures: A Look at Seepersad Naipaul's Stories PURABI PANWAR	67
6.	The Indo-Caribbean Short Story: Negotiations between Social Identity and Self-Concept SUDHA RAI	78
7.	The Politics of Historical Reconstruction: A Study of V.S. Naipaul's *The Loss of El Dorado* and *A Way in the World* VISHNUPRIYA SENGUPTA	94
8.	Negotiating V.S. Naipaul CYRIL DABYDEEN	116
9.	Metaphors of Disintegration in Shiva Naipaul's *The Chip Chip Gatherers* MADHURI CHATTERJEE	126
10.	Rites of Passage: George Lamming's *In the Castle of My Skin* NIDHI SINGH	135

11. Race of Races in Sam Selvon's *Those Who Eat the Cascadura* 142
    M. ROSARY ROYAR

12. Conflict and Resolution: Selvon's *The Plains of Caroni* 152
    SUPRIYA AGARWAL

13. Creating an Independent Reality: Sam Selvon's *An Island Is a World* 164
    CHARU MATHUR

14. Diverse Cultural Icons and Codes in Paule Marshall's *Praisesong for the Widow* 175
    ASMA SHAMAIL

15. Negotiating Interstitial Spaces: Itwaru's *Shanti* and *The Unreturning* 191
    MINI NANDA

16. Cultural Transformation in Diaspora: Arnold Harrichand Itwaru's *Shanti* 205
    INDIRA BABBELLAPATI

17. Re-locating Alter(native) Voices of Silence in Lakshmi Persaud's *Raise the Lanterns High* 219
    JAYITA SENGUPTA

18. 'I Cannot Always Be a Little You': Daughter-Mother (Country) Relationship in Jamaica Kincaid's *Annie John* 235
    PUNAM GUPTA

19. Identity, Subjectivity and Voice: A Reading of Austin Clarke's *The Polished Hoe* 247
    C. VIJAYSHREE

20. An Interview with Ramabai Espinet 257
    ELAINE SAVORY

    Appendices: M.K. Gandhi's articles on Indentureship 275

    Notes on Contributors 287

Introduction

Two writers, V.S. Naipaul at one end and Jean Rhys at the other, have largely been the ones responsible for the attention of the academia to the Caribbean. The West Indies, as the collectivity of islands is called, has long been known on account of cricket, but now its writers have begun to create another point of worldwide interest. Another writer with a place in the popular imagination is Eric Braithwaite, whose novel and later film *To Sir, With Love* has been seen and admired by generations of school children, but they may not have necessarily delved into Caribbean pasts and histories. Then came another signal that the Caribbean was important, and was alive and kicking when Derek Walcott was awarded the Nobel Prize in 1992. Yet despite these associations the Caribbean that we know is only of the surface.

Histories are important and histories have a way of travelling. West Indies is one example of a society constructed artificially of imported populations who have gone on to build their own power structures, political histories and national identities. They have also gone on to migrate to other parts of the world taking with them large chunks of their Caribbean background. Today we read Jamaica Kincaid, Wilson Harris, Arnold Itwaru and others like them as writers with 'hyphenated' identities and even with doubly hyphenated ones. We read in their work histories of race relations and power struggles that constantly remind us of their Caribbean background.

Why is the Caribbean interesting? To my mind, there are a host of reasons for that : it is one living society where multiculturalism has been put to test. Given the circumstances of common oppression and numerical majorities, it could have led to a better acceptability of cultural differences. The creolisation that it resulted in, through intermixtures of races and languages, could itself have become a term of a wider range and greater respectability. Instead all this has not happened. The people of the Caribbean, like Naipaul, often turn round and say, that it is a place without a history, or migrate to other lands, or engage in the process of retrieving lost histories and voices for entirely personal reasons. It is only now with diaspora studies capturing critical imagination that lost histories have become important. Going back to the limited application of the word creole – at times negative, at other times neutral – its limits are embedded in imperial history and in the failure of mankind – a failure to capitalise on this human experiment – in terms of human progress and peace.

These populations of the erstwhile slaves and indentured workers were spread in different islands with the result that local histories and politics have intervened to shape their literary work in ways one does not immediately recognise. In fact so little attention has been paid to the history of islands, that very few of us have located their literature within other freedom struggles. Uprisings in the Caribbean, the British slave trade and the profits that flowed into society were all interconnected movements. The last forty years of the eighteenth century were the peak period of the slave trade with British ships carrying this human cargo. London was one of the largest slaveship ports with Bristol a close second. Politicians and public figures freely invested in slaveships and even church bodies owned slave plantations. Both the wealth and the industry of Britain were sustained by this slave trade.

It is important to closely examine this period of imperial history in order to understand the successive colonisations of other countries. The full significance of both *Mansfield Park* and *Wide Sargasso Sea* in terms of culture, gender relationships, patriarchy and author-work relationships can only be realised against the historical setting. Before India acquired the reputation of the right place for a second son of an English aristocratic family to make a fortune in, West Indies had already earned that reputation. Today it is easy to condemn the German persecution of the Jews but in no way was slave trade less of an atrocity. It resulted in the death of thousands of slaves in the overcrowded ships, the values of kinship were severely damaged and more than 3,00,000 African slaves were brought over to different lands, depopulating a whole continent and destroying indigenous cultures.

Slave rebellions in the Caribbean have a long history but it was only when British political figures like John Wilberforce and religious leaders like John Wesley brought this to public attention that the anti-slavery campaign caught on in England. Women too joined this movement and one of the features was the boycott of sugar. It was only after 1832 that slavery was abolished with the rider that the slaves would be labelled apprentices for a period of six years. The law came into effect in 1834.[1] In America slavery was abolished only as late as 1865.

Abolition of slavery and the beginning of export of indentured labour are interconnected events. Britain, as a colonial master, looked around for substitution of the slave market and found it in the Indian worker. Shiploads of 'coolies', with a mere scattering of women, were exported to Trinidad, Jamaica, Guyana and Fiji. Also to South Africa. These were contractual labour but the conditions were no better than that of slavery, except for a couple of minor exceptions. Actual sales did not take place and if there were families, they were not divided. But the completion of the contract did not necessarily mean freedom or a return home. Shiploads carried this human cargo to their destination right through the nineteenth century and even the beginning of the twentieth, indifferent to the after effects of the dislocation in psychic, cultural and political terms.

Gandhi's stay in South Africa sensitised him to the condition of these workers, the imported labour force, who were permanently locked up in a sense of inferiority and subjected to continued humiliation. Gandhi led a systematic campaign against this government-assisted emigration, conducted for the benefit of its own economic gains. After his return to India in 1914, he addressed several meetings and wrote articles about indentured labour in order to arouse popular consciousness. Some of these have been included as appendices to this volume in order to establish the long history of emigration and the concern of the home country for its emigrated population that finally led to political intervention from native leadership.

The origins of the Caribbean writers, despite the limited size of the whole group of the islands, are as mixed and varied as those in a country the size of India. No two writers, no matter from where they come, have similar histories or backgrounds. They have also travelled in different directions both literally and metaphorically. David Dabydeen refers to it as a 'dazzling variety' ranging between naturalistic narrative and fragmentary prose, working through calypso/folk tale, biblical lyricism and histories of cultures in fictional narratives.[2] It is not for nothing that these scattered islands with varied histories, several religions, an assortment of imperial masters and a plethora of languages have featured twice on the Nobel Awards for Literature. This factor, in itself, calls for a closer look at the Caribbean experience. What is it in that culture which gives birth to a nostalgic carrying forth of past cultures, a constant interweaving of the personal and the political, a need to open out interstitial spaces, to travel abroad, to look at oneself through the eyes of the other and then go on to deconstruct both self and other? White, black or brown, they turn their rootlessness into roots but these too find a ready soil in different lands. If the Caribbean people have a collective memory, it is a memory of lost homelands, of broken families and of utopian dreams more often than not destined to remain unfulfilled. Each also relates differently to the Caribbean. Some have a sense of belonging and a return home is important to them, others are only too happy to find themselves elsewhere. Power structures at home (the Caribbean), resulting in racial inequality and social prejudice deny one the space to grow. Arnold Itwaru's *Shanti* and *The Unreturning* bring this out in sharp colours. Bissoondath likewise captures the sense of being persecuted in his collection *Digging in the Mountains*.

For the Caribbean 'home' and 'origin' may work at odds with each other. Having been brought there to populate the islands, their histories bring with them memories of other origins. But it would be wrong to come to the conclusion that they have no sense of home. Ramabai Espinet in a recent interview said that the Caribbean was a home to which she often went back. The atmosphere of the landscape haunts their writings and memories, as the writings of Jean Rhys, Sam Selvon and Shiva Naipaul demonstrate. Uma Parameswaran once observed that the Caribbean collectivity was a stronger presence in the academia than the South Asian.[3] Such observations and expressions of feeling are also expressions of a collective memory, and in some measure, a collective history. And memories are reflected not merely in autobiographies, travelogues or in autobiographical fiction but find an expression in the dreams of nation-building as in several novels of Sam Selvon.

Caribbean writing in its landscape, plantation backgrounds, use of folk lore, creole speech, slave histories and the memory of transmitted cultures, its political world that attracts interference, and its presence in different parts of the world has become a travelling culture being lived through in multiple ways. It takes upon itself the responsibility of validating the very act of living. It is the Caribbean that has replaced memories of earlier pasts as a home of return. Identities, homes and sense of belonging have all travelled new routes.

How does one read Caribbean writing? As self-contained, experience related texts or as national and cultural histories? As oppositional strategies for freedom of the self or a continued colonialism symbolised by the stereotype of a victim? As narratives of self-exploration or of self-pity? Or of an acknowledgement of the simultaneity of a localised space and a world beyond geographical boundaries? Whichever way we choose to read, the literature rooted in the Caribbean past needs to be placed against that background to be given its legitimate place not merely through its Nobel awardees but through a host of other writers who are subjecting their past to scrutiny and are in search of the underside of history.

The essays in this volume have taken up several representative authors of the Caribbean, either by addressing their work or through contributions by the writers themselves. Two notable omissions are (regrettably) Derek Walcott and Neil Bissoondath, solicited essays on them failed to meet all successive deadlines. The attempt has been to provide a chronological history of the Caribbean and give representation to writers of different affiliations living now in different host cultures. A fair amount of women writers are also taken up for discussion.

Several of these essays were presented at a seminar in Jaipur on Indo-Caribbean Writing. But we felt the need to look at other writers like Paule Marshall, Jean Rhys, Austin Clarke, Caryl Phillips, Jamaica Kincaid and, above all George Lamming, in order to understand Caribbean histories, patterns of migration and race relations and went on to request essays on their work. It was felt that though Caribbean writing has been centre-stage for quite sometime, it has been so mainly in a non-historical way. Naipaul's India connections and India travelogues have received a disproportionate attention and Jean Rhys' *Wide Sargasso Sea* has had to live in close relationship with *Jane Eyre*. The need was to free them from these fixed locations and to place the writers right in their Caribbean location.

Cyril Dabydeen's description of life on a sugar plantation offers a valuable insight into the landscape and the community life. He has highlighted the literary constructs of self, time, place and space reaching back to the first migration from India. In this sensitive memoir, the freedom and innocence of childhood are underlaced with a sense of temporariness that only a nostalgic memory can reflect. This essay was first published in *The Caribbean and Environment* (2005) and is included in this volume with the permission of the author.

David Dabydeen's article, already published in *Studying British Cultures*, is also included here with the writer's permission. West Indian literature occupies almost a similar position in India as in England in terms of filiation and affiliation. It was felt that David Dabydeen's argument and insight are equally relevant to the teaching of West Indian literature in India as in England even if Indian students may not look at it with expectations similar to the ones English students may have. Dabydeen stresses the need to locate the text in the cultural context of its origin and tradition and points out the significance of the oral tradition for the West Indian writer. Using pedagogical strategies he opens out the texts to interpretations that are not thwarted by western theoretical frameworks.

The essays on the three Naipauls – the father and his two sons – trace a family's experimentation with form, narrative and theme. Incidentally the volume also contains three essays on short stories and the special demands the form makes both on the writer and the reader. Purabi Panwar, Sudha Rai and Manveen Brar take up the different experiments in terms of gender, landscape, social concern and form. While Panwar takes up the senior Naipaul's stories, Rai works with writers ranging from Naipaul to Shani Mattoo and Brar's concern is with the portrayal of the Carib in Jean Rhys's stories. The Naipaul explorations are visible in Vishnupriya Sengupta's essay where Sengupta takes up the politics historical reconstruction and the search for *El Dorado*. Madhuri Chatterjee, as a counterpoint, works with the image of a house and the need to anchor in Shiva Naipaul's *The Chip Chip Gatherers*. A valuable addition to the Naipaul discourse is Cyril Dabydeen's essay on Naipaul, where one can trace a dialogue between two different generations from the Caribbean.

Suddenly one has begun to realise that there are writers other than the Naipauls who have Caribbean origins. Sam

Selvon is the focus of attention of three different essays, each dealing with a different novel and a different aspect. Selvon, a contemporary of Naipaul, presents a contrasting attitude towards the islands. Rosary Royar unfolds the meaning of the *Those Who Eat the Cascadura*, Supriya Agarwal *The Plains of Caroni* and Charu Mathur *An Island Is a World*. Working with images, loyalties, infidelities and conflicts, the novels are about a journey towards a modernisation that is perceived simultaneously as a desirable one as well as a threat to value structures.

Some papers are gender-oriented and locate the position of the woman in the West Indies. C. Vijayshree in her study of Austin Clarke's *The Polished Hoe* has taken up the issue of the black woman's exploitation and problematised the question of voice and identity. Similarly Jayita Sengupta reflects on defeatism and oppression faced by Indian origin women in Caribbean Writing with special focus on Lakshmi Persaud's work *Raise The Lantern High*.

Indira Babbellapati and Asma Shamail in their essays have worked on the issue of identity. While Asma Shamail has concentrated on the Black Literature of Paule Marshall, Indira Babbellapati has taken up Arnold Harrichand Itwaru's *Shanti* as the background material to throw light on the different cultural components that go into the shaping of the Indian identity. Asma Ismail has considered issues of gender and class, contrasting physical and material survival in Eurocentric space and the spiritual affirmation that can be acquired through cultural connections. Mini Nanda's essay on Itwaru takes up a contrastive study of *Shanti* and *The Unreturning* working through the complexity of interstitial spaces. Nanda explores the subversive strategies that rise out of the interstitial habitation.

The work of George Lamming *In the Castle of My Skin* is used as a medium by Nidhi Singh to study the psyche of the colonised people and Singh goes on to explore writing as an act of redefining the self by confronting the past. In her essay on Jamaica Kincaid, Punam Gupta works on *Annie John*. Equating relationship with one's motherland to the biological relation of mother and daughter she has dealt with the question of nation construction.

One rarely remembers that Eric Braithwaite, the author of *To Sir, With Love,* is also of Caribbean origins, or that Caryl Phillips is a fellow Guyanese. Jasbir Jain works with the two writers in her essay, "Inventing Auto Narratives". Jain explores the impact of political locations both on the construction of the self and the form of autobiographical writing and works out the connections between personal histories and ancestral memories.

In the detailed and analytical interview that Ramabai Espinet has given to Elaine Savory, the writer's work is explored from multiple angles. Elaine Savory, herself a poet and one who has worked on Caribbean literatures both intensively and extensively, opens out several dimensions of Espinet's writing. Both the writer and the interviewer travel a distance in memory and history, evaluating, critiquing and reflecting on Caribbean identities and realities.

Encompassing the work of known figures, Nobel Prize Winners, theorists who have written about exile in terms of its pleasures like Lamming, or engaging with writers who have won the hearts of more than three generations like Eric Braithwaite and those who are now making history like Caryl Phillips these essays go on to explore the potential and the ongoing struggles of writers who are just beginning to be noticed. In this lies the value and the strength of this volume.

* * *

We take this opportunity of expressing our deep sense of gratitude to each one of our contributors who have generously responded to our claims. There are several of them we have known and interacted with earlier, met at conferences abroad or hosted them at Jaipur. We are privileged that of the three creative writers from the Caribbean both Cyril Dabydeen and Ramabai Espinet have visited us. David Dabydeen has been a fellow seminarist first in Germany then in Bangladesh. Yet there are others we have only corresponded with. We thank them all and hope someday we'll sit together at the same table. This is only a beginning towards a new friendship. We also thank Cyril Dabydeen, David Dabydeen, Ramabai Espinet and Elaine Savory as well as their first publishers for permission to use the material.

This volume is for Frank Birbalsingh, who with his charming wife, visited us at Jaipur and opened a dialogue on Caribbean writing. Thanks, Frank, this anthology is a way of saying, 'Thank you, very much'.

Endnotes

[1] See http://www.bbc.co.uk / BBC history-Abolition of slavery.
[2] See David Dabydeen, "Race and Community in Anglophone Caribbean Fiction," *The Toronto South Asian Review*, p. 139.
[3] Meeting with Jasbir Jain at Jaipur.
[4] In conversation with Jasbir Jain at the seminar held at Jaipur Feb 17-19, 2007.

1

Shaping the Environment: Sugar Plantation or Life After

CYRIL DABYDEEN

Resonances, not unlike residues of memory, as I conjure up cane-ash like tarantulas floating in the air, then slowly coming down on us standing on the balcony of our house in the village. Everything relived, perhaps not unlike being reborn: such was plantation life and its ambience as cane-harvesting came upon us; and it seemed excitement was always in the air, akin to frisson. As children how we tried catching the strands of ash coming down, almost in arrested time. Then the ash disintegrated, became sheer dust! But fires kept emblazoning, in our minds and consciousness, maybe in mine most of all, with the sky always lit up, picturesque, yet also frightening. And indeed the sugar plantation was all for us in Guyana's coastline (we called it the coastland) – as if it were all the landscape of the country situated a few feet below sea-level: a place we knew intimately with ubiquitous palm trees and other lush flora, interminably variegated; and the rest of the country was the interior, or hinterland, like unknown territory (though this gradually began changing). And a seawall was built to protect the coastland – especially around Georgetown – from the Atlantic Ocean at high tide. And hadn't the Dutch when they occupied the region also built canals, kokers, forts: the most famous being Kyk-over-al, not unlike what occurred in Holland itself? Dutch emblems, colonial residues as they were, combined with other European legacies that helped forge a place, a country, even a people's memory: all I would dwell on and write about in my growing up. The spirit of the place it was, always forming, became ingrained in us: everything intertwining, more than just geography of the imagination, or what destiny had in store for us.

Adelphi, our village, situated in the Canje district – the same district where the Rose Hall sugar plantation is located in the county of Berbice; and the plantation indeed, now thriving under 'different' ownership, was where I established, seminally, my own indelible sense of the environment; and Rose Hall is still one of the largest sugar plantations in the country, perhaps emblematic or symbolic of the life lived in other areas of the coastland also. And for one like myself the name "Rose Hall" began to gradually have its own resonance, being more than English since everything was located in the so-called 'ancient county' of Berbice, one indeed founded by the Dutchman Abraham van Pere in 1600. The county's main town, New Amsterdam, would have as its principal novelist Edgar Mittelholzer who wrote of the place's unique lore with his own sense of history and drama: all in his Kaywana series, which I would regularly read, as 'things moved among them.' Make-believe it all was, too, stirring the fervid imagination, if Mittelholzer's only. Not much later, it was Wilson Harris I also read to help form the spirit of the place: he too was born in New Amsterdam, but the locus of his imagination was the interior, the same elusive or mysterious Guyana hinterland. The polarities of place: always coastland and hinterland, with other juxtapositions of feelings, sensibility, indeed kept shaping the environment as it also seemed like hallowed time itself in us, with us. Would I deny it? Would I want it any other way?

The sugar plantation often carried the sense of an overwhelming empire, as the local place-names suggested diverse origins, influences, always combining European and English; later would come distinctive African and Asian elements, and all other influences too because of who we were becoming as 'a people,' all of which permeated my consciousness with the sense of otherness, maybe; and other landscapes, environments, as everything kept coming closer in a genuine potpourri world of races, creeds, transforming or reshaping in odd or mysterious ways. Beings, presences, all here in the outpost of empire; and this coastal ground was now all as the ocean's waves lashed, with mangrove and courida spread out along the Corentyne coast – not a seawall – in the same Berbice county.

Maybe like prehistory itself too it seemed, everything being imprinted on us in continually remarkable ways. And the Corentyne was not far from the Canje: the former where my father was born and raised, an environment itself always suggestive of the sea: it was my time spent there as a child, a place etched in my memory and redolent of seaweed, mollusc, mullet, shrimp, crab; and seabirds hovering: all with the sense of an extended family, if only my father's; and insects, sandflies mainly, hurling themselves at us at nights even as we burned coconut husks, shells, to generate smoke in the air to thwart the pesky flies and mosquitoes from attacking us, like the Eumenides (in my creative writing I sometimes alluded to this). While living in the Canje, we indeed kept visiting my father's district, like compelling ground, as a way to escape the sugar plantation's hold on us. Underlying too was the sense of salt-water and fresh-water merging in more immediate ways. A riverain territory it was on this coastal belt, as Guyana is indeed known by its indigenous name, 'the land of many waters.' This consciousness it was for me, literally, but metaphorically too no less.

It was the fifties and sixties, you see; and my own particular village, Adelphi, formed part of the Rose Hall sugar plantation – the village's name hinting at what was classical (note the Greek, Delphi), and somewhere was a hidden oracle? The adjacent villages like Goed Bananen Land, with Dutch echoes, as the name Canje itself suggested, and then the town of New Amsterdam also. But Rose Hall carried the sense of the metropolitan world because the plantation's representatives – managers, overseers from the Bookers-McConnell Co., of the UK – all lived in palatial homes with well-manicured lawns displaying abundant flowers, choice vegetation: everything almost picturesque, idyllic, far removed from the gritty life we lived in the villages. Our houses were built on stilts, and tenements too they were, all here on the coastland. When the rains came, inevitably, it was like a further assault on the senses, reminding us always that we were in a region known for equatorial downpours: all being part of the wider Amazon basin, didn't we know?

And the plantation world with its physical and social structure wasn't unlike an apartheid system – the way it was all formed or arranged, though we never thought of it as such, never consciously. And our lives, with the customs circumscribing language: speech patterns deriving from Scotland, Ireland, Wales, England, and West Africa, India, and elsewhere: everything associated with lore, as if from long ago; and dialectal formations as if stemming from the soil itself, integrated and simultaneously demarcated our spaces.

Language: the verbs, nouns – of doing, naming things, working-peoples' expressions, sprung rhythms, with no abstract phrase, but metaphors rife in everyday expressions, poetic use at best with unforgettable or rhythmic cadences everywhere along coastal Guyana; and it seemed that our Indian ancestry was yet intact the more I intuited it. Feelings see-sawed, as I felt fated to be here in this 'outpost'. A creole-sustaining time too it was, as cultures intermingled. Our being Guyanese with a nascent nationhood forming here in South America – far from Africa or India. Yet surprisingly it was also an India inspiring images of Kipling, as I conjured up Mowgli riding an elephant, and my being a mahout, then being with a Bengal tiger – though Guyana is more amenable to the jaguar – untamed, even chthonic, the mysterious Amazon jungle inspiring myths reflective of Amerindian beliefs which Claude Levi-Strauss would write about [which I later tried to capture in my collection of poems *Born in Amazonia* (Mosaic Press, Canada, 1995)]. And cosmologically, the jaguar represented the forested middle ground, the anaconda the watery world below, the eagle soaring the world above the forest canopy – all according to lore, as I conceived it in my imagining.

Time and place were all, with more myths forming, or juxtaposed with the sense of an ancestral past and present time, but invariably associated with the spirit of the place and environment, being immanent the more I thought about it, the indelible imprint of the land no less. And my own family's sense of place, if only a faraway one, was somehow associated with a religious sensibility: my grandmother's Hinduism and lore drawn from the Bhagavada Gita, Ram and Sita, and the monkey-god Hanuman, or a distant Lanka, sometimes gripping us. And who was the fierce figure of Rawana, the evil-doer? Everything still indelibly linked, inescapably with cane-fires, didn't I know? Didn't I think too as I watched the sky light up once more of a dragon spitting fire, and it was St. George with a long-bladed sword engaged in an epic battle, everything active in the febrile imagination? The coastland somehow engendered it all.

In the Canje, far down the river by the same name, at a place called Magdalenenburgh – there where the region's first slave rebellion (called a Revolution) occurred, I also reflected on, if only subliminally. Cuffy and Akara: slave figures-turned heroes, all that riveted my consciousness, as if the environment itself spawned the uprising; it was what I grew up with, as I recreated or experienced lurid dreams: palpable images of slaves actually struggling with irons on against whiplash; and their own deep longings for Africa as they dwelled in dark hovels – the ordeal of plantation life. But counterpoint: there were smells, aromas, cane-blossoms amidst other flora forming an ambience while the sugar factory kept grinding, and heady molasses smells rose in the air. All I breathed in, inhaled.

But a different reality returned. The adults, villagers – including some who were relatives – would again go out in the fields to harvest the cane, backbreaking work that had to be done: their wielding the machetes – literally cutlasses – across whole fields of cane in the searing tropical heat. In the afternoon I watched the workers coming home, faces blackened with ash, unrecognisable as they seemed. Next punts – long narrow iron barges really – filled with neatly tied bundles of cane clanged thunderously as they snaked along in the network of canals, taking the harvest to the giant factory. King Sugar was lord and master: its economic impact was world-wide–with its own particular social and political consequences or resonance, always shaping the environment, if only ours; and maybe in faraway England, also.

All the while I kept increasingly being imbued with the self: in the new place, with a new identity forming, including reflecting on current or past anxieties as Guyana's lurid world also spawned fears of the ole higue, jumbie, backoo, massacouraman, moongazer. All echoic, evil spirits haunting with shadows – indeed moving among us. Past and present seemed one in the village in backwater South America, adding to the fears growing in us as children. Sinews of body and mind too, the more I contemplated it, as I again watched the workers wending their way home, their faces veritable masks...far more than idylls one read about in poems by Cowper and Wordsworth. This was no romantic setting, but inescapable reality. And maybe we hoped that the socio-economic order would change, far more than simply expressing romanticism of 'ownership' of the sugar plantation with Guyana becoming independent in the mid-sixties, and not long after to assume a dubious socialist republican status; and would democracy be all, we hoped, as the races, cultures, creeds co-existed, or simply clashed? Upheavals in the new place, after 'empire'.

The throes of labour strikes followed, and political rivalry with changeover. Corruption, acrimony. Everything festered. Mistrust, tinged with a deterministic Marxism, and then Guyana seemed to be an almost ungovernable land despite the vast potential around: the environment itself seeming to take its toll, because of the vexed or troubled human spirit in a post-independent land. Crime inexorably reared its ugly head: all despite the promises of the vast hinterland resources (Guyana being part of the greater Amazon with untapped forestry and mineral wealth) which we often extolled, or lamented.

For me during this period it was yet primarily the apprehension of a coastal life, coastal memories – as if I wanted it to always remain that way – the sugar plantation being supremely all. And the coastland wasn't yet swallowed up by the vortex of waves as the mangrove provided a barricade. All the while the two main races – Africans and Indians – competed or integrated with more than symbolic expressions of holi, phagwah, Eid, festivals all; and Christmas-time as masquerade too, and Easter's kite-flying celebrating Jesus's ascension to heaven. Indian weddings welcomed entire villages, as pujas with the pundit's nasal chants rose in the puri-filled air in the tropical 'paradise' – in the land once thought to contain El Dorado, as Walter Raleigh would have it.

Que-que, too: such distinctive African outpourings, as everything appeared immediate or authentic, as expressions of who we were indeed becoming. Underneath it all was the quest to survive as more cane-fields were set ablaze, fires burned. And there was the logie, like the village's own: this makeshift narrow wooden building, not unlike a stable, where workers were 'housed' during the cane-cutting season, you see; and twenty or thirty men would cook, sleep together: blacks and browns, a veritable creole gang; and there seemed to be no sense of racial difference or animosity in congested space with the legacy of a slave past or indentured-labour angst; maybe it was only what was in the imagination, in the spirit's quest to survive above all else.

In odd ways I interacted with these workers in the desultory setting of a grandmother's cakeshop. Faces with more longings I contemplated: these same workers, with families left behind – as everyone seemed bent on eking out a living doing truly mind-and-spirit-numbing work in then British Guyana. Overhead cirrus clouds drifted by, and coastal birds like the kiskadee, robin redbreast, and blue-sackie skirted the air, or flitted about on the ground, especially during the rice-cutting season – this other form of subsistence, in sparse lands, or swamps adjoining the sugar estate – the villagers with a determined instinct to survive forging on with a memory of continents far away or close up. This I also cogitated on, and made my own experience and intimation over time.

II

Spaces imbedded in us are often tied to family: in my case of a grandfather, who was a 'driver' – someone perhaps unique. He was called 'Albion Driver': Albion being synonymous with a romantic England I conjured up, but ironic in the sense of outpost and empire; and he was tasked with getting the able-bodied locals to go with him to set the cane-fields ablaze, whole acres at a time in order to eliminate the hazardous cane thrash, insects and rodents, all which impeded the harvesting of the cane as the workers wielded their machetes against cane-bark. (I sometimes imagined him in other sugar plantations everywhere across Guyana.) It was also rumoured that the fire's intense heat actually improved the sucrose content of the cane's yield; but this was never proven. Looking back, I wondered if my grandfather had a particular management zeal in marshalling the most dependable villagers to go with him to strategically set these fires; and how quickly the flames rose up as I yet stood on the balcony of our house, like recurrent time, and watching it all imagined an apocalypse – the entire world ablaze, including England, Africa and India. Heraclitan!

The term 'driver' might have derived from the time of slavery – an overseer who 'drove' the workers with a whip into spirited action. But did my grandfather really have such a status, illusory as it was? Six or seven I might have been when he was struck down with a stroke in our bottom-house, and he would die after a long and debilitating illness, leaving my grandmother to assume a matriarchal role: she now had to raise us, children and grandchildren alike, such being her 'lot' or fate, as she lamented: all according to customary Indian belief; and her sense of grief seemed mixed with a wilful forbearance. And when the Driver was alive, wasn't she called a 'maharajin,' the female counterpart of a 'maharajah' (of sorts): all that the environment spawned with ongoing mimicry, in the time of empire with the Raj appearing to somehow pantomime us in South America. Never mind Mahatma Gandhi and other Indian freedom fighters agitating for India's independence, and their also wanting to dispense with a caste system. For us, tradition and the indentured life were mixed with pain and penury.

My grandfather's presumed maharajah status was role-playing at best, I knew, a way for him to find refuge or solace from the hard life we lived. Imagine the heroes of Magdalenenburgh also mimicking: seeing themselves as Dahomey kings as they rebelled...and longed for freedom, not unlike what would later occur in Hispaniola. Toussaint, Dessalines, Henri Christophe: Look out!

Our village cakeshop was where the workers often congregated after the day's work was done: their bodies sore, and I'd sense that they simply wanted to sustain their beings, in a manner of speaking; and our place was like a community centre fostering a camaraderie of spirit among people mostly of Indian heritage (though there were also some of African backgrounds), all who desultorily discussed religion and politics, mixing Kalidas with Savaji and Gandhi, everything being interchangeable because of the mood they were in; and their awkward references to Aesop also, or legends invented by Homer. African anancy stories too I listened to, as east and west, north and south coalesced, or past and present came together. Everything ubiquitous, or a seeming melange. Mantras also recited, though without sustained piety, yet with incorrigible ethnicity. A growing confidence, no less.

One or two villagers asserted themselves with intellectual finesse, I remembered, or it was just their pretension as they quoted the German scholar Max Muller on Indian thought and philosophy, or the sage Ramakrishna. And did Max Muller really say 'If I am asked under what sky the human mind has most fully developed some of its choicest gifts, has most deeply pondered on the greatest problems of life and has found solution of some of them..., I shall point to India'? Inherent paradoxes, as seen in Warren Hastings' foreword to the East India Company's English rendering of the Bhagavada Gita. Did Hastings actually say that the 'writings of the inhabitants of India will survive when the British dominion in India shall have long ceased to exist, and when the sources which it once yielded of wealth and power are lost to remembrance'?

Fate's hand at work, or life's inevitability: the same that brought the indentured workers, my ancestors, to these distant shores of the Caribbean and the Amazon, I pondered. And wasn't sugar first crystallised in India long before the West knew about it...long before Columbus came to the so-called New World? Economic circumstances underpinned it all, in extolling King Sugar; and no one in this faraway land, especially those who toiled long in the fields, would ever forget their origins: with the Ganges or Ghana somewhere in the air. Novelist George Lamming I would later listen to in Trinidad concede that 'we are endowed with a racial consciousness': this too like undeniable or ineluctable reality. Lamming would go on about fears held by some, mostly Africans, as 'a strategy for conquest,' and that 'Indians' is not a monolithic word; that the two major races, East Indians and Africans, come from a 'common history of exploitation.'

Always recall in me, as I pondered the image of that first ship that came to British Guyana in 1838 bringing my ancestors after the abolition of slavery, and the last such ship that came in 1917 – the jahajis as the ships' occupants called themselves – which I dwelled on particularly, since my maternal grandfather, whom I didn't know well at all, might have been on it: he was a boy when he arrived; and then a great grandmother whom I indeed knew – she, as a woman, had crossed the dreaded kala pani!

My memory of this great grandmother was of a bundle of a woman, without knowledge of English, who irascibly rebuked us with Hindi words – she seemed caught in the umbilicus of time, and was now forever removed from Bombay or Uttar Pradesh where she might have come from. And the environment inflicted itself on her senses; and her great grandchildren would now be also separated from Bharat – the land of her birth – even as we innocently or wilfully mocked her in her dotage, because we were becoming 'British' in a way. In her kernel of silence she might have recreated a whole tradition as she literally talked to herself, deep in her veins. I would observe her, like a relic; and later when I went to India – something she might never have imagined – and saw a bunch of old women in a side street in Bombay nattering together, their faces creased or corrugated-looking, yet distinctly lively or animated as they seemed, I immediately recreated my great grandmother.

Vestiges all, the environment's grip always – the same sugar plantation life, as I relived it; and such a great fear was experienced in coming to Guyana and the Caribbean as Atlantic waves rose over a hundred feet high, I conjured; and my young grandfather's own pulverizing fear as a boy, and the lifelong insecurity it engendered because of that first traumatic experience – the same insecurity in us all, subsequently, a perpetual anxiety about survival. Would there be another time or another place for us?

A new mythos forming it also appeared, in our mixing with other races and cultures, and not without the sense of serendipity: this interacting mostly with the descendants of African slaves leading to a creolisation that seemed unrecognisable, unplanned or unrehearsed, as time went on; and dialectal impulses sometimes tinged with the rhythms of calypso (later reggae), which we would accept or simply deny because of almost different lifestyles we manifested. Zeitgeist, all. And were there different values associated with work and play too, and sentimental attitudes to family stemming not least from religious customs and beliefs? Committed politicians would berate us about our common social status and working-class background, and how to forge unity, despite distinctive racial consciousness, which the Europeans never had a stomach for anyway: this divide no less; and it always came down to how best to wrest better living conditions from the sugar-plantation's powers that be. The struggle was on, integrally associated with the spirit of the environment.

And who were the oppressors, colonisers: all visions we carried with us, and in us? In awkward or amorphous ways I yet remained in the cakeshop in my personal reverie and watched the workers sometimes expressing themselves with bawdy laughter, or observed their frustration and frenzy giving way to rum-shop indulgences, or their idling time away by playing card-games mostly, even as some surprisingly argued the poetics of religion: again the *Bhagavada Gita* or *Gitanjali* (Tagore), or formulated associations with the Prophet Mohammad and Christian ideals. Judaic, if also with a touch of the Hellenic. Didn't they also quote Aesop, willy nilly? Wayside evangelists – hot gospellers – came too, and the children of the same sugar-cane workers huddled under a 'bottom-house' and lustily sang hymns led by a zealous grandmotherly African type eager to make 'converts.' How we looked forward to receiving a pristine religious card with a picture of Jesus on it, or one with an image of the Garden of Eden – my own favourite – because it seemed immediate to our environment.

Unconsciously I began cherishing my own sense of faith and belief, as if the environment was dictated by destiny itself and was making it all happen, as I also longed for an immediate salvation, like time to come. Did I just then again contemplate the cane fires? Our district with sluices, canals, kokers, the way irrigation itself circumscribed us: this too like a miracle because of man's will to dominate his place, the alluvium and clayey ground. And more of the individual spirit came into us as the mammoth cane-factory hummed, throbbed: like a giant heart beating.

Like my very own.

III

Hibiscus, sunflowers, lily and bougainvillea: these were always in the air, in the hedges around the village houses; and how our minds worked ceaselessly in such arresting surroundings, the environment's almost romantic or idyllic appeal, yet with an unmistakable sugar-plantation air as canefields wavered their tassel-like tops in the trade winds blowing. I kept looking out from the balcony of our house, in Adelphi village or settlement (as it was also called); and maybe in a day-dreaming cocoon I found myself in, I waited for an oracle of sorts to appear, not unlike how Wilson Harris evoked a classical Hellenic world with Agamemnon and Hector in his early poems as he saw correspondences while exploring the hinterland, as I'd begun reading about, numinously experiencing it all. And like counterpoint, I'd also begun listening to drama serialised by BBC on our KB radio, and recreated Victorian worlds, or just Jane Austen's. Opera also came over the radio, and other forms of classical music, such renditions, while those congregating at the shop scoffed, their being unaware of my own changing self. Maybe it was their own sense of an uncompromising identity, or will not to succumb to European culture.

The cane workers preferred Bollywood music as simple recreation for their minds too tired to think of anything else. Occasionally more classical Indian tunes stirred them to deeper thought: deeper longings, not without nostalgia or forlornness upon hearing the nightingale-like voice of Lata Mangeshkar over the radio. Jukebox time too it was with calypso, everything seemingly juxtaposed. But *bhajans* – such religious songs – with *Bhagavada Gita* appeals often transported them to a far time, a far place. Distant horizons, or new shores yet in the making, rivers or seas crossed, not far unlike the Arabian Sea. A fleeting sense always. Cirrus clouds kept moving overhead. A spectacular sunset also, more than cane-fires ever created. Auguries, only.

Then the canefields for a while disappeared altogether with a further blaze of fire. Tarantulas no longer floated down like ash, and maybe other worlds converged as I was growing up, my own feelings and emotions being on a tightrope. And did I begin to express concerns about saving the pristine, yet unspoiled environment because of the factory's potential for causing pollution? No determined ecological sense was in me, then – only later this was formed, as my awareness and consciousness grew. Then a sense of solitariness or solitude prevailed in me, and in others too. I recall one African villager, an old man, who brought his guitar to the cakeshop and plucked out a few recognisable tunes. His blues, you bet; and he and my grandmother conversed in a strange, mute rhythm. Voices of ancestry, lore, with other indwelling spirits stemming from the immediacy of plantation life, including a semblance of backoo, ole higue and other jumbie spirits, as the environment itself inspired–all new fears. And then the moongazer, or the massacouraman – this latter a malignant water-spirit, which I would write about in my short novel *Dark Swirl*. Water indeed being everywhere, in our 'land of many waters' with creeks, canals, rivers. Torrential rains poured down once more, everything appearing as an elemental onslaught, adding to the sense of forlornness and lore.

I yet mingled with everyone, watched and listened to their incessant jabber, being immersed in their body talk, laughter, the pain and still penury of daily living all around, our always trying to make ends meet because of paltry wages. More twisted, bent bodies: the human environment no less. But underneath it all there was also a zest for life, as seasons changed, or manifested as life's grinding monotony. Visions yet in me, as I imagined more places far away. And sugar was indeed the lifeblood, akin to my own beating spirit. Sugarcane, and rice-paddy fields, all around; and a heartbeat became more emblematic of where I now was, even in my vicarious return to the place of origins, and felt I'd never left. Left where?

The Canje district or the village and country as a whole with the sense of empire never truly disappeared, I figured, because of who lived here first a long time ago, and those who never wanted to be here in the first place but who finally inhabited the land and occupied spaces interpreted as authentic belief.

More waves rising up: a young boy, the same grandfather as he turned out to be, in dire fear, as the ships kept crossing the 'dark water,' rocking in mid-ocean, but now for the last time. It was 1917. And that old woman, still the bundle, vicariously began returning to India in my imagination and being in a side street in Mumbai, as she cast a wayward glance at me, like an evil eye. Recognition it was; and did I now perhaps come from a new place called Canada with its own Great Spirit, or wherever else I happened to be?

Everything akin to the transmigration of souls, in the old woman's wavering consciousness no doubt due to what was believed by the ancient Greeks being subliminally in her, or what she might have conceived of Alexander the Great's designs on more than northern India (Punjab), but also on the whole wide world. Adelphi, like all other villages on the coastland Guyana not without oracular echoes, I also conceived, and with Dutch, French and English legacies, or what else I also vicariously coped with, but tried to deny because of my individual spirit forming.

Ships in all the world's oceans, in all corners of the globe too, more than Walter Raleigh or Francis Drake ever dreamt about. And Alexander the Great's ancestor, Heracles, being at it, with the sense of simply being reincarnated, not just transmigrated. Ashes floating down the Ganges, the wheel of fate or destiny turning because of the flame of fire in a coastland sugar-plantation – and who first lived here, or the last, in spaces carved out of real memory, all working together to shape the land – a new environment palpably in the making.

2

Teaching West Indian Literature in Britain*

DAVID DABYDEEN

The West Indies, in the words of the Nobel Laureate Derek Walcott is 'The world's most accessible fuck.'[1] Not surprisingly, courses on the region's culture are considered 'sexy', they are swamped by eighteen to twenty-one-year-old white undergraduates who come seeking excitements other than the intellectual. Some have black lovers, or have smoked marijuana. All have danced to Bob Marley. The richer ones have lain under the sun of Barbados. Speaking generally, they attend West Indian Literature classes because they find their own culture jaded, lacking frisson and danger. To be a West Indian Literature student is to be cool, hip and subcultural, like the subject of their enquiry, the blacks who inhabit the ghettos of Kingston or Brixton.

The teacher's business is to disabuse them of their expectations and to police their enthusiasms. The teacher is killjoy. The teacher instructs them to read the unreadable,

---

* From *Studying British Cultures*. Ed. Susan Bassnett. (London: Routledge), 1997.

to speak the unspeakable: post-colonial and postmodernist theory. The student in an early class on Sam Selvon who exclaimed, 'but Trinidad is such a *vibrant* place, all that music and rhythm and sand and simple speech. Whoever would want to live in England!', by the end of the course speaks of West Indian culture in sombre, terrorist terms - it subverts canons, it interrogates the great tradition, it challenges the direct authority of the dominant, it contents the ideological hegemony of cultural precepts, it mugs the Queen's English. At the end of the day, West Indian culture equals mugging, in spite of the high-falutin' rhetoric. And the students' initial innocence has been lost to the more mature pleasures of mastering the technochip jargon of theory.

The fault is partly ours. We are West Indian teachers in single numbers inhabiting the margins of the Western academy. Our jobs were not necessarily created out of the academy's desire to enlarge and enrich its humanities curriculum by being more fully representative of humanity, but out of post-imperial guilt, or the social pressure exerted by street-blacks. Our centres are handouts, forms of welfare cheques. The Centre of Caribbean Studies at the University of Warwick, the first of its kind at a British university, was after all, created in the wake of the Brixton and Toxteth riots, and the American invasion of Grenada. The West Indies, in the words of George Lamming, is 'a unique experiment', characterised by fantastic survivals, hybridities and amalgamations.[2] Through immigration multicultural societies emerged; a complex mixture of Amerindians, Africans, Asian and Europeans living together with the varied legacies left by Spanish, English, French and Dutch colonisers and now within the shadow of the United States. There is scarcely an ideology in the Third World that does not have a Caribbean provenance, the most striking expression of which is perhaps the Cuban revolution.[3] The Western academy, however, remains to be convinced of the intellectual potential of 'Caribbean Studies'. Hence the marginal status reflected in marginal and precarious funding.

The survival and career enhancement of the marginal and tokenistic West Indian scholar in the Western academy depends on mastery of the Western idiom. The same goes for other 'Third World' scholars in their own countries. As the Indian academic, Meenakshi Mukherjee puts it, 'a generation ago, when I began to study literature as an academic discipline, I submitted to the central ideologies of power in the literary and intellectual domain which at that time were Anglo-American in origin and male in outlook'. European critical traditions have since displaced the Anglo-American, but the problem remains that validation is the business and privilege of the 'Centre'. Thus the radical ideas of a critic like Edward Said have had to 'pass through the Centre...in order to return to the periphery'. If, as Mukherjee argues, the most crucial terms and concepts of the new critical discourse are 'historically linked with certain phases of literary development in Europe', then their inapplicability to 'Third World' literature should be evident. Yet the West Indian teacher, with minor and vulnerable status in the Western academy, knows with what his bread is buttered. And it's French butter. Instead of devising a West Indian poetic in which to read West Indian literature, the teacher reaches for brand names and market leaders - Lacan, Derrida, et al. The result is, as Mukherjee states memorably, 'mime and ventriloquism'.[4]

The writers have done what they can to sneer at the new theoreticians, none more brilliantly than Derek Walcott in arguing for chaos, paradox and nonsense as sources of creativity :

> A lot of dead fish have beached on the sand. Most of the fish are French fish, and off their pages there is the reek of the fishmonger's hands. I have a horror, not of that stink, but of the intellectual veneration of rot, because from the far off reek which I get from the stalls of the academy, there is now a school of fishermen as well as schools of fish, and these fishmongers are interested in examining the disembowelled entrails of poetry, of marketing its guts and its surrounding conversation of flies. When French poetry dies the dead fish of French criticism is sold to the suckers. 'Moby Dick is nothing but words, and what are words, and what do I mean when I say Moby Dick, and if say Moby Dick what exactly do I mean?' It convinces one that Onan was a Frenchman, but

no amount of masturbation can induce the Muse.... I cannot think because I refuse to, unlike Descartes. I have always put Descartes *behind* the horse.[5]

Walcott's is an ancient Romanticist charge against the critic that is 'murdering to dissect'. Wole Soyinka's charge is more contemporary; it is against the atomic white light of theory which threatens abstraction and annihilation:

> We have been blandly invited to submit ourselves to a second epoch of colonisation - this time by a universal - humanoid abstraction defined and conducted by individuals whose theories and prescriptions are derived from the apprehension of *their* world and *their* history *their* social neurosis and *their* value systems. It is time, clearly, to respond to this new threat.[6]

The challenge to the West Indian teacher then, within the Western academy, is to abandon Western critical theory as being inappropriate to an understanding of West Indian literature, and to take the consequences in terms of career, or in terms of being seen to be unfashionable or intellectually backward. The West Indian teacher will then have to offer for analysis a set of propositions about the history and culture of the region - a particular region, *derived from the body of creative writing* itself. The primacy of the writing must be restored, otherwise the centuries-old struggle for self-expression will be denied. The work of Pauline Melville, to cite but one writer arbitrarily, emerged from the plundering and silencing of her Amerindian ancestors. We can either be alert to her writing – its specific body of ideas, its specific form and texture – or we can drown her living voice – and the voices of the past – in a chorus of *their* (French, Anglo-American) techno speak. And if we are to quarrel with Pauline Melville's ideas or craft, then that disputation is best served by positioning another West Indian literary work against hers. The books should speak with each other, the task of the teacher being to host the dialogue. The criteria for literary judgement should be derived from the works themselves and not from Plato and his footnotes.

II

The problem with postmodernist theories is that they tend to dismiss 'presence' as a kind of metaphysical conceit and valourise 'absence', 'aporia' and 'kenosis'. Such approaches may be suited to an exploration of such a novel as *Flaubert's Parrot*, but they should be anathema to students of literature written by blacks. Take Olaudah Equiano, for instance, the eighteenth-century African-British writer, whose central concern was with textual presence – placing himself before the audience, asserting his humanity ('am I not a man and a brother?') at the height of the slave trade, the philosophical justification of which was the designation of blacks as a species of lower primates. Post-Structuralism thinks of literature as a dance of the pen. For Equiano, it was anything but. Writing for him was a deadly serious business. It was bound up with his own personal salvation as well as with the Abolitionist cause. As a slave in the Americas, his mastery of the English language saved him from beatings and brutalisations, since he could argue eloquently against 'violence and injustice', quoting biblical precepts to his Christian persecutors. When he published his autobiography in Britain in 1789, he lived by its revenues, travelling all over Britain reading from it and in the process selling thousands of copies to a new market of readers – the Abolitionists. Equiano had found a niche in the market for books and out of his blackness he created a text which exploited that niche and became, literally, a best-seller. Equiano made such a fortune from the sale of his book that he became a moneylender, his clients being white Englishmen! The wide currency of the book, as well as its literary merit, ensured that it became a potent weapon in the hands of Abolitionists.

A postmodern, a historical approach, which for good measure also kills off the author, is patently inappropriate to a reading of Equiano. Deconstruction, for instance, mocks the notion of referentiality and representation, it sunders the link between word and world. In the words of Sukhdev Sandhu, 'this is most pernicious. Equiano emerged from and wrote of social milieux which he knew about with a kind of painful intensity. To say that his book stems from a particular period and body of social circumstances is not to deprecate its literary qualities, but to make the point that you cannot fully appreciate his work without a firm grasp of the social and historical materiality that underspins it.[7]

To illustrate, I quote in full a story Equiano tells of a venture in which he was involved, with a fellow slave, both of them sailors on ship trading between the Caribbean islands:

> ... and at our sailing he had brought his little all for a venture, which consisted six bits' worth of limes and oranges in a bag, I had also my whole stock, which was about twelve bits' worth of the same kind of goods, separate in two bags, for we had heard these fruits sold well in that island. When we came there, in some little convenient time he and I went ashore with our fruits to sell them but we had scarcely landed when we were met by two white men, who presently took our three bags from us. We could not a first guess what they meant to do, and for some time we thought they were jesting with us, but they too soon let us know otherwise, for they took our ventures immediately to a house hard by, and adjoining the fort, while we followed all the way begging of them to give us our fruits, but in vain. They not only refused to return them, but swore at us and threatened if we did not immediately depart they would flog us well. We told them these three bags were all we were worth in the world, and that we brought them with us to sell when we came from Montserrat, and showed them the vessel. But this was rather against us, as they now saw we were strangers as well as slaves. They still therefore swore and desired us to be gone and even took sticks to beat us, while we, seeing they meant what they said, went off in the greatest confusion and despair. Thus in the very minute of gaining more by three times than I ever did by any venture in my life before, was I deprived of every farthing I was worth. An insupportable misfortune! but how to help ourselves we knew not. In our consternation we went to the commanding officer of the fort and told him how we had been served by some of his people, but obtained not the least redress: he answered our complaints only by a volley of imprecations against us, and immediately took a horsewhip in order to chastise us, so that we were obliged to turn out much faster than we came in. I now, in the agony of distress and indignation, wished that the ire of God in his forked lightning might transfix these cruel oppressors among the dead. Still however we preserved, went back again to the house, and begged and besought them again and again for our fruits, till at last some other people that were in the house asked if we would be contented if they kept one bag and gave us the other two.

We seeing no remedy whatever, consented to this, and they, observing one bag to have both kinds of fruit in it, which belonged to my companion, kept that; and the other two, which were mine, they gave us back. As soon as I got them I ran as fast as I could, and got the first Negro man I could to help me off, my companion, however, stayed a little longer to plead; he told them the bag they had was his, and likewise all that he was worth in the world, but this was of no avail and he was obliged to return without it. The poor old man, wringing his hands, cried bitterly for his loss, and indeed he then did look up to God on high, which so moved me with pity for him that I gave him early one-third of my fruits. We then proceeded to the markets to sell them, and Providence was more favourable to us than we could have expected, for we sold our fruits uncommonly well; I got mine for about thirty-seven bits. Such a surprising reverse of fortune in so short a space of time seemed like a dream to me, and proved no small encouragement for me to trust the Lord in any situation.[8]

Over the years, in teaching this passage, I have stressed the following:

- The pathos, consciously created by alliteration, rhythm and repetition, designed to appeal to an age of sentimentality ('we told them that these three bags were all we were worth in the world').
- The story's conscious mimicry of the structure of biblical parables (including a powerful moral ending), designed to appeal to an age of religious seriousness.
- The emotional and symbolic power of the goods of oranges and limes (as opposed to meats, which Equiano would have also traded in), in line with the tastes of an age of romanticism.
- The careful and rational arguments ('we told them...we showed them...') Equiano uses to regain his goods, appealing to an age of enlightenment.
- The deft shifts of linguistic registers, revealing something of Equiano's command of narrative in an age of narrative. (The line 'An insupportable misfortune! but how to help ourselves we knew not', moving from the rhetorical flourish to quick pragmatic monosyllables, recalling Robinson Crusoe's apostrophe to money; the shift from the rhetorical to the realistic is repeated later, Equiano's voice swelling to Old Testament proportions to damn the

cheats – 'the ire of God in his forked lightning' - then quickly returning to earth with 'still however we persevered').

- The exceedingly polite and literary turn of phrases, revealing Equiano's adoption of the mask of an eighteenth-century gentleman, in an age of slavery which sought to prove the inferiority of blacks by reference to their inability to arrive at language. ('He answered our complaints only by a volley of imprecations against us, and immediately took a horsewhip in order to chastise us, so that we were obliged to turn out much faster than we came in.')

Other linguistic strategies in this brief passage include the questioning of the moral authority of whites to rule and subjugate. The use of the religious word 'chastise', for instance ('took up a horsewhip in order to chastise us'), evokes a topsy-turvy world in which the sinner is confused with the sinned against. The white man plays God when he is mere thief and wielder of a callous whip. The world-turned-upside-down is of course the 'moral' of Equiano's tale ('such a surprising reversal of fortune in so short a space of time...'), as it was of many eighteenth-century pieces of white writing, but in Equiano's case the trope is deeply painful since it originates not from the philosophical imagination but from the weals on his black skin. The 'moral' of Equiano's tale may read like an ordinary piece of Christian wisdom, but its consciously conventional tone disguises a profound 'existentialist' sorrow at the day-to-day experience of black people: its uncertainties, aborted hopes and cruel vicissitudes. As a slave, Equiano knew the condition of non-being; he knew that *being*, in the context of an age of commerce, depended on owning *something*, and on making it subject to his will (hence the measuring of his life according to the worth of his oranges and limes, and his freedom to dispose of his goods). Equiano saved £40 and purchased his own freedom. He bought his own life, then sold it in the form of an autobiographical publication, making a massive profit out of the 'existentialist' transaction. The 'moral' of his tale, 'to trust the Lord in any situation' is massively ironic when we consider the commercial meaning of the word 'trust'. In God he trusts, everyone else must pay him cash.

I teach Equiano as an artful storyteller and writer, one who is always conscious of the moods and trends of his age, and exploits these for the sake of money-making and for the liberation of his fellow blacks. The exploited becomes the exploiter, with a moral and ethical purpose, thereby undermining the very foundations of eighteenth-century commerce: the bifurcation between ethics and business, expressed in the eighteenth-century dictum, 'religion is one thing, trade another', was the very rationale for slavery.[9] Above all teach Equiano as an eighteenth-century travel writer, one who knew the 'tricks' of contemporary travel writing, its mixture of money-making, exotic adventure and Christian zeal; one who mimicked the 'tricks' so as to expose their hollowness and hypocrisy.

Such approaches to Equiano are very different from those of some of my white students who impose upon the writer their own secondhand theories, thereby trivialising the literary genius of the man. Hence the student who took a pseudo psychoanalytic view, describing Equiano's longing for his mother (from whom he was separated as a boy, and enslaved) as an Oedipal concern; who argued that the oranges presented Equiano's testicles, and that their theft symbolised the persistent emasculation of the black and white supremacists since the seventeenth century. Westerners whose idea of liberation is the arousal of the clitoris, and who meditate upon their genitalia for the meaning of emancipation, obviously have utterly different perspectives and lifestyles from Equiano and the mass of his descendants. By all means they should wank over their own texts, but to do so over ours is to repeat the sexual patterns of slavery in which the black could be violated in silence (the silence of the Letter of the Law), word and world severed in a manner prophetic of postmodern theories.

III

How to avoid Western theory, which will exoticise, capture and Calibanise the black subject, is the challenge before the West Indian teacher in Britain. Suspicion of Western theory must go hand in hand with a reconceptualisation of the nature of West Indian-ness, one which foregrounds the existence of cultures only partially affected by contact with the European. Teachers of Caribbean Studies in Britain still tend to focus on the ways Britain impacted on the economy, social and kinship institutions and psyche of African slaves and their descendants. The prevalent view still is that the region was made (or to use Walcott's imagery, *laid*) by Britain. In other words we are mulattos and mimic men and women; we play cricket, but with sufficient exuberance and flair to make us a little distinctive; we speak English, but with sufficient grammatical oddities to justify our different colour. Little attention is paid to the myriad ways in which Africans altered British manners and thinking, even in the era of slavery. The creative impact of African languages, philosophies and cultural practices on the day-to-day lives of white masters and overseers is hardly understood. No one denies the massive erasure of African cultures in the era of slavery, but few investigate and document the ways in which the British became 'Africanised' in the process. Caribbeanists remain habituated to reading colonial history as a one-way traffic of values, in which British culture supplanted and superseded that of the African while remaining 'unadulterated' by anything African. The Western academy also appears unable to read non-Western Caribbean traditions in their total or partial survivals, preferring to focus instead on the Western effort to eradicate these traditions. As a result, notions of coloniser/colonised, centre/periphery, and so on continue to dominate descriptions of the historic relationships between British and West Indian cultures.

Of Caribbean intellectual, it is the Guyanese painter Aubrey Williams who is most explicit in his championing of the non-Columbian values of the region. He confesses that working in Europe, and with a European education, the images of his canvas are inevitably 'glossed over with European angst, European psychology, European everything because I am still a captured individual'. He is also trapped in the materiality of Europe in that he uses canvases and oils; he cannot 'go back' to grinding pigments and using fats. And yet his whole life's struggle, as a Guyanese of Amerindian, African, Indian and European ancestry has been to banish the European aspect from his art. He concludes on a confused note of defiance and despair, 'all my life I have been trying to get rid of it, but I don't know whether I can. If we can get rid of it in ourselves it will be a great achievement. I don't think that getting rid of economic structures, or changing them, is enough. We have to find new values, new directions, which we can now do only with the coming generations. Not so much with ourselves'.[10] Williams's position is open to the charge that it evokes the very notions of ethnic purity and essentialism which underpinned the imperial project and which wreaked such havoc upon the very pre-Columbian peoples who inspire his art. I think, however, that Williams simply wanted a downgrading of the role of Europe in our making, in favour of a greater recognition of our native resources, the communities of native values which survived in spite of the conquistadors, planters and missionaries.

I would suggest that one of the ways of fulfilling William's quest for 'new values and new directions' in the region is by engagement with what is oldest in the region, namely our Amerindian cultures. In Guyana we have many such living cultures - Wai Wai, Macusi, Arawak, Carib - but Western Caribbeanists know next to nothing of Amerindian languages, oral and written expression, myths, religions, art, music, diet, political economy, gender relations, and so on. Evidence of the wilful neglect of Amerindian cultures is stark: I know of no anthology of West Indian oral and written literature (and there are many, produced by such specialist publishers as Longman and Heinemann) which include a single Amerindian poem, chant, song, prayer or proverb. There is correspondingly a total ignoring of Amerindian ideas in books that purport to deal with the intellectual traditions in the region. There is not even a footnote in such books, explaining the absence. The simple fact is that the scholars who produce such texts – which form the basis of teaching Caribbean Studies in the Western academies – have rarely travelled into the interior to meet Amerindians, never mind studied their languages and cultures. To do so demands effort – the effort to *know* the subject. The dismal truth is that Caribbeanists are still very much timid external observers of the cultures of the region. Herskovitz's injunction that they should 'get down from their verandas' and live among the peoples they study falls on deaf ears. If the region has always been prey to piracy and quick plunder, today it endures new pirates from the metropolis – people who make quick visits, observe hastily and in fright of the native preference presence, then return to pronounce with authority in the centres in Britain.

The Amerindians, the most invisible of West Indian peoples, are paradoxically signposts of the future. What distinguishes their existence is the absence of recognition of boundaries. They carry no passports, seek no visas, observe none of the territorial imperatives and protocols of the colonial legacy. They have no sense of centre or periphery. Maps, colonial in conception, which demarcate the land, are alien to them. Amerindians cross over at will to Venezuela and Brazil, irrespective of the fact that the landmass was divided up by the Portuguese, the Spanish and the British. Similarly their sense of time is not linear and periodic but circular and continuous.[11] They are postmodern in the movements of their own lives without the bureaucracy of theory to inform them of the fact, or to validate their condition.

Another way of realising Williams's desire for originality rooted in native form and native content is to attend to Asian cultures, another neglected aspect of Caribbean Studies. Among immigrants to the region, Indians proved to be the most resilient to Christian conversion. H.P.V. Bronkhurst, the nineteenth-century Methodist missionary, confessed to utter frustration at the stubbornness of Indian beliefs: 'In preaching to the coolies, whether in sugar estates, in the yards, villages and publicly, in large numbers or privately in their houses, we meet with endless objections brought before us again and again'.[12] So successful were they in resisting colonial brainwashing that today, 155 years after their first arrival, Indian cultures, centring on the mosque and Hindu temple, flourish in Guyana and Trinidad, in original and creolised forms. The resistance to Christianity was, of course, never total, and in addition Indian cultures were open to change within the slowly dissolving framework of tradition.

In a recent essay on the influence of Indian classical and folk music on the making of West Indian literature, Sasenarine Persaud, a Guyanese writer, has this to say of Sam Selvon: 'Sam Selvon's work is not without the influence of these rhythms and closer examination may well show that much of his often touted calypso rhythms are actually the rhythms of *chowtals* or *taans*'.[13] Persaud invites us to listen to the orality of Selvon's narrative with more subtlety and greater awareness of Indian songs, song-games, tales, proverbs, riddles, charms, oaths and jokes which constitute a distinctive Indo-Caribbean orality. Needless to say, critics of Sam Selvon have wholly ignored this dimension to his writing. Persaud proceeds to reveal how a West Indian novel can be Indian in structure and technique by reference to one of his own works, in which the division into three sections and the varying length of each section correspond to the three rhythms of the classical Indian raag, with the reversal of rhythms informed by the yogic view that there is no beginning and no end, just cycles to and from pure consciousness. The exploration of the nature of memory, which constitutes Persaud's fiction, also has a distinctive Indian motive. The nature of memory is a central Afro-Caribbean concern, given the metropolitan efforts to erase the Africanness of the African and the counter efforts of writers like Equiano to remember the dismembered body of the past by the fusion of the living imagination and scholarly recovery of data. Persaud's project differs in that he is not concerned with the materiality of history within a particular time-span. Persaud is concerned with 'essence of the reality of reincarnation, which is memory. If the individual can sit down and train the consciousness to retrieve what the consciousness has recorded, then he can see past, present and future. This is the essence of yoga'.[14]

I would venture that Persaud's essay, if developed and magnified, can offer completely new ways of reading certain works by West Indian writers, East Indian or otherwise. The critical terminology used, derived from Sanskrit literature and Indian classical and folk music, is refreshingly different from the jargon critics use today, which is almost entirely derived from the West. If we are to deconstruct West Indian fictions, then let us attempt to use a vocabulary and concepts derived from Indian aesthetics that are native and alive and present; because they are still being used in every day and ritualistic life by a substantial proportion by our Indo-Caribbean peoples. If we learn the vocabulary, and the cultures that create and sustain that vocabulary, we may well find surprising correspondences with Western concepts we take on board with such ready mimicry. Why are we, for instance, so engrossed with Paul de Man's rejection of a metaphysics of presence, when closer to home we have critics and priests who also reject the notion of origin, but from a native yogic philosophy? And if that yogic philosophy, which speaks of seamlessness, contradicts the Afro-Caribbean search for specific roots and origins, how can we embrace that contradiction to forge a sense of national unity? Such Caribbean questions are possibly beyond solution by the use of European conceptualisations, as Aubrey Williams intimated.

Since 1838 we have had in the West Indies a body of texts of staggering physical bulk and philosophical dimensions, which have been almost completely ignored by Caribbeanists. I refer to the Hindu epics. The *Aeneid* of Virgil runs to 12,000 lines; the *Iliad* of Homer to double that number; the *Ramayana* rolls on to 100,000 lines, while the *Mahabarata* quadruples that sum; the *Vedas*, when collected, form eleven huge Octavo volumes, while the *Puranas* extend to 2 million lines. I mention quantity so as to highlight the fact that the act of ignoring these texts is an act of monumental bias. These native texts are available, they have existed in English translations for decades, and are regularly performed on stage and village grounds by the common people (as Derek Walcott reminded us in his reference to the Ramlila Festivals at the opening of his 1992 Nobel Prize speech).

The *Ramayana*, narrated, sung and dramatised by Indo-Caribbeans from the days of indentureship to today, was important for several reasons. The story of banishment, exile and displacement and perilous new encounters among strange tribes, the story of a fall from grace into a prison-house of misery, served as an allegory of the experience of indentureship. We don't have to keep imposing a Homeric grid on native life, or agonise over Western theories of tragedy, to express the character of our West Indian historical and individual selves. Exile and homecoming are the *Ramayana's* themes.

The *Ramayana* ends with the rule of Rama, the Golden Age, or Ram Raj, the Age of Light. The absence of poverty, petty jealousies, diseases, hunger and death was, of course, the antithesis of life in nineteenth century United Provinces and Bihar from where Indo-Caribbeans originated, as well as the life that awaited them in the colonial plantation. Scholars like Clem Shiwcharan have argued that the shame of the actual past, and the guilt of severing family ties and abandoning traditional duties in fleeing to the colonial plantation, encouraged Indians to forget their specific origins. What replaced the sense of history was a sense of the *Ramayana*, and as direct contact with India diminished with time, it was the *Ramayana* which represented India to the descendants of indentured workers. 'It was an India that was as opulent, magical and epic as the fables of the *Ramayana*; a land on the brink of a Golden Age (a view strengthened, incidentally, in the 1940s, when India fought for and won independence from Britain; the second colony to do so)'.[15] In other words, India existed in the realm of the imagination and as a result the image of India was susceptible to manipulations in order to fit specific exigencies. India (the past) was made and remade with the same freedom with which the *Ramayana* was constructed – the *Ramayana* having no single authorship but being a product of writings and rewritings, accretions and transformations. The *Ramayana* existed in different versions, and not merely as a printed text. The *Ramayana* had an oral existence – for the common people it existed as stories and songs and dramatic performances which could be altered according to the nature of the audience or the nature of the performances or the nature of the landscape and environment, or simply the contingencies of the moment. If we want to identify postmodernism in the West Indies we can look at the ancient *Ramayana* and to its reception and enactments in the region. The coolie, wielding his cutlass before the cane in the nineteenth-century plantation, was, in a peculiar way, at the cutting edge of critical theory.

To conclude, to teach West Indian literature in the Western academy will be flawed and partial until the Amerindian and the East Indian, with their particular cultural and philosophical dimensions, are placed at the centre of our considerations. To do so will involve recognition that West Indian peoples are not merely creatures of Britain forged by British cultural values. It will involve, therefore, redefinition of the character of the West Indian, with emphasis on the cultural values and practices that survived British colonisation. Caribbeanists will have to be retrained, at the very least in terms of learning Sanskrit, Hindi or an Amerindian language. A concomitant redefinition of Britishness will emerge inevitably, one that recognises Britain's historic inability to penetrate 'other' cultures; and one that qualifies the belief that still prevails, about the crumbling of 'native' cultures before Britain's superior imperial might.

Endnotes

[1] Address to Association of Commonwealth Language and Literature Studies, University of Kent, 1989

[2] George Lamming, "The Indian Presence as a Caribbean Reality", in F. Birbalsingh (ed). *Indenture and Exile: The Indo-Caribbean Experience* (Toronto: TSAR, 1989), pp. 45-54.

[3] Alistair Hennessy (London: Macmillan, Warwick University Caribbean Studies Series, 1994/5).

[4] Meenakshi Mukherjee, "The Centre Cannot Hold: Two Views of the Periphery", in S. Slemon and H. Tiffin (eds), *After Europe* (Sydney and Aarhus: Dangaroo Press, 1989), pp. 41-8.

42 David Dabydeen

[5] Derek Walcott, "Caligula's Horse", in *After Europe*, op. cit. pp. 138-42.
[6] See Diana Brydon, "Commonwealth or Common Poverty?", in *After Europe*, op. cit., pp. ix-xiii.
[7] Private communication with author, August 1995.
[8] Paul Edwards (ed.) *The Life of Olaudah Equiano* (London: Longman, 1983), pp. 80-81.
[9] See D. Dabydeen, "Eighteenth Century English Literature on Commerce and Slavery", in D. Dabydeen (ed), *The Black Presence in English Literature* (Manchester: Manchester University Press, 1985), pp. 26-49.
[10] Aubrey Williams in conversation with Rasheed Araeen, in Anne Walmsley (ed.), *Guyana Dreaming. The Art of Aubrey Williams* (Sydney and Aarhus: Dangaroo Press, 1990), pp. 43-61.
[11] I am grateful to George Simon and Pauline Melville for insights into Amerindian perspectives, and to various essays by George Mentor, Jannette Forte, Anne Benjamin and Desrey Fox, published by the Amerindian Research Unit, University of Guyana. See, too, Andrew Sanders, *The Powerless People* (London: Macmillan, Warwick University Caribbean Studies Series, 1987).
[12] I am grateful to Clement Shiwcharan's excellent study of Indo-Guyanese history, "Effort and Achievement" (unpublished Ph.D dissertation, Centre for Caribbean Studies, University of Warwick, 1989) for information on this and other subjects.
[13] Sasenarine Persaud, "Extending the Indian Tradition", in *Indo Caribbean Review*, vol. 1, no. 1, 1994, pp. 15-28.
[14] Ibid.
[15] Clement Shiwcharan, op. cit., pp. 39-49.

References

Appiah, K.A. "Is the Post - in Postmodernism the Post - in Postcolonial?" *Critical Inquiry*, Vol. 17, Winter 1991, pp. 336-57.

Ashcroft, Bill, Gareth Griffiths and Helen Tiffin. *The Empire Writes Back: Theory and Practice in Post-colonial Literatures*, London: Routledge 1989.

_____. *The Post-colonial Studies Reader*, London: Routledge, 1995.

Barker, Francis, Peter Hulme and Margaret Iversen. eds. *Colonial Discourse/Postcolonial Theory*. Manchester: Manchester University Press, 1994.

Baugh, E. *Critics on Caribbean Literature*. New York: St. Martin's Press, 1978.

Chrisman, Laura and Patrick Williams. eds. *Colonial Discourse and Postcolonial Theory: A Reader*. London: Harvester, 1993.

Cudjoe S.R. ed. *Caribbean Women Writers*. Cambridge, MA: University of Massachusetts Press, 1999.

Dabydeen D. and B. Samaroo. eds. *India in the Caribbean*. London: Hansib, 1988.

Dabydeen, D. ed. *The Black Presence in English Literature*. Manchester: Manchester University Press, 1985.

Dirlik, Arif. "The Postcolonial Aura: Third World Criticism in the Age of Global Capitalism", *Critical Inquiry*, Vol. 20, Winter 1994, pp. 329-56.

Fanon, Franz. *Black Skin, White Masks* (1952). London: Pluto Press, 1986.
____. *The Wretched of the Earth* (1963). London: MacGibbon and Gee, 1965.
Gilroy, Paul. *The Black Atlantic: Modernity and Double Consciousness*. London: Verso, 1993.
James, C.L.R. *Spheres of Existence*. London: Alison and Busby, 1980.
King, B. ed. *West Indian Literature*. London: Macmillan, 1979.
Lazarus, Neil. "Disavowing Decolonization: Fanon, Nationalism and the Problematic of Representation in Current Theories of Colonial Discourse", *Researches in African Literatures*, Vol. 24, No. 4, Winter 1993, pp. 69-98.
Maes-Jelinek, H. *Wilson, Harris, The Uncompromising Imagination*. Sydney and Aarhus: Dangaroo Press, 1991.
Miyoshi, Maso. "A Borderless World? From Colonialism to Transnationalism and the Decline of the Nation State", *Critical Inquiry*, Vol. 19, Summer 1993, pp. 726-51.
Mohanty, Chandra. "Under Western Eyes: Feminist Scholarship and Colonial Discourse", *Feminist Review*, Vol. 30, Autumn 1988, pp. 61-88
Mudimbe V.Y. *The Invention of Africa*. London: Currey, 1988.
O'Callaghan, F. *Women Version*. London: Macmillan, 1993.
Ramchand, K. *The West Indian Novel and its Background* (revised edition). London: Heinemann, 1983.
Rao, Venkat. "Self-formations: Speculations on the question of post-coloniality", *Wasifiri*, Spring 1991, pp. 7-10
Said, Edward. *Culture and Imperialism*. London: Chatto and Windus, 1993.
____. *Orientalism*. London: Routledge, 1978.
Tiffin, Helen. "Postcolonialism, Postmodernism and the Rehabilitation of Postcolonial History", *Journal of Commonwealth Literature*, Vol. 23, No. 1, 1988, pp. 169-81.

3

Inventions of Auto-Narratives in Braithwaite and Phillips

JASBIR JAIN

Writing is never a one-way communication. Its multiple directions are both self-directed and other-directed. Very often the process of self and social interrogation is a continuous one. More than a generation apart, and writers entirely of a different kind, Braithwaite and Phillips also have something in common. Their origins are Caribbean, their host culture, in large measure, has been British and their exposure and early educational training along British traditions. E.R. Braithwaite's first volume of autobiography, *To Sir, With Love* (1959) won a degree of popularity and was made into a film in 1967. It has appealed to readers across cultures and carries within it the humanistic idealism of the fifties. Braithwaite was born in British Guyana in 1920 and, in the words of Caryl Phillips, had a comfortable childhood as the child of Oxford educated parents. As a young man Braithwaite quickly 'absorbed the conservative, middle-class manners of the Caribbean intellectual'.[1] Writing an Introduction to a new edition of the novel in 2005, Caryl Phillip's observes that then (1959) as now (2005), British society remains wedded to its age-old racial prejudice. Braithwaite went on to write five other volumes of autobiography with two appearing in 1962 another in 1965 to be followed by a fifth book in 1972. The final volume *Honorary White* appeared in 1975 and marked the end of his faith in liberal ideology. On the surface all these volumes take up Braithwaite's personal experiences and social encounters and are, in the main, representative of an 'objective and controlled protest against race prejudice and colour discrimination'.[2] But at another level Braithwaite raises several other questions; the sociocultural context of the birth of a 'self', the 'marginality' of being, the whole pedagogy of learning and the puncturing of stereotypes are only some of these.

Born just a year before the publication of *To Sir, With Love* (1959) in St. Kitts, Phillips arrived in England as a young baby. His rootedness in British society is much more thorough than Braithwaite's. It is no longer a dream chased from across the ocean through textbook exposure, and accepted with all its flaws and heartaches, but a probing of cultural roots and colonial exploitation as Phillips takes up the issues in several of his novels but more particularly in *Crossing the River* (1993) and at a metaphorical level through transference to a Jewish psyche in *The Nature of Blood* (1997).[3] Phillips's work reflects an altogether different aspect of the writer's self as it is located in the sociocultural context. Apparently it is not possible to ignore Aime Cesaire, Frantz Fanon or even Derrida while reading Phillips. His generation has grown up on the idea of negritude and has turned the whole question of racial discrimination inside-out highlighting the long history of colonial oppression in its many guises of religious conversion, the civilisational discourse and then the marginal location in metropolitan societies.

Both Braithwaite and Phillips can be considered representative writers of their generations in ideological and attitudinal terms even as they raise different questions in relation to racial discrimination and examine the issue from different angles. As the meaning and experience of exile are different for each of the two, the narrative embodiment necessarily becomes different. Braithwaite, brought up on British educational system, British history and ideas, is deeply influenced by the liberal ideology of accommodation and tolerance. His arrival in England in 1939 had led to the feeling that, at long last, he was 'personally identified with the hub of fairness, tolerance and all the freedoms' (*To Sir, With Love* 39). Personal loss and anguish are transmuted into an ideology of commitment and involvement. The children of the economically and socially disadvantaged East-Enders become a parallel construct for his own salvation. It is a long struggle: first against social injustice, then against being fitted into a stereotype and then later against his own emotional relationship which he strives to put on an even keel. The sombre tone is relieved by several factors. There is first the white man in the park who persists in conversing with him and offers him advice at a time when his spirits and his funds both have dipped (45-48). Men like the conductor in the bus in the very first chapter, men who assert the dignity of the individual offer him another support structure. The school Headmaster with his unflinching faith in the children shows him another aspect of the human struggle. In fact, alongside the rejections and rebuttals, the refusal to treat him as an equal, the refusal to recognise his competence and qualifications, are a host of gestures of friendship and human warmth.

To Sir, With Love is an autobiographical novel with a difference. It is located in the 'present' and takes up only the span of a year or so. Though Braithwaite's journeys to USA and his experience in the RAF are mentioned, the West Indian reality does not feature in the novel. It also does not travel very much beyond the school. As such it foregrounds pedagogy and the human involvement any worthwhile pedagogy demands. Thus the autobiography, despite the narrative centredness, becomes in the end a collective and a collaborative venture which seeks to work out the themes of dislocation and exile.

Exile has been variously framed by different writers. Frank Birbalsingh distinguishes between the sense of exile felt by white emigrants to the colonies (as in Australia, Canada and New Zealand) and the West Indian's sense of exile. Exile as it is experienced by African and Asian populations of the erstwhile colonies is markedly different. Over and above the sense of cultural displacement, the African and Asian populations have the consciousness of being oppressed and exploited and of being reduced to a total objectification. The cultural imposition of colonialism has erased their languages and cultures. Their sense of exile, the transplantation to other 'homelands' constitutes a distinguishable category in itself.[4]

One dominant outcome of this sense of uprooting is the need to belong to a more stable, permanent and cohesive unit. In the case of V.S. Naipaul, one can perceive the attempt to return to India, which ended in failure, and then the desire to relocate himself in England. *An Area of Darkness* (1962) and *An Enigma of Arrival* (1987) are the two ends of this journey. Others like Braithwaite, Caryl Phillips's parents, Cyril Dabydeen, David Dabydeen and a host of others have veered towards Britain, Canada or the US but belonging extracts it own price entailing acceptance and submission. Often also a total new self-education. Naipaul works towards it through identification with its landscape, its inheritance and its history.[5] Braithwaite does so through acceptance of the racial discrimination and adopting the line of least resistance. The past is a closed door. Colonial history does not find a place even as the stereotype of a negro is deconstructed. Both the strategy and the narrative structure in *To Sir, With Love* work towards this. The foregrounding of the bus ride right in the beginning, the encounter with the smartly dressed (obviously white) woman who refused to occupy the vacant seat beside a black man and Braithwaite's disembarking from the bus at a point when the encounter could have led to an ugly scene are a preparation for the rest of the story. Throughout there is a gradual erosion of his faith and of the romantic belief in a just society, a deepening awareness of the struggle that lies ahead in the very existence of a negro and his inclination to sidestep an encounter and the setting for this is laid out right at the beginning.

This sidestepping of a direct confrontation structures the narrative. First, the white woman in the British bus, then the train journey during the visit to the Victoria and Albert Museum, later still the waiter in the restaurant are all public events. Besides this there are also the classroom encounters : Denham and the boxing match, the embarrassment of the class to join the funeral of a fellow-student's father and Braithwaite's experience in house-hunting are all skirmishes of a more intimate nature, happening amongst people one happens to know. Gillian's resentment against him is against this passivity of behaviour, this refusal to take on an attack headlong (147). His colleagues attribute this to the servility of the slave and Gillian perceives in this a subtraction from his masculinity.

But even in this sidestepping Braithwaite is deconstructing the stereotype. The negro is perceived as inferior to the white race. To many he is just a 'darky' or a 'nigger' or a 'black'; identified in their minds with inexhaustible brute strength.... They expect of him a courteous subservience' (41).[6] The word 'native' was widely used as a generic term for all coloured peoples (100). When he goes looking for a room the prospective landlady refers to him as a 'darky' (102). One of the students is surprised that his blood is red (109-110). His desire to avoid creating a scene is not necessarily an act of cowardice. He does take on Denham, conquers his own resentment of the students' hostility and goes on to assert a dignified code of behaviour. He works outside the average construct of a negro who is otherwise perceived as an unrefined, aggressive being. None of this, however, really takes away the hurt of discrimination. Mrs Pegg's behaviour, the non-recognition of his individual competence, the emptiness of all professions of British belief in fairness, the petty snobberies of people like the waiter, his daily sense of fear on meeting his class – none of this is denied or forgotten. The consciousness of colour which is thrust upon him in 1943 stays with him. He also recognises the constraints the white society imposes on negro behaviour. Looked upon as a race with extraordinary sexual prowess, they are to be denied relationships of love across the barrier of colour.

There are three parallel discourses in Braithwaite's account of his experience in the East End school : first that of racial discrimination, second of pedagogical experiments and third of a personal relationship. But the resolution for all three is the same : reaching out. The whole class turns up at Seales's house for his father's funeral, his teaching methods win him respect and Gillian's parents accept him. There is no escape from the colour of his own skin; he needs to associate it with personal dignity. These three discourses are, however, framed by the discourses of colonial exploitation Braithwaite recognises the extent to which British education has deracinated him without owning him – he is British but not a Briton; it generated a dream but denied its reality. The people at home, that is in Britain, he is aware, have given no thought to the way colonial people across the world, different in colour, 'assiduously identify' themselves with British loyalties and traditions. When war broke out, he had unhesitatingly volunteered for service with the Royal Air Force. But when in Britain, he realises that it is all an empty bubble. Outside academics it is all prejudice and hate. The Briton at home takes no responsibility for the colonial. Inequality defines all relationships[7] (40-41). Braithwaite's revenge works through pedagogy. He opens up the horizons of Britain's underclass, allowing them to taste, if not the great debates, the meaning of being human. Pedagogy comes full circle through this reversal.

The book cannot be read as a straightforward autobiography; its surface simplicity underplays the conflict as well as the structure. Rising above the stated theme, it is also a narrative about the 'self' and the 'other'. Frantz Fanon in *Black Skin, White Masks* devotes two chapters to the sexual relationship across colour. In the second of these "The Man of Colour and the White Woman" he refers to the black man's attraction towards a white woman as a journey towards self-realisation based upon a denial of colour, of becoming the other. Very often such a relationship has also been placed within the metaphor of rape. Quoting from a novel by René Maran, *Un homme pareil aux autres* (1947), Fanon points out that the relationship also needs to be authorised (in Braithwaite's case Gillian's parents play this role), because this authorisation signifies the final acceptance. It makes the 'other' one of 'us'. This 'us' also separates the coloured man from his kind. The sexual myth of the quest for white flesh is not perpetuated as he is fully aware of the rough course that awaits a mixed marriage and the children of such a marriage.

Caryl Phillips, in a very different move from Braithwaite, steps outside individual memory to seek recourse to the collective memory of oppression and exploitation formulated through a combination of objectification, religious conversion and dislocation. Ashcroft, Griffiths and Tiffin in *The Empire Writes Back* and Birbalsingh in *Guyana and the Caribbean* refer to the 'ancestral exile' of the West Indian. In the Caribbean the European imperial enterprises 'ensured that the worst features of colonialism throughout the globe would all be combined in the region' (Ashcroft et al 145) In Birbalsingh's view this dislocation from an ancestral homeland 'frustrates the emergence of a national identity' and prompts more 'psychic feelings of not belonging anywhere' (Birbalsingh 170). Phillips's confrontation with this sense of loss is not through nostalgia or rebellion but through a journey into the hinterland of individual and collective psyches.

Crossing the River has four parts framed by an unnamed prologue and epilogue. Each part is located in a different setting and a different time of history. What is seen as a truncated family, at one level, of a father and his three children, works at another level as a fragmented account of African lives of pursuit and persecution, of loneliness and suffering. The echoes of the prologue which frames the four parts pervade the rest of the narrative but are most dominant in the third part "Crossing the River". A family which is forced into separation through poverty is further fractured and separated through their owners and their circumstances. The shifting landscapes – the interiors of the forests in Liberia, the snow-covered roads in the second, the sea in the third and an urban stretch of war-affected England in the fourth are also travels to and fro across time from the mid-eighteenth to the mid-twentieth century. The prologue in itself is an unspoken dialogue between the African father who is compelled to sell his children and the white slave traders; it is both personal and historical and it juxtaposes the two worlds of the white man and the black man, with greed marking one and need the other. The sentences are short and brittle as if unable to carry the burden of the meaning:

> A desperate foolishness. The crops failed. I sold my children.... My Nash. My Martha. My Travis. Their lives fractured. Sinking hopeful roots into difficult soil. For two hundred and fifty years I have longed to tell them : Children I am your father. I love you. But understand. There are no paths in water. No signposts. There is no return. To a father consumed with guilt. You are beyond. Broken-off, like limbs from a tree.... The crops failed. I sold my children.
>
> (*Crossing the River*, 1-2)

There is no return. Instead there is a finality about everything. History has no fluidity. It only moves in one direction. The cover on the 1994 Picador edition depicts three human faces merging into each other signifying the common origins, similar fate and the archetypal suffering of the black man.

Nash (in the first section), when he is sent back to the pagan coast, carries with him the teachings and the value-structures contained in the teachings to Liberia but when his letters go unanswered, those values begin to be defunct. Loyalty, Christian charity, 'civilisation' values, monogamy – all begin to seem redundant when mortality and poverty stare them in the face. Christianity acquires a white face. There is a feeling, not of a mission, but of a second dislocation. The guilt of his master, as he makes the journey to Nash with his own fever-ridden body and his own sense of isolation does not compensate for the human betrayal and fails to bring him back to life. The white man is now placed in the hostile landscape not as a powerful purchaser of slaves but as a vulnerable human being. "The Pagan Coast," through the character of Williams' wife and the villainous role she plays, exposes the unlearnt lessons of Christian ethics. Nash has absorbed them much more deeply than his white mistress who breaks all laws of affection and morality by not allowing Nash's letters to reach her husband.

Martha's story – the briefest of the three narratives – takes us to America and the slave-owning masters who even as they promise freedom to loyal slaves are compelled to sell them or bequeath them to other claimants. As the aged body makes it way towards the warmth of friendship, death catches up with her. There is no return. It is only in Travis, the third child's narrative, that there is hope for redemption. The war-narrative moves back and forth between 1936 and 1963 and uses two races, two backgrounds – England and America – and places war at the centre. Personal histories, mother-daughter relationship, woman-woman friendships all come to the fore. The narrative voice is that of a white woman who first marries Len and then Travis. Her marriage to Travis has its own constraints : she cannot live with him in America. Mixed marriages would mean trouble. In any case Travis dies in the war leaving behind a 'coffee' coloured son. Travis is rehabilitated, though ever so briefly, by a white woman. And this woman comes, like Braithwaite's school children, from the lower social scale. Travis, like Braithwaite, feels no hesitation in joining the defence services. The loyalty the unwanted coloured man offers the white society is amazing. Its like laying down all your personal defences and walking into a deathtrap. Braithwaite works with the First World War and after; Phillips' fourth section works through the Second World War. How does the black man, otherwise not equal, become more than equal in times of war?

In the midst of these slave narratives told from the outside (none of the three has the voice of the black, though the first part has letters by Nash), the third part is a white man's logbook as he travels to purchase slaves. It also contains a letter to his wife. Contrasted with his own love and affection for his wife is the entire objectification of the slave as a commodity. His cargo of slaves is like any other inanimate cargo except that they can conspire and rise against him. Violence, inhumanity, anger and interrupted dreams lie between the white and the black world.

Caryl Phillips's novel disturbs one while E R Braithwaite's offers a positive hope and indications of social acceptance. Phillips means to disturb while Braithwaite offers a survival strategy. Phillips charts racial history, Braithwaite works through experience, yet at heart both the works are about racial discrimination, the shallowness of the white civilisation and its value structure. Both are conscious of the oppression that goes to construct power in different scales, one personal, the other racial; one focused on a limited time span, the other spread over centuries, space and generations; together they compel the reader to open out histories of imperialism and the meaning of progress. In fact all professed civilisational values are placed under the scanner as the see-saw of human relationships is now governed by the oppressed. They are auto-narratives in the manner they construct the self through a questioning of the very system that has framed them, rendered them homeless and rootless and in large measure blinded them to the oppression and injustice till adulthood. They are acts of remembering and reconstructions. It matters little how much of it is experience, how much history and how much imagined. When lives have to be put together, the narrative design itself becomes a part of the effort of reconstruction.

Both the narratives easily lend themselves to psychoanalytical frameworks. They defy both the purely experiential or the confessional autobiography; none of the heroism of public autobiographies is there; further, the pain and the frustration are also not directly articulated. Braithwaite retains the first person narration but places his experiences in a dominantly neutral frame. The teacher-student relationship de-individualises the issue. But both the bus journey, right at the beginning, and the visit to Gillian's parents towards the end are deeply marked by the question of race. Phillips adopts a purely fictional framework and works on a large canvas, analysing strategies of expansion – expansion of territory, of commerce, or religion, of power – and the dislocations of family, of individual and of values. In order to be free of the burden of the past, it has to be explored as Phillips proceeds to do; in order to continue to live a decolonisation of the mind has to take place as it happens with Braithwaite. The stages are awareness/consciousness, making inroads into the other's territory and finally creating a space of one's own across colour and time. Else how does one cope with truncated families, loss of roots, language and name, loss of origins and separated siblings? How does one cope with the anguish of being and with existential loneliness?

Endnotes

[1] Caryl Phillips, "To Ricky with Love", *The Observer*, July 23, 2005.
[2] Frank Birbalsingh, "The Autobiographical Writing of E.R. Braithwaite," *Guyana and the Caribbean*. Ed. Frank Birbalsingh, Chichester, West Sussex : Dido, 2004, p. 177.
[3] Through this strategy not only does he draw a parallel between Blacks and Jews but also crosses the gender boundary as Eva, the Jew character, is a woman. The rootlessness, the violated bodies and separated siblings all resurface in this and function within the constructs of identity and nation. The Jews are also in search of a country.
[4] See Frank Birbalsingh, "Exile and Autobiography : The Caribbean Experience," *Guyana and the Caribbean*, pp. 169-170.
[5] See my forthcoming article, "Landscapes of the Mind : Naipaul's *Enigma of Arrival*", *Journal of Caribbean Literatures*.
[6] Also see p. 88.
[7] *Black Skin, White Masks* (1952) Translation 1967, London : Pluto Press, 1986.

References

Ashcroft, Bill, Gareth Griffiths and Helen Tiffin. *The Empire Writes Back*. London: Routledge, 1989.
Birbalsingh, Frank. "Exile and Autobiography : The Caribbean Experience," *Guyana and the Caribbean*. Ed. Frank Birbalsingh. Chichester, West Sussex : Dido, 2004.
_____. "The Autobiographical Writing of E.R. Braithwaite," *Guyana and the Caribbean*. Ed. Frank Birbalsingh. Chichester, West Sussex : Dido, 2004.
Braithwaite, E.R. *To Sir, With Love* (1959) London : Coronet, 1993.
Fanon, Frantz. *Black Skin, White Masks* (1952 English translation 1962) London : Pluto Press, 1993.
Phillips, Caryl. *Crossing the River* (1993). London : Pan Macmillan, 1994.
_____. *The Nature of Blood*. London : Faber and Faber, 1997.
_____. "To Ricky with Love", Extract from Phillips's Introduction to a 2005 Vintage edition, *The Observer*. July 23, 2005.

4

Images of the Caribbean in the Early Works of Jean Rhys

MANVEEN BRAR

Jean Rhys, best known for her novel *Wide Sargasso Sea*, is the author of many short stories and novels, writing almost throughout the twentieth century from 1927, when her first short story collection *The Left Bank* was published, till 1979 when her autobiography *Smile Please: An Unfinished Autobiography* was published posthumously. Rhys's writing centres around themes of colonial identity, isolation, the sense of things falling apart, the female psyche, dependence and loss. She uses poetic language, irony, and a concern for subjectivity and language to develop her themes of anxiety and loss. Rhys uses a cosmopolitan setting for her writing like many of her contemporaries and is compared to Sylvia Plath by Helen Carr in *Jean Rhys* (1996) for she 'uses her life experiences, the pain, the rawness and the wounds as the material from which she writes her fiction'(3).

V.S. Naipaul in the *New York Review of Books* (1972) was the first to suggest that Jean Rhys thirty to forty years ago identified many of the themes that engage us today and also that her creative writing should be reread in terms of her colonial origins. In fact, until the publication of *Wide Sargasso Sea*, Rhys's Caribbean origins went unnoticed. Subsequently, Rhys has been included in the world of postcolonial literature and her novels and short stories are reread through these theories. The present paper explores the depiction of her homeland Dominica in Jean Rhys's early short stories, "Trio", "Again in the Antilles", "Mixing the Cocktail" in *The Left Bank* (1927), and the more substantial depiction of the same island in her novel *Voyage in the Dark* (1934). The representation of Dominica in her early writings reveals her relationship to her native island, her unique position in modernist writing, as well as her complex cultural location.

Jean Rhys's deepest identification was with her Caribbean childhood. In an interview with David Plante, published in his article "Remembrance" (1995), Rhys said that unlike many children of expatriate families, she was very sure that she was not English even though she lived most of her life in England, and had earlier lived in and written about Paris before the war. Writing about her sense of rootlessness in her autobiography *Smile Please* she confessed: 'I knew in myself that it would never happen. I would never be part of anything. I would never really belong anywhere and I knew it and all my life would be the same, trying to belong and failing.' (*Smile Please* 124) Ultimately she always felt an 'outsider', fundamentally homeless, and it was this social and existential marginality which provided a powerful edge to her writing.

Ford Madox Ford's preface to her first short story collection, *The Left Bank* (1927), introduced Rhys to the literary scene. Ford strategically placed Rhys as an exotic writer from a new world who can interpret the old world in innovative ways. In the preface he comments on Rhys as follows:

> And coming from the Antilles, with a terrifying insight and a terrific - an almost lurid! - passion for stating the case of underdog, she had let her pen loose on *The Left Banks* of the Old World.... What struck me on the technical side...was the singular instinct for form possessed by this young lady.... Her business was with passion, hardship, emotions: the locality in which these things are endured is immaterial. So she hands you the Antilles with its sea and sky - 'the loveliest, deepest sea in the

world - **the Caribbean!'** - the effects of landscape on the emotions and passions of a child being so penetrative...

[*Tigers are Better Looking* 148-149)

In this remark Ford uses the words such as *instinct, passion, emotion, and child*, the very words that were used to categorise the nature of the black people, to describe Rhys and her writings. What he admires as a quality in her writing is a new innocent way of writing the 'old world'. Ford accentuates the exotic characteristics in her writings, but in doing so, he constructs Rhys as the 'other' of the European culture and demonstrates the unconscious stereotypes of the race that postures itself as somehow superior and objective.

In *The Left Bank*, three short stories depict the image of the Caribbean: "Trio", "Mixing the Cocktail" and "Again in the Antilles". "Trio" is a brief sketch of a night at a Montparnasse restaurant where the narrator encounters three "compatriots from the Antilles", a man with a coal black skin, a young attractive girl with lighter complexion whom the narrator assumes had some white blood in her veins, and a fat coffee-coloured woman with the Martinique turban. On seeing them, the narrator experiences an acute feeling of home sickness and describes the girl using stereotypical images:

> The fuzzy, negress' hair was exactly the right frame for her vulgar, impudent, startlingly alive little face: the lips were just thick enough to be voluptuous, the eyes with an expression half cunning, half intelligent... supple, slender, a dancer from the *Thousand and One Nights*... (35)

However the girl ironically sings 'F'en ai m-a-r-r-e,' in other words, 'I am fed up' as if she is fed up with the narrator's framing description of her.

According to Sue Thomas in *The Worlding of Jean Rhys* (1999), these short stories intrinsically use the discourses of pre-established images of Dominica in travelogues, in which the people of Dominica are portrayed to be under the 'enervating influence of the sultry climate'. They demonstrate the effects of 'lack of robustness' and 'excessive appetites, especially for alcohol, sex and spicy food; idleness; and a luxurious life on the islands'. (54)

"Mixing the Cocktails" describes a young girl's vague awakening into the adult world amidst the contrast of a British colonial upbringing and the lush, sensuous world of Dominica. Every evening she serves up the mix of angostura, lime and gin, measuring it out with 'uncanny intuition' for the colonial cocktail hour. But this ritual in no way dims her awareness of the exotic world which surrounds her, where, 'the moon does bad things to you if it shines on you when you sleep' (38). Both the incidents and atmosphere from this story recur in Rhys's novel *Voyage in the Dark*.

The narrator who is the young girl herself in the story uses the myth of the pirate Morgan's treasure, the blue sea, drowsiness, the obeah: the tropes that were used to describe Dominica by the travellers, 'A wild place, Dominica, Savage and Lost. Just the place for Morgan to hide his treasure in' (38). But the narrator also tells us that she is described as 'gone native' by her mother who is anxious to define her daughter as English. The mother exclaims: 'you must break yourself of your habit of never listening. You have such an absentminded expression. Try not to look vague' (38). As a result, the narrator feels cut off from her family as well as their Englishness, and she thinks:

> I long to be like Other People! The extraordinary, ungetatable, oddly cruel Other people, with their way of wantonly hurting and then accusing you of being thin-skinned, sulky, vindictive or ridiculous. All because a hurt and puzzled little girl has retired into her shell. (38)

"Again in the Antilles" is the story of a quarrel between the editor of the *Dominica Herald* and *Leeward Island Gazette*, Papa Dom and Mr Hugh Musgrave, a white plantation owner. Papa Dom is described as a 'born rebel' and 'a firebrand' and 'He hated the white people, himself not being quite white, and he despised the black ones, not being quite black... "coloured" we West Indian calls the intermediate shades' (40), while Mr Musgrave is regarded as a dear, but peppery old man, who is 'neither ferocious nor tyrannical' as a plantation owner (40).

When Papa Dom wrote an article, accusing Mr Musgrave for his atrocious act of tyranny, he misquotes a poem. Mr Musgrave takes this opportunity to assert his superiority of race, pointing out that the poem Papa Dom quotes from was not from Shakespeare but from Chaucer, and comments:

> It is indeed a saddening and a dismal thing that the names of great Englishmen should be thus taken in vain by the ignorant of another race and colour. (40)

Papa Dom is not discouraged by this and questions the authorship of the poem. He continues:

> I fail to see that it matters whether it is Shakespeare, Chaucer or the Marquis of Montrose who administers from down the ages the much-needed reminder and rebuke. (40)

According to Sue Thomas, Papa Dom existed in reality but his characteristics were in contradiction to Rhys's portrayal. The real Papa Dom, Augustus Theodore Righton, was not known to be a firebrand. However, by giving Papa Dom a different image and accentuating the conflict between the two racial groups, Rhys foregrounds the colonial situation of Dominica, which is far from the exotic stereotyping image of Dominica portrayed in travelogues.

Together these three short stories mark the imaginative inception of West Indian material, which was integrated into her later work, reaching its fullest development in *Wide Sargasso Sea*. Jean Rhys does not write or use the Caribbean image after her collection *The Left Bank*. Although there are indirect allusions to the tropics in *Quartet* (1929), *After Leaving Mr Mackenzie* (1931) and *Good Morning, Midnight* (1939) Rhys uses West India as a literary trope only in the *Voyage in the Dark* (1934) where the Caribbean background anticipates the fully developed exoticism of *Wide Sargasso Sea*. In this work, Rhys sets the home of the semi-autobiographical heroine, Anna Morgan, in an island of the West Indies. Although she does not directly mention the name of the island, the latitude and the longitude of the island of Dominica are described:

lying between 15 10' and 15 40' N and 61 14' and 61 30' W. A goodly island and something highland, but all overgrown with woods, that book said. And all crumpled into hills and mountains as you would crumple a piece of paper in your hand - rounded green hills and sharply - cut mountains. (17)

In the *Voyage in the Dark*, nineteen year old Anna Morgan comes to England from West Indies and gets a job as a chorus girl with a provincial touring company, falls in love with a wealthy young man in London and becomes his mistress. She is eventually disposed of by him and, through naivete and lack of initiative, falls into compromising circumstances, attracts a succession of lovers, becomes pregnant, and gets money from her first lover to have an abortion. Throughout the novel the warm memory of her childhood in a West Indian island is contrasted to a cold English landscape. Juxtaposing the image of England and Dominica, Rhys seems to question the binary between dreams and reality, and the issue of the mother country for the white Creole colonial.

A series of beautifully constructed memory-frames blend into the narrative and set up a cumulative and complex process of awareness, giving depth, richness and a moral focus to the novel. Anna's memories are exclusively of her life on the island and they are characterised by a sharpness of detail which forms a careful contrast to the dreamy quality of her present life in England. The story opens with the depiction of Anna's alienation in England. For Anna, going to England was not just going to another country, but rather an experience of being born again.

> It was as if a curtain had fallen, hiding everything I had ever known. It was almost like being born again. The colours were different, the smells different, the feelings things gave you right down inside yourself were different. (7-8)

Right from the beginning she tells us that the contrast for her is far deeper than the matter of simple and obvious opposites. The entire psychology, the deeper structures of civilisation are fundamentally opposed. The strong olfactory images which dominate these initial memories underscore the primal nature of Anna's island experience and her deep attachment to her motherland that endures in the cold and darkness of England.

> ...it was funny, but that was what I thought about more than anything else - the smell of the streets and the smell of frangipanni and lime juice and cinnamon and cloves and sweets made of ginger and syrup, and incense after funeral or 'Corpus Christi processions', and the patients standing outside the surgery next door, and the smell of the sea breeze and the different smell of the land breeze. (7-8)

The memory of the island and the smell is so pervasive that she feels 'sometimes it was as if I were back there, it was as if England were a dream' but 'at other times England was the real thing and out there was the dream, but I could never fit them together'. (8)

Gradually Anna gets used to England, except the cold and monotonous cityscapes that looked exactly alike to one another. The landscape of the city that Anna depicts is swarmed with identical house streets and people, and she cannot hide her disappointment at the difference of the image of England that she had read about in books during her childhood.

> I had read about England ever since I could read - smaller meaner everything is never mind - this is London, hundreds thousands of white people rushing along and the dark houses all alike frowning down one after the other all alike, all stuck together, the street like smooth shut-in ravines and the dark houses frowning down. (7)

This depiction of London is similar to that of her contemporary writers from the West Indies. For example, V.S. Naipaul depicts London as the city where everyone shuts their doors behind their backs (*The Mimic Men*). And Samuel Selvon describes it as a city where people with pale stricken faces swarm like insects (*Lonely Londoners*).

The disappointed love for the mother country (England) is not experienced by Rhys alone, other West Indian writers have written about it and it is not specifically the experience of the white Creole. The alienation in England where people keep themselves behind closed doors stays as Rhys's impression of the country.

The binary opposition of England and Dominica is intensified by the confrontation of Hester and Francine, a black servant in the family, the former incarnates England whereas the latter incarnates Dominica. Hester is Anna's stepmother recently arrived from England whom Anna views as the epitome of Englishness:

> She has clear brown eyes which stuck out of her head if you looked at her sideways, and an English lady's voice with a sharp cutting edge to it. Now that I have spoken you can hear that I'm a lady. I have spoken and I suppose you now realize that I'm an English gentlewoman, I have my doubts about you. Speak up and I will place you at once. Speak up, for I fear the worst. That sort of voice. (7)

The relationship between the two is hostile since Hester is suspicious about the racial background of Anna's natural mother often referring to her as a person of 'colour', a derogatory term for a Creole with mixed racial background, she also addresses Anna's maternal Uncle Bo as 'Uncle Boozy having illegitimate children all over the island'. Hester voices the European fear of degeneration, that the European settlers are degraded and dishonoured in many respects if the family stays for five generations in the tropics, and that they become closer to the natives and lose English traits, regress back into barbarism and are thus inferior to the English people.

Anna's attachment with Francine, on the other hand, is akin to the one she has for her own mother. She identifies with her like any little girl would and voices her wish to be like her, 'I wanted to be black, I always wanted to be black. I was happy because Francine was there.... Being black is warm and gay, being white is cold and sad.' (13)

Francine teaches Anna songs and stories, something which feminists like T. Minh-ha Trinh in her book *Woman, Native, Other : Writing Postcoloniality and Feminism* (1989) refer to as subversive forms of patriarchal linear history that connect to orality and the circular time of women. Francine is connected to that orality or the physical domain of Anna when she says, '...when she wasn't working Francine would sit on the doorstep and I liked sitting there with her. Sometimes she told me stories, and at the start of the story she had to say

'Timm Timm,' and I had to answer Bois Seche' (68). Anna confides in Francine and is soothed by her when she has her first menstrual period, fortifying her attachment with Francine further, even at the cost of alienating Hester.

Francine is the one who is connected to the place of maternal *chora* a term used by Julia Kristeva in *New French Feminisms: An Anthology* (1981) for the semiotic pre-oedipal phase, a state of language anterior to the word, the undifferentiated state of continuity with the womb or maternal body. Rereading *Voyage in the Dark* from this perspective opens up the field for displacement and deconstruction and Kristeva's call for a new discourse on maternity that acknowledges the importance of the maternal function in the development of subjectivity and culture. Anna is acutely sensitive to the issue of race that separates her from Francine and ultimately results in Francine's hostility towards her. She realises that they are divided by a discourse based on categorisation created by deep-rooted myths based on superficial differences.

In this sense, Rhys demonstrates through her fiction, the deep fissure created by colonialism and she refutes the idea of easy reconciliation amongst the races, despite the fact that her heroine feels more akin to the culture of the oppressed. In doing so, she does not reiterate the modernist's representation of black culture as European "Id" in Freudian terms or a dark side of the modern European man's psyche. Anna knows she is white and being white means for her to be subsumed in the linear time: 'being white is getting like Hester, and all the things you get – old and sad and everything. I kept thinking 'No... No...No'. And I knew that day that I'd started to grow old and nothing could stop it'. (72)

The figure of mother/land is an absence: just as Anna's real mother is dead, the maternal link to the land is lost. Francine who represents Dominica and Hester who represents England are figures of substitute mothers but they are unable to fill the void left by her mother's absence. Towards the end, after she has an abortion, Anna dreams of crossing the sea and going back to her home in Dominica. What she dreams of is her native island Dominica although the trees are all wrong as they are English trees. She attempts to go back to her motherland by holding on to the branch of one of the English trees, but the deck of the ship expands and prevents her from landing. Then she hears that somebody has fallen overboard and sees a child coffin in which the boy bishop 'a little dwarf with a bald head' with 'a priest's robes and a large blue ring on his third finger' is sitting. He is alive, and commences the summoning, saying 'In nomine Patris, Filli...' Anna thinks that she ought to kiss the ring but she cannot take her mind off from someone who has fallen overboard. Then she notices that the boy bishop has large light eyes in a narrow cruel face rolled like a doll. The bishop could be a caricatural representation of the church which justified slavery. Anna tries to get ashore without success, powerless and tired among confused figures.

It becomes clear in this dream scene that Anna cannot go back home. Her return is blocked in her dream as well as in her mind, just as she cannot be like Francine. In other words, Dominica is her lost homeland where she is denied a return, and she cannot, as the sign of her obedience, kiss the ring of the bishop, who represents Christianity, the patriarchal order as well as England, and she tries incessantly to get ashore. She cannot go either way and is trapped in the sea. This dream scene reveals that Anna is not allowed to identify with Dominica as her home, even though she loves it and feels as an outsider in England.

Rhys's sense of displacement and cultural rift created a curious racial identity with blacks and an affinity for exile. Rhys's own attitude towards blacks as revealed in her work is complex and is further complicated by her own Creole background. She identifies herself as a Dominican 'I am the real West Indian, I am the fifth generation on my mother's side.' However, she cannot return to Dominica which she loves so much, nor can she become like Hester. Home is lost just as Anna's mother is lost.

Rhys's literary legacy as a Caribbean writer is important for many reasons. Firstly, her fiction sensitises us to the complex ways in which different groups at different times have tried or not tried - to be at home in the islands. Secondly, it recreates the peculiar insider/ outsider perspective of the white Creole, and the representation of their multiple layered responses fill a gap in the historical record. Thirdly, it subtly reveals connections and visions of the crucial interdependence of black, brown and white women in the Caribbean and the interculturation that results. Fourthly, it unsparingly examines the cost of colonial and patriarchal domination of the Caribbean. The past can never be fully recaptured or redressed, it can only be revisited. Rhys's work facilitates such imaginative revisiting and enables the reader to experience a different sense of relationship to the past, and thus a different way of thinking about cultural identity.

The state of exile and loss of the fixed national identity in Rhys's fiction can be compared to the other modernist writers. Rhys's sense of home and exile is different from that of Hemingway, who in an epigraph, a letter to a friend in *A Moveable Feast* (1950) considered, exile as a beneficial experience that enriches one's life. 'If you are lucky enough to have lived in Paris as a young man, then wherever you go for the rest of your life, it stays with you, for Paris is a moveable feast' (Letter to a friend). The position which Rhys takes on dislocation and exile is different from the one conceptualised by modernists like Hemingway whose idea of exile was not only race-neutral but inspiring. Rhys's position, situated between England and Dominica recalls Said's definition of exile in his *Reflection on Exile and Other Essays* (2000). According to Edward Said, 'Once an organic bond between nationhood and citizenship is broken it cannot be reconstituted, and nationalism and exile become opposites that cannot be reconciled; exile, unlike nationalism, is fundamentally a discontinuous state of being'. (360)

For Said, the potential of exile lies not in its ability to raise the hardship of exile into poetic inspiration but in its ability to transform the foundation of humanistic belief. In this sense Rhys's inability to identify completely with any one nationality and her chosen state of in-betweenness can be considered as a statement against the logic of nationalism, or sharp boundaries that separate self from the other in a critique of colonialism and the war. Rhys's chosen state of exile is a political statement that questions the prefabricated values of belonging at a time when nationalism was prevalent in Europe.

References

Bryan, Edward. *The History, Civil and Commercial of the British Colonies in the West Indies* (London 1793-1801). Vol 2: 7-16 quoted in Thomas *The Worlding of Jean Rhys*.

Ford, F.M. "Preface" to *The Left Bank's* selection from *The Tigers Are Better Looking*. London: Andre Deutsch, 1968.

Gregg, Veronica Marie. *Jean Rhys's Historical Imagination: Reading and Writing the Creole*. Chapel Hill: University of North Carolina Press, 1995.

Hemingway, Ernest. "Epigraph, a letter to friend", *A Moveable Feast*. (1950) UK: Penguin, 1973.

Kristeva, Julia. "Woman Can Never Be Defined". Trans. Marilyn A. August in *New French Feminisms: An Anthology*. Eds. Elaine Marks and Isabelle de Courtivon. Brighton: Harvester Press, 1981.

Naipaul, V.S. "Without A Dog's Chance", *New York Review of Books*. 18 May 1972, pp. 29-31.

Plante, David. "Remembrance." 275-76 quoted by Veronica Marie Gregg in *Jean Rhys's Historical Imagination*.

Rhys, Jean. "Again in the Antilles", *The Collected Short Stories*. New York: Norton & Company, 1992.

___. "Trio", *The Collected Short Stories*. New York: Norton & Company, 1992.

___. "Mixing the Cocktail", *The Collected Short Stories*. New York: Norton & Company, 1992.

___. *Voyage in the Dark*. New York: W.W. Norton, 1982.

___. *Smile Please: An Unfinished Autobiography*. New York: Harper and Row, 1979.

Said, Edward. *Reflections on Exile and Other Essays*. Cambridge, Massachusetts: Harvard University Press, 2000.

Thomas, Sue. *The Worlding of Jean Rhys*. Connecticut: Greenword Press, 1999.

Trinh, T. Minha-ha. *Woman, Native, Other: Writing Postcoloniality and Feminism*. Bloomington and Indianapolis: Indiana University Press, 1989.

5

Between Two Cultures: A Look at Seepersad Naipaul's Stories

PURABI PANWAR

Seepersad Naipaul, V. S. Naipaul's father, was a journalist on the Trinidad *Guardian* until his death in 1953. He published a collection of stories titled *The Adventures of Gurudeva* on his own in 1943. The book did reasonably well. Later, V. S. Naipaul published it in 1976 with an Introduction so as to put the stories in their context. A look at the sociocultural milieu in general, the indenture in particular as well as *"Prologue to an Autobiography"* which is the first of the two narratives in V.S. Naipaul's *Finding the Centre* is in order as they reveal a lot about Seepersad Naipaul's creativity.

The indenture or forced labour system was a special feature of the colonial regime to recruit labourers from colonies in Asia and Africa to cane/sugar/ coffee/ tea plantations in countries like West Indies, Fiji, Guyana etc, which were also colonies. This system of forced labour or indenture prevailed from 1845 to 1917 when recruiting agents went to the interiors of India and lured poor, mostly landless peasants to work on the plantations. Since most of these peasants lived considerably below the poverty line, they thought they would lose nothing in trying out this career option.

A trip to Kolkata (then Calcutta) where the formalities were completed and the long and uncomfortable sea voyage began for people most of whom had hardly ever stepped out of their village earlier. Crossing the *kala pani* was a traumatic experience and many died on the way. Those who survived made friends on the ship, establishing bonds that survived a lifetime and transcended differences of caste, creed and religion. They called each other *jahazi bhai,* and remained like blood brothers throughout their lives. Since the voyage across the *kala pani* was bound to bring them into close contact with *mlecchhas*, it was better to be fortified with religious texts like the *Ramacharitmanas* and the *Mahabharata* as well as the *Gita* in some cases, which would sustain and inspire these poor people on alien soil in the hours of grief. Public readings from these texts would relieve the gloom of their existence and bring some light into their lives which were full of hardships. Most of them liked to imagine themselves in *vanavasa* or exile like Rama and Lakshmana, from which they would emerge as better and purer human beings. Another thing that kept their spirits up in the darkest hours was the chanting of the *Hanuman Chalisa* which is supposed to ward off evil in any form.

Since most of these people were poor and illiterate unlike their latter day counterparts in countries of the west, they could not maintain any links with India, nor did they have any papers to prove where they had migrated from. Once they had signed the agreement or *'girmit'* as they called it, they had signed away their freedom as indentureship was no better than slavery. They called themselves *'girmitiyas'* and worked on plantations, living in pitiable conditions, hardly better than the African slaves in the USA. The only difference was that indentureship was for a period of five years. After that they could go back to India or sign up another period of indenture. When some of them made an attempt to come back to India after five years, they found that whatever little land and small cottages they had owned here, had been grabbed by relatives/ neighbours. So they went back to the country of adoption and served another term or two, finally settling down there itself.

If we attempt to theorise diaspora, never mind which time frame it belonged to, we need to be conscious of the ways in which mourning and grief acquire historical depth along with blurred racial memory. In the words of Vijay Mishra, 'Without memory, without a sense of loss, without a certain will to mythologise, life for many displaced persons will have become intolerable and diaspora theory would lose its ethical edge' (Mishra 44). The diasporic sensibility is valuable to bridge culture through a widening of experience. Experience might be widened but bridging cultures, especially for one who has been away from the mother country and usually not in touch with it, is almost impossible. In the process of diasporan experiences a sense of loss and unhappiness especially when he or she has no ways or means to keep in touch with the country of origin is inevitable.

'The ambition to be a writer was given me by my father,' says V. S. Naipaul in 1984 in "Prologue to an Autobiography" (*Finding the Centre*). This is the first time that he spoke about his family, his childhood in Trinidad and his early years in England. As for his father's works, one is left with only a slim volume of stories and can attempt to analyse his works from them and what his son has to say about him. How was it received when it was first published? V.S. Naipaul says in his *Introduction* that the book was a success from the financial point of view. A thousand copies were printed and almost all of them were sold out, though the price, one dollar, 4 shillings was steep by Trinidad standards. As for the reader response, there were one or two letters of abuse from people who thought the author had written damagingly about the Indian community.

Seepersad Naipaul was a bit of a rebel from what one reads about him in the *Introduction*. His own father called Naipaul, or Naipal or Nypal, was brought to Trinidad from eastern Uttar Pradesh, somewhere near Gorakhpur, as a baby some time in the 1880s by his mother. This brings me to a fact that I had not mentioned earlier. When colonial migration started, those who ventured beyond the *kala pani* were all men. After some time the colonisers realised that unless women migrated along with men, they would not settle down in the country of adoption. So, a quota of 40 per cent was fixed for women. Still, only the very brave or desperate women opted for migration as they had nothing to look forward to in India. Naipaul's grandmother who belonged to the Panday (or Parray) clan, migrated with a small baby. To quote V. S. Naipaul, 'She must have been deeply disgraced, because she was willing to go alone with her baby to a far-off island to which other people of the region were going...she intended her son to be a pundit; and in the district of Diego Martin she found a good pundit who was willing to take her son in and instruct him' (*Finding the Centre*).

So Naipaul's grandfather became a pundit, an important and respected vocation in Trinidad even today. Why and how did his son become a journalist and nurture an ambition to become a writer? According to V.S. Naipaul, 'It was a version of the pundit's vocation' (ibid, 67). One can read in this ambition a desire to remain exclusive and different in a society where there was a lot of manual work and very little reading and writing. Seepersad Naipaul could never get out of Trinidad which he would have liked to, one feels. Trinidad society was a closed one, it did not permit too much liberal thinking or writing, something he found out as a journalist. Yet this was the only society he knew, the only society he could portray authentically in his writing. V.S. Naipaul puts the stories in their context when he says, 'They are a unique record of the life of the Indian or Hindu community in Trinidad in the first fifty years of the century. They move from a comprehension of the old India in which the community is at first embedded to an understanding of the colonial Trinidad which defines itself as their background, into which they then merge.' (Introduction, *The Adventures of Gurudeva*)

The character of Gurudeva, a village strong man who might well have emerged as a politician at district level, is based on a relative, someone who had married into V. S.

Naipaul's mother's family but had been turned out from it, the mention of his name forbidden. Incidentally, V.S. Naipaul's mother's family, the Capil Deos of Chaguanas, were rich and powerful, a family on which the Tulsis in *A House for Mr Biswas* is based. Seepersad Naipaul remained dependent on them throughout his life. He did not like it and tried to make fun of them in his works, an attitude that is carried on by Mr Biswas in *A House for Mr Biswas*.

Generally a writer's initial creative works are based on his or her personal experiences. Seepersad Naipaul's father was a very cruel and mean person, who treated his wife very badly. One finds Gurudeva, the protagonist, treating his wife Ratni in a similar fashion. He would not let her laugh because he said it was bad manners in a newly married girl. If she did laugh, he would silence her with a look or a slap. One can read it as a trope for the coloniser-colonised relationship. In a colonial set up a woman faced exploitation on two counts – for being a woman and for belonging to the colonised race. Of course Ratni put up with everything, including the battering which she accepted as her lot.

Ironically, even her parents did not complain about it but took it as something she had to go through so as to cleanse herself of sins she had committed in her previous birth. In fact the father was rather happy, even gleeful at the way in which their daughter put up with all the ill treatment and saw in it the exemplary way in which a woman could go anywhere, do anything. The mother took all the credit herself and marvelled at the way in which her daughter put up with all this, concluding, 'Thank God for that. It says a lot for the exemplary upbringing I have bequeathed her.' In these lines the discriminating reader would find not only a mother's word of praise for a daughter who fulfilled the role of a passive wife as she had been taught in a patriarchal society, but praise for the way in which the colonised had been conditioned to put up with the exploitation of the coloniser, without so much as a word of protest. One finds a similar situation in literary works written in Indian languages in the colonial era in which colonial principles are upheld directly as well as in an implied manner as in the case of Gurudeva and Ratni.

There are times when the colonised wanted to switch roles with the coloniser even as one realised that it was nothing but wishful thinking and far from reality. So Gurudeva craved for fame, 'He wanted to be looked upon with awe by the whole village. He hankered to be popular, but to be popular in a spectacular way.' This desire for fame and success in the world was something that Naipaul's father craved for, could not attain and transmitted the same to his son. The main reason that made Naipaul disassociate himself totally from his kin in his ancestral village in eastern Uttar Pradesh when he visited it, was because they were poor people. To come back to Gurudeva, his desire for fame and power found an expression in acquiring a number of mounted sticks, the sort that lathaits or stick fighters use. No one was supposed to touch the sticks as that made them want to draw blood. As time passed '...almost everybody in the village, knew that Gurudeva was a man who kept mounted sticks; and they respected and feared him for that as much as they respected and feared the sticks themselves.' I have read that in the 18th and 19th centuries when zamindars had stick fighters to suppress their tenant farmers, it was believed that some of them had mounted sticks that would do as they were asked by their master, on their own. In distant Trinidad this became part of racial memory and is used to convey an illusion of strength and authority.

Gurudeva's adventures as a stick man were bound to land him in jail and they did. As one reads about his experiences in jail, one compares it with the experiences of the *girmitiyas* when they signed the bond. However, when he came out of prison, Gurudeva was very philosophical about it. He told his family 'If it wasn't for the family you miss in jail, you won't find jail bad.' Of course this was bravado; he had had a bad time in jail. He had never really worked and the hard labour there was too much for him. But somehow by chanting a prayer when he was supposed to be working, he escaped some of it. On being admonished by the warder, he did not sing while at work but every morning before the jailor came, he would sing in his cell. Ironically, this is how he became religious, though he did not know much about religion. One feels that this was how the *girmit* people became religious, holding their copies of the *Ramayana* and the *Gita* close to themselves, chanting verses from them or the *Hanuman Chalisa* to ward off evil in an alien land where circumstances were anything but congenial.

Talking about his father, V.S. Naipaul said, 'He belonged, or was sympathetic, to the reforming movement known as the Arya Samaj, which sought to make of Hinduism a pure philosophical faith' (*Finding the Centre* 79). The differences between Sanatanis and Arya Samajis in northern India in late 19th and early 20th centuries, were sure to have an impact on Indian society in Trinidad and they did. So, Gurudeva became religious because he liked the exclusivity that went with being a pundit and the respect that commanded. I am told that in Trinidad even today a Brahmin commands immense respect, especially if he happens to be from India. A friend who had served there for a two-year term under the Indian Council for Cultural Relations (ICCR) sponsorship , told me that someone he knew went there on a similar assignment, found the knowledge of Sanskrit and the ability to perform pujas and be a priest at marriages, much in demand. Ultimately he left his teaching post in Delhi and settled down in Trinidad as a pundit. This long digression only goes to show how the Indians in Trinidad held on to their religious beliefs. It also suggests why Gurudeva turned to religion, particularly to Sanatana Dharma, as a security.

Under these circumstances, he turned to all those things that would give him a 'Hindu Brahmin' identity. Ironically all those things were superficial like tying a dhoti instead of wearing trousers, living in a kuti, a thatched hut, eating food cooked on a chulha cleansed with a daubing of cowdung, not letting persons who ate fish, meat or pork or who had not bathed, enter his hut etc. with a lot of effort he learnt Hindi. Irony is Seepersad Naipaul's forte, something that he passed on to his son. It is not difficult to make out whose side Naipaul senior was on, though he did not spell it out clearly in these stories.

One can trace a link between these stories and a column that Seepersad Naipaul occasionally wrote for Trinidad *Guardian* with the byline 'The Pundit' instead of his own name. V.S. Naipaul feels that MacGowan, the editor of Trinidad *Guardian* rewrote these columns, something that his (V.S. Naipaul's) mother refuted. He also felt that '...some of the material was plagiarised by my father from the reformist Hindu literature he had begun to read.' (*Finding the Centre* 69). I have not been able to access any of these articles so as to be able to compare them with the stories. One can only take V.S. Naipaul's words for the influence that MacGowan exercised on Naipaul's writings. This is how he puts it, 'The Hindu who wants to be a pundit has first to find a guru. My father wanting to learn to write, found MacGowan. It was MacGowan, my father said, who had taught him how to write; and all his life my father had for MacGowan the special devotion which the Hindu has for his guru' (*Finding the Centre* 67).

I have referred to some of the autobiographical elements in the stories earlier. There are others worth a mention. Seepersad Naipaul married Draupadi who came from the clan of Capil Deos, a rich and influential family in Chaguanas. It was a close-knit family where decisions were taken at the top, by Seepersad's mother-in-law and her two elder sons-in-law, decisions which everyone was supposed to accept. While on one hand it did keep the family together, it also bred a simmering discontent among the younger members. On a microcosmic level it was a coloniser-colonised relationship which Naipaul's father had to accept as his financial instability made him a dependent on his wife's family, something he resented. Another reason behind this resentment was the fact that he himself empathised with the Arya Samaj movement, having read about it, while his wife's family maintained a strict Sanatani stance, as they were orthodox pundits.

This found an expression in the string of invectives that Gurudeva hurled against his wife Ratni's parents as well as other members of the family. Even later, in *A House for Mr Biswas,* Mohun Biswas displayed a similar resentment for Mrs Tulsi, his mother-in-law, and all the others who wielded power in the Hanuman House where Mrs Tulsi lived with the family. The resentment was transmitted from father to son who fictionalised it and later remarked, 'To grow up in a family or clan like ours was to accept the ethos of the feud' (*Finding the Centre 77*). This again, can be given a wider interpretation.

In a large family made up of all kinds of persons, some are bound to be economically, socially and politically stronger than others. In such a set up the politics of power is very similar to that in a colony, albeit on micro level. Seepersad Naipaul's position in the joint family with his wife's mother as the matriarch, was rather precarious. It is possible that that he thought his association with MacGowan would enhance his position professionally and by implication in the family hierarchy as well. Unfortunately MacGowan left and without a mentor his career nosedived. Gurudeva's liaison with Daisy Seetoolal, a relationship from which he expected a lot and hoped it would enhance his status on all counts, ended disastrously. Ratni had already left for her parents' home earlier and Gurudeva was on his own. Though his mother did console him in the way all mothers do, saying, 'Let she go beta; you goin' get plenty more.' The reader is not so sure. Though Gurudeva faced the Panchayat bravely, the fact that he was not able to make Daisy a proper Indian wife and the very suggestion made her leave him, made him socially vulnerable.

The use of language in the stories is political and therefore significant. Seepersad Naipaul is writing about people who are first or second generation immigrants from the interiors of India, namely eastern Uttar Pradesh and Bihar. When they left their villages to work in plantations in distant colonies they knew only Hindi or, more specifically, the dialect they spoke at home. Their exposure to English speaking plantation owners made them pick up a smattering of the language. However, in keeping with their mindset, they retained the idiom of their mother tongue even while they spoke English. This comes alive in *The Adventures of Gurudeva* making it an authentic Caribbean-Indian text. In the colonial and post-colonial set up, English became the language of power even when this involved adapting it to one's sociocultural milieu. Thus the standard blessing when someone touched the feet of an elder was 'live', a literal translation of its Hindi equivalent 'jiyo'. I quote a short passage to convey the way Indian words and ideas were retained though English was the language generally used.

> 'You will know just now,' said Gurudeva... 'You know a Brahmin must look on a cow like he is looking on his own mooma?'
> 'I know that.'
> 'You had a red-and-white cow?'
> 'I had a red-and-white cow. Chitkabari.'
> 'It was a bahila – a cow that don't put down?'
> 'If you say a cow is like your own mooma, you shouldn't call it bahila. Is not a good word. It don't sound nice,' Ramdas said.

It is the skillful use of language which makes the lives of the *'girmit'* people and their children come alive, especially to an Indian reader who is familiar with the sociocultural milieu and the religious debates which were politicised at home as well as overseas, among the Indian diaspora. Much later, in 1981, Salman Rushdie experimented with the English language in *Midnight's Children* and brought it down from its pedestal. But one must remember that Seepersad Naipaul was not experimenting, he used the language which was actually spoken by the *'girmit'* people. Some of V.S. Naipaul's early works, even parts of *A House for Mr Biswas* have strains of it, but in the stories of Gurudeva one savours this patois, part of the attempt made by those people of Indian origin to make themselves at home in an alien land and empower themselves with the coloniser's language, modifying it to their own need and taste.

The contemporary reader needs to consider this linguistic aspect of the stories very seriously for along with an urge to empower themselves with the coloniser's tongue, it also indicates an inclination to retain links with the mother country.

Thus the conversation of the characters often reads as if it had been literally translated from Hindi. It takes the diaspora one or two generations to feel at home in the country of adoption, longer if there has been no premigration sociocultural orientation regarding the country of adoption, which might serve as some sort of a familiarisation process. Till then the negotiation between two cultures, two languages, is always uneasy and nowhere is it perceived clearly than in the literature produced by the first or even second generation diaspora, especially when migration has been a more or less coerced process as in the case of the indentured labourers, the *'girmit'* people. Caribbean literature like anything else in the Caribbean region, is more or less a fusion today. However, within this fusion there are different ethnic groups who like to retain their exclusive identity, their culture, language etc. I realised this when I heard descendants of the *'girmit'* people speak about themselves, their struggle to forge a distinct ethnic identity and the exploitative attitude of the colonisers, at a seminar organised on the anniversary of the Indian Arrival Day, an occasion that is still celebrated on a large scale in Trinidad. This is the context in which the modern day reader should read Seepersad Naipaul's stories so as to comprehend them and the circumstances in which they were written.

References

Mishra, Vijay. "The Art of Impossible Mourning", *In Diaspora: Theories, Histories, Texts*. Ed. Makarand Paranjape. New Delhi: Indialog Publications, 2001.

Naipaul, Seepersad. *The Adventures of Gurudeva* (1976) New Delhi: Buffalo Books, 2001.

Naipaul, V.S. *Finding the Centre : Two Narratives*. Andre Deutsch Ltd., 1984.

6

The Indo-Caribbean Short Story: Negotiations between Social Identity and Self-Concept

SUDHA RAI

Stuart Hall in his essay "Negotiating Caribbean Identities" (Hall: 281-292) puts forward the thesis that: 'the Caribbean is the first, the original and the purest diaspora,' since 'everybody there comes from somewhere else.' Its people bear the 'stamp of historical violence and rupture' because of the nature of their physical severance from their countries and cultures of origin, and the circumstances of deceit and exploitation, that surrounded them in their new promised land of plenty. Hall argues further that 'the way Caribbeans negotiate their identities has a message for the rest of the world....for wherever one finds diasporas one always finds precisely those complicated processes of negotiation and transculturation which characterize Caribbean culture' (284).

Researches in social psychology in the areas of prejudice and discrimination, especially racial discrimination show us that for identities to be successfully negotiated and established, social contexts of 'reciprocity' and 'receptivity' (negated when there are conflicting and hostile polarisations into the 'we' and 'they'), need to be strengthened. In the absence of these nurturing attitudes, ethnic groups in the Caribbean who lost their self-esteem under colonial rule, continue to negotiate the colonial legacy of racism and marginalisation. As Baron and Byrne observe in their study of the origins of prejudice:

> Prejudice stems from a number of different sources. According to *realistic conflict theory*, it derives from competition between social groups for scarce resources. The *social learning view* suggests that children acquire prejudice from parents, teachers, friends and mass media. *Social categorization* suggests that prejudice stems from our strong tendencies to divide our social world into "us" and "them". (230)

The contribution of *stereotypes* – 'cognitive frameworks involving beliefs about the typical characteristics of the members of social groups' in the practice of discrimination, that continues to keep communities apart, needs to be further taken into account.

Through the two frameworks outlined here – Stuart Hall's theory of the distinct nature of Caribbean identities characterised by 'multiple origins' and 'multiple essences' and Baron and Byrne's study of the diverse causes of 'prejudice', – the present paper compares selected Indo-Caribbean short stories from three collections: Seepersad Naipaul's *The Adventures of Gurudeva* (1943), *A Flag on the Island (1967)* by V.S Naipaul and *Jahaji* edited by Frank Birbalsingh *(2000)* briefly dwelling on themes and issues in the first two volumes to problematise the transition from Old Hindu India and the colonial Caribbean, to move to a more detailed focus on recollections of the Caribbean sifted by the Indo-Caribbean diaspora, (while renegotiating their identity in a climate of racism and prejudice in foreign parts), in the third collection. The stories address the leading questions: 'Where am I from?' and 'Who am I after all?' and are tested in the real world as much as in the fantasy world. My paper examines the specific problematic of the contemporary Indo-Caribbean diaspora in its serious, and anguished attempt to negotiate the 'I' by opening the hidden chests of memory, by gathering histories, and by confronting the shifting boundaries of the 'us' and 'them', or the 'we' and 'they'.

Tracing the history of the Indian migration to the Caribbean, Frank Birbalsingh (Introduction to *Jahaji* vii-xxxiv) observes that four lakh Indians came under contract or indenture to the Caribbean between 1834 and 1917. With the freeing of the blacks, the original labour force on the plantations, under the Emancipation Act of 1834, Indians 'occupied the lowest rung of the ladder in Trinidad' (Dr. Eric Williamson, quoted in Birbalsingh: 2000). In his historical sketch, Birbalsingh identifies the period of great political turmoil and instability that ensued after the independence of Trinidad and Tobago in 1962 and Guyana in 1966, caused by rivalry between the Afro-Caribbean and the Indo-Caribbean desire for political power. The dominance of the Afro-Caribbean in post-independence nationalism, precipitated the large wave of Indo-Caribbean migration to Britain, Canada and the United States in the 1970s and 1980s.

The term 'coolie' itself stuck to Indians as a stereotype coming from prejudice, even when Indians had improved their social status considerably. It is this set of historical factors that contributed to themes of 'marginalisation, insecurity and homelessness,' in Indo-Caribbean writing (Birbalsingh :2000).

The first collection of short stories by an Indo-Caribbean writer Seepersad Naipaul titled *The Adventures of Gurudeva* was published in 1943. V.S. Naipaul in his 'Foreword' to the 1976 edition, attributes his father's wish to be a writer, to '... the caste sense, the Hindu reverence for learning and the word, awakened by the beginnings of an English education and a Hindu religious training' (14). Naipaul find the stories to be significantly concerned with Hinduism and the practices of Hinduism (15) as his father was a keen student of Hindu thought.

As a journalist Seepersad Naipaul was already covering Indian or Hindu topics for the *Trinidad Guardian* and the same observation of cultural behaviour, eye for detail, dramatic narrative, control over language and down to earth style is evident in his stories. Naipaul observes that his father's stories: 'are written from within a community and seem to be addressed to that community : a Hindu community essentially ...' (18). He commends the stories as 'the valuable part of the literature of region,' showing 'unusual knowledge and unusual breadth of sympathy' (24).

The Adventures of Gurudeva develops the individual identity of Gurudeva, within the Brahminical joint family of the 1930s and 1940s Carib, projecting a progression from a totally given identity of cultural Brahminical masculinity to an unconscious protest against the lack of choices regarding the formation of the individual self. The first story concludes in fourteen-year-old Gurudeva's conceding to the wishes of his father Jaimungal to marry twelve-year-old Ratni. His school education is rudely interrupted as education itself is viewed as destructive to Hindu caste values and prerogatives. In his journey of caste approved masculinity, other stories in the collection depict Gurudeva hardening into a wife beater, a stick fighter, being sent to prison for a year for attacking a *gatka* player and a policeman. On his return home, he 'transforms' himself by becoming a vegetarian and a teetotaller, fitting into the role model of an austere Pundit identity, even constructing a separate *kuti* for his orthodox pujas. He takes to his career as a Pundit, dispensing with western trousers and learning how to tie a dhoti, in a delectable scene of male cultural bonding, described by Seepersad Naipaul in slow motion: 'So Gurudeva remains a Hindu, and was proud of his being a Hindu, though he hardly knew what Hinduism meant' (76).

Gurudeva sees himself as defender of the *Sanatan Dharma* – the eternal religion. He also stops using the Creole English of the Caribbean, consciously using Hindi in all situations to win respect from family and the village community. At the age of 22, Gurudeva had cherished an ambition to be noticed. His progression from Gurudeva the 'bad-John', to Gurudeva the Pundit who delivers discourses, defending Aryan Hinduism against the attempts by the rival Pundit Biswas, the Hindu reformer preaching in the village, about the need for widow remarriage and freedom from caste practices, to dislodge its worth.

The picture of a traditional Hindu society that accepts arranged marriage, cruelty towards women, patriarchy and the Hindu belief in karma is rendered with wit, involvement and sympathy by S. Naipaul, each story a reflection of his own Hindu predicament of enclosed life within the joint family. With Gurudeva falling in love with Daisy Seetoolal, a Christian convert, modern in her dress, vivid lipstick, and refusal to comply with purdah, there is a turmoil created within the family and village community for Gurudeva has decided to take a second wife and Ratni, his first wife, has chosen to leave him.

The final story in the collection, "Gurudeva is a Bachelor" shows that despite Gurudeva succeeding in convincing the panchayat that he is entitled to take a second wife, (quoting the example of King Dasharatha and his three wives from the Ramayana), as Ratni has not been able to give him a son, the tables are turned on him when Daisy, the new woman, walks out on him, refusing to comply with the orthodox Hindu norms for a wife. His sympathetic portrayal of situations as much from the woman's point of view, as from the Hindu patriarchal consciousness, is a strength in Seepersad Naipaul's narrative technique.

Seepersad Naipaul's stories interweave observation on the situational propriety of using Hindi. When Gurudeva returns from jail, he fumbles in acknowledging Ratni his wife, from whom has been separated for a year. He says 'is orright, is orright,' to her rather than speak in Hindi : 'He ought to have touched her on the head or the shoulder and given her his benediction. He ought at least to have said 'Live'! in Hindi. The movement and the occasion demanded Hindi. But he was shy, as shy as Ratni herself. He felt acutely embarrassed and awkward and found it difficult to say the right words in the right way and in the right language' (79).

As an episodic linear narrative, centred around a single major male protagonist, *The Adventures of Gurudeva* represents the life of the patriarchal Hindu community in the Caribbean village, seeking to consolidate old India, but already, the centred way of life is seen to be eroded by Christianity, the war and the presence of American soldiers, that brings in rapid changes. The faithful rendering of the Hindu community and its caste practices, man–woman relationships, canonical religious texts and the struggle to preserve India in an entirety makes this first collection of Indo-Caribbean short stories a marvelous achievement in representing the social history of a period, as well as the existence and fancies of individuated characters.

Moving to V.S. Naipaul's only volume of short stories *A Flag on the Island*, stories belonging to the 1950s and 1960s, we find a similar centering in Hindu India in the Caribbean. The centre however is now much more exposed to a 'monologic, self-critiquing, philosophic mode that extends the short story as a form of knowledge', and exhibits a position of empowerment 'to life-choices outside the trapped situations of (Caribbean) colonial history.' (see Rai in Panwar ed. *V.S. Naipaul*: 114-125). In this collection, the surging post-colonial consciousness offers an intellectual and psychological explanation of Caribbean society – the separation of African from Indians, and Indian from Chinese, despite their shared history of indentured labour.

In "The Baker's Story" from this collection for example, a confessional narrative about a black man, who attempts to rise from mediocrity and poverty by running a bakery, the light bulb moment occurs for the black, when he realises that to succeed, he has to appoint a Chinese to deal with buyers across the bakery counter. Trinidadians do not accept blacks as bakery shop owners. In the Caribbean social categorisation of that period, the 'us' and the 'them' are differentiated in absolute terms. The narrator of the story wakes up to his new insight about Trinidadian society exclaiming : 'And then I see that though Trinidad have every race and every colour, every race have to do special things. But look man If you want to buy a snowball, who you buying it from? You wouldn't buy it from an Indian or a Chinese or Potogee. You would buy it from a black man ... If an Indian in Trinidad decided to go into the carpentering business the man would starve. Who ever see a Indian carpenter? I suppose the only place in the world where they have Indian carpenters and Indian masons is India' (121). Even his marriage to a Chinese woman, does not permit the black male narrator to be socially acceptable or visible. The inner world and the outer, social identity and self are subjected to separation (in the codified social categorisation in the Caribbean) under the influence of stereotypes and the prejudices that go with them.

Naipaul writes in *An Area of Darkness* of the unwritten social code, the lack of 'dramatic confrontation of opposed worlds' in the West Indies, for Hindu families like his own. While these families registered 'difference,' no attempts were made to intermingle with the members of the other communities. 'To me the worlds were juxtaposed and mutually exclusive' observes Naipaul, defending his Hindu, Brahminical perspective from George Lamming's charge that Naipaul has not paid, 'sufficient attention' to 'non-Indian groups' in his works. The many Indian identities and the many Indian realities that Naipaul problematises through his West Indian experience, indent the smooth surface of the 'imaginary homeland' essentialised through artifacts in his grandmother's home. He eventually describes himself as 'robbed of loyalties' because of his relocation in England.

Naipaul's travelogue *The Middle Passage: The Caribbean Revisited*, incorporates the voice of Naipaul who is a first class passenger on the Spanish ship Francisco Bobadilla bound for the West Indies, who learns that the ship has just brought in between 700 and 1200 immigrants to England. The dream of making it good in a second land of peace and plenty – England – has been sold to immigrant clients. 'Like all good West Indians he was unwilling to hear anything against England,' Naipaul remarks of a fellow passenger on the ship. Having been away for almost a decade in England, Naipaul is perturbed to hear Indians denounce Negro in racist terms and condemn miscegenation. He writes: 'Believing that racial co-existence, if not cooperation, is of urgent importance to the West Indies, I was disturbed by these Indian views and wanted to explore them further'

(22). However the multicultural collectivity of the West Indies is under siege, from within because of the competing interests of Africans and Indians, and from without, from diasporic non-European populations, each seeking economic advancement and political power.

In his short stories, Naipaul dramatises the multilayered cultural identities within the 'we' and the 'they'- of religious affiliation particularly. Family histories as in the story "My Aunt Gold Teeth" are sketched with familiarity and wit, homing in on the contestations of Presbyterian Christianity with orthodox Hinduism. The humiliations of poverty, experienced so keenly by Naipaul's father, as a trainee pundit, are sounded out in the story "The Mourners" from a social class perspective. The rejection of Hindu religion for its 'animistic rites, its idolatry' reported by the schoolteacher Randolph after conversion to Christianity ("A Christmas Story"), the forbidding colonial school casting traditional Hindu identity afresh ("The Raffle"), the 'we' of the mother's side of the family and the 'they' of the father's side ("The Enemy"), inter-racial marriages, the American presence firing new dreams of prosperity, the upsurge of religious revivalism like the Aryan leadership and swamihood (caricatured in his novels *The Mystic Masseur*, *A House for Mr Biswas* and *The Mimic Men*), and the babble of dialects and the corruption of purist languages – each shift in an essentialist community identity Naipaul depicts, breeds confusion and violence for the self, and the urge to seek another firmer foothold, that in turn proves futile.

"A Flag on the Island", the title story in the collection focuses on an American soldier Frankie, revisiting his past in the Caribbean, setting up a narrative perspective an interesting interplay of past and present, imagination and reality, converging on the native and the American experience in the past, and that of the native and the tourist in the present. Forced to interrupt his voyage on a liner with a stopover because of an impending hurricane, the narrator can no longer secure himself within attitudes of detachment. He is compelled to negotiate his friendships on the island and to dwell on all the games that are being played out under the idea of postcolonial Caribbean identity. It is significant that the book in the reception lobby on display that Naipaul directs the reader to on Frankie's arrival on the Island is titled *I Hate You: One man's search for identity* by one Mr Blackwhite. The narrator observes in the course of the narrative of flux and redrawing of political attitudes that the Caribbean is in the vortex of, that 'interests only seem to coincide' and that 'what changes changes' (184). Frankie's journey of understanding of identities is concluded with his return to the liner, and the illusion of a return to home.

In his short fiction, Naipaul initiates the representation of the shifting sands of hybridity through the intermixture of genres that negotiate the void at the heart of the self, interrogating the loss of a central philosophical and aesthetic tradition, and the absence of an audience for his works. His later works expand the meditations of the diasporic narrator sounded out in the long short story "A Flag on the Island", refining a narrative technique that dwells on the ironies of 'we' and 'they', set in motion by colonial history. Layer upon layer of oral histories, researched histories, autobiographical histories and subliminal memories negotiate the silences and erasures within families and between communities sifting the lies, the partial truths and the struggle to survive under a new cultural order, while demolishing orthodoxies. The absent self in Naipaul's stories is constructed through tropes that represent the experiences of exile, violence, exploitation, alienation, and in-betweenness, setting up an aesthetics of fragmentation, haunted by the compulsive need to obtain the whole picture.

Other patterns of negotiation of the Indo-Caribbean identity by the diaspora in Canada and the U.K. are etched out in the diversity of perspectives collected in the anthology of Indo-Caribbean fiction *Jahaji*, edited by Frank Birbalsingh (2000). The title *Jahaji* refers to the new identity of Indians forged in the course of their arduous ship journey to the Caribbean. Singh traces the history of the Indian *jahaji* and the subsequent history of the stigmatisation of Indians as *coolies*.

My attempt here is to analyse how the protagonists in the stories from *Jahaji* negotiate the tentative uprooted identity forged in the Caribbean and its reconstitution abroad, through the agency of religious revivalism, fantasy and the esemplastic power of the diasporic imagination, sifting cultural and racial stereotypes of social identity so as to formulate the troublesome, absent self. The stories in *Jahaji* fall into three categories. First, the stories about individuals who have lived only in the Caribbean. To the second category belong the stories, about people who have lived in the Caribbean and migrated at a later date. In the third category are the stories about those individuals who have never lived in the Caribbean but have at least one Indo-Caribbean parent. (Birbalsingh xxviii)

How far apart are the 'we' and the 'they'? Can they come closer and if so how? The stories in the collection chalk out the pathways of interrogation taken by the protagonists, leading sometimes to a retreat behind the wall of the 'we' or occasionally, in attempts to redefine the notion of community by forging friendships across the divide, though the attempts are usually unfruitful.

The story "Pooran, Pooran" by Ismith Khan captures the theme of 'the harsh, rural living conditions of the earliest indentured immigrants, as well as their first experience of change as reflected in the educational opportunity which Pooran has of attending secondary school in the city.' (Birbalsingh xxviii). The story concludes with Pooran appealing to his father: 'Babooji can I go with you to plant the sugarcane fields? I don't want to go back to learn any more in the big college' (14). In this story the boy withdraws to the safe sanctuary of the 'us'. Tradition and the small warm circle of security provided by his labourer father, and mother who cooks delicious fried fish and egg plant in coconut oil, contest the aspiration towards the negotiation of a new multicultural identity through the agency of colonial education, a system that proves irrelevant, forbidding, and alienating.

In Rabindranath Maharaj's story "Swami Pankaj", a successful plantation owner of coconut and papaw trees, Pankaj, who has developed his own secret formula for countering the plantation disease caused by the red beetle, migrates to Canada, after his wife's death and his own illness, to take up a job as a taxi driver. He confides in the male narrator of the story, who is virtually the only friend he trusts, that his dream is to master certain spiritual techniques like the sadhus in the Himalayas. He eventually decides to make the return migration to India, in order to fulfil his dream.

Other details of his life that are mentioned tell the reader that his children have left him to his whims and to a solitary struggle in Canada. In Trinidad before his migration to Canada, he had been subjected to racial hostility: 'I was the enemy (he says), not because I do harm to anybody, but because I didn't fail' (47). Pankaj feels he has taken ill because he has been subjected to a lot of 'bad-mind' in Trinidad. It is both ironic and significant that he decides to journey by ship to India. The words he quotes from his favourite Swami – 'wherever we go we leave a piece of ourselves,' punctuate Pankaj's negotiation with his Caribbean past, a journey that concludes in the separation and endorsement of his orthodox, cultural Indian layer, in an essentialist fashion. Both the Caribbean and Canada are constituted as the 'they', constructed as domains marked by mistrust and hostility.

Other stories in the collection *Jahaji* grapple with the tensions between opposed cultural groups in Canada or England and the concerted effort to revisit the past and its traumas, to consciously test one's loyalties by setting up a dialogue between the past and the present. In the story "Going to Guyana" by Cyril Dabydeen, Chris who is on a plane bound for Guyana, takes stock of his cultural affiliations: 'I'd been living in Canada much too long, and now I felt compelled to return' he muses and admits that he'd 'put off returning until now, wrestling with an awkward but prolonged alienation, in the county, as with women in infatuation or love' (108). Anxiety ridden about renewing contact with the tensions of his Caribbean past, which are already simmering in the cross-fire of conversation he consciously listens to, between African, Chinese and mulattoes on the plane, Chris learns that 'Guyana now blasted bankrupt.' A new identity is projected in the story by representing Chris's divided loyalties and fluctuating emotions between Nicole, a Canadian whom he's currently dating, (both Chris and Nicole work for the Canadian Government) and Arabella, the African air hostess from Guyana, who attends to him on the plane.

Perceptions of the racial body are at variance, constituted by the community the viewer belongs to. While Nicole finds his looks are 'not Asian at all', Arabella proudly displays him to her family claiming that the west (America) has made no change in him all these years (117). Chris is accommodated in a plane bound for New York as violence erupts in Guyana. The reflective journey through family ties, spatial attachments, ideological positions, psychological conflicts and situational pragmatism is juxtaposed by Dabydeen within the six hour long actual spatial and temporal journey Chris takes, to and fro, on the plane. As he leaves Guyana his home of origin, waving to his family and Arabella, he rationalises '... one more time, not believing it was my final parting: my disappearing act' (120).

For the third generation Indo-Caribbean diaspora born in U.K., the United States or Canada, the door they wish to open to a newfound identity is repeatedly slammed in their faces. In the story "The Interview" by Christine Singh, Kris (short for Krishna) (his father works in the post office, his mother is a nurse), is the butt of veiled racial insults and stereotyping. Christine Singh suggests that the 'here' of U.K. and the 'there' of the Caribbean are equally problematic for Kris. He is caught between parental impositions and expectations of conformity to a Hindu-Trinidadian heritage on the one hand and the otherness of an English society on the other. The story initiates in its structure of the 'interrogations' that Kris is constantly subjected to in British society – about where he comes from, and if he doesn't like it here what is he doing in London and even why doesn't he go back then

– the structure of the interview that he faces later, for an intern's summer job with IBM computers. At the interview, when he is asked where he's from, Kris can only respond with the stark truth: 'I really don't know.' He realises that he is a mismatch to all categories he is labelled with – each of the identities thrust on him is partial, fixed and stereotypical while he is groping towards a new identity, of 'Englishness,' hoping to contribute to the country through his highly developed computer skills. Since the real world cannot accept him for who he is, he has a virtual friend in the reality of a computer diary. The entries are addressed to 'Dear Krishna' a solitary space wherein he can accost his real identity, as his friendships with English boys and girls have fizzled out under parental strictures or white racism.

In Shani Mattoo's story "Sushila's Bhakti" the Caribbean is referred to as a zone of 'national cultural chaos' (174). Sushila, the artist, interrogates her Brahmin roots, Indo-Trinidadian generational history and her present obfuscated identity of Indo-Caribbean Canadian. She achieves this through the making of a painting, using the 'substances' of Indian green mehndi and African metanil yellow. The journey of the diasporic self as a complex of multiple histories and worldviews is represented through the bright colours, and their unique cultural associations which enable her the brief ecstasy of bonding with her roots, though the roots themselves are fragile : 'Having Brahmin roots somewhere deep in her, Sushila knew she had buried connections to that higher self, connections that could be excavated and polished up. She would embark on a revival of her distant past to take control of her present' (174-175).

Negotiation of identity involves the process of selecting identities, trying on selves. Brahminical men, because of their patriarchal privilege cannot be selected, as Sushila embarks on the arduous task, almost out of reach, of connecting with her point of origin. For Sushila, art becomes a process of interrogation that enables her to play with ideas. Perceptions gathering within her tell her that self-concept is not a fixed result but constantly subjected to modification, through relocation, the contexts of relocation and the stage in ones life when one relocates.

Language itself and speech is subjected to loss, erasure or intermixing overriding purist considerations. The rhythm of everyday female rituals such as the kneading of the dough are picked up and given a new thrust as Sushila kneads the green mehndi and the yellow metanil. For the diasporic person compelled to journey from one self-image to another, the symbolic spaces of art are cathartic: 'She played and fretted and worked and invented until she came to a junction where she could take a turn that skirted needing to be pinned down as Hindu, or as "Indian" or as Trinidadian (in themselves difficult identities to pin down) in favour of attempting to write a story of her own using her own tools' (180). Quite an exception to most other stories in the anthology *Jahaji*, the story "Sushila's Bhakti" ends on a note of 'delight'.

"The Propagandist" is the nickname given to Ramkissoon an Indo-Guyanese cane worker (married to Afro-Guyanese Joyce) who works on a plantation owned by the British concern, Briggs and Company. The narrator, a twelve-year-old boy, who is the son of Ramkissoon's neighbour, exposes the Propagandist's greed and miserliness and the shrewd political skills he uses in exploiting all parties during the first elections in the West Indies where the PFP (People's Freedom Party) was likely to oust the British. The PFP with Indian leaders and members finally wins the elections. However the narrator comments: 'The end of the election was the end of an era: nothing in Guyana would ever be the same again. The old serpent of politics had made its fatal entrance into our young and green Caribbean garden of colonial innocence; and we would pay dearly for it' (28).

Ramkissoon's internalisation of colonial racist attitudes towards Africans is highlighted, when Ramkissoon supports Indian cricketers on the Indian team's first tour of the West Indies in 1953, rather than the West Indian cricket team which is composed of Afro-West Indians : 'Since when yuh hear monkey can play bat and ball?' It was a standard colonial jibe – labelling Africans or people of African descent as 'less than human' (19). As Ramkissoon degenerates into a schemer and a drunk, the curtain comes down on his life when he fatally injures himself under the influence of drink. Elahi Baksh emphasises the upheavals that Ramkissoon invites, because of his loss of roots. The finger points at the psychological damages caused by colonialism – the divided self, unable to bond with one's Indian roots or with one's brethren – the Afro-West Indians. In their shared condition of the void within one's identity, the Indo-Caribbean narrator, now member of the diaspora in Canada, and Ramkissoon are connected: '... the world that drove him to death has also driven me in to exile, and I can no longer deny an indissoluble bond between him and me, one that links much more than the two of us together' (30).

The Indo-Caribbean short story through the samples discussed here does not optimistically project the forging of brotherhoods, sisterhoods, or communities that have successfully negotiated the task of rebuilding themselves out of the shambles of history and migration, power and violence in the Caribbean, or in their new diasporic formations in the development world. The focus is on the soul-searching of a central, individual consciousness testifying to the dispersal and fragmentation of communities.

Such a perspective is distinctive from those found in other fictions, which George Lamming identified in his essay "Colonialism and the Caribbean Novel": 'Where community and not person, is the central character' (Lamming: 273). V.S. Naipaul's stories, belonging to the post independence 60s phase of Indo-Caribbean short story, are renderings of the Hindu perspective on the life of communities in the Trinidad, and their partial linkages with other communities, their comedies of rivalry, the ironies of their separation, as well as the beginnings of processes of dispersal and further migration of these groups.

The achievement of the Indo-Caribbean short story to sum up, is the recovery of the ways of life of the Indian community in the Caribbean, representing a pattern of social cohesion with a three-generational span, its origins in the harsh history of indentured labour. Social identity is explored through the issues of religion, caste, gender, language, oral narratives and songs, ethnic difference, rural and urban facts, food, drink and clothing, and through migration. Self-concept is tested against all these aspects of social identity and what the fertile spaces of imagination make of the self. The negotiations of identity are rendered from the perspective of the human aspirations of transplanted Indians, caught in the hegemony of imposed systems of education and religion while battling to preserve the Hindu faith, or Hindi as a language. The nurturing of fancy and of fantasies, of heroism, fame and success within the possibilities offered by a postcolonial momentum of history, make these vividly fleshed out narratives, witness to the oppositional pulls of tradition and modernity, essentialisms and pluralisms. The regional and diasporic stories of West Indian identity, shaped by colonisation, neocolonialism and race stand as witnesses on the threshold of the negotiation of prejudices and hatred, often redrawing the lines between 'we' and 'they', skeptically cross examining the illusion of 'in group' and 'outgroup homogeneity' (Baron and Byrne: 230).

References

Baron, Robert A. and Donn Byrne. eds. *Social Psychology* (1997). New Delhi : Prentice Hall of India Pvt. Ltd., 1999.

Birbalsingh, Frank. ed. *Jahaji: An Anthology of Indo-Caribbean Fiction.* Toronto: TSAR Publications, 2000.

Hall, Stuart. "Negotiating Caribbean Identities", *Postcolonial Discourses.* Ed. Gregory Castle, Oxford: Blackwell Publishers, 2001.

Lamming, George. "Colonialism and the Caribbean Novel," *Postcolonial Discourses.* Ed. Gregory Castle, Oxford: Blackwell Publishers, 2001.

Naipaul, Seepersad. *The Adventures of Gurudeva* (1976). New Delhi: Buffalo Books, 2001.

Naipaul. V.S. *A Flag on the Island* (1967). Harmondsworth: Penguin Books, 1969.

_____. *An Area of Darkness* (1964). New Delhi: Penguin Books India, 1968.

_____. *The Middle Passage: The Caribbean Revisited* (1962): Harmondsworth : Penguin Books, 1969.

Rai, Sudha "Postcolonial Parables of Survival : V.S. Naipaul's *A Flag on the Island"* in *V.S. Naipaul.* Ed. Purabi Panwar. New Delhi : Pencraft International, 2003.

7

The Politics of Historical Reconstruction: A Study of V.S. Naipaul's *The Loss of El Dorado* and *A Way in the World*

VISHNUPRIYA SENGUPTA

In the Foreword to *The Loss of El Dorado* Naipaul writes:

> I was born in 1932 in a small country town called Chaguanas, a mile or two inland from the Gulf of Paria, in the house my grandfather had built in 1920. Chaguanas was a mainly Indian settlement. Hindu and Muslim festivals were celebrated; Hindi (or its Bhojpuri variant) was the first language I heard.¹

Naipaul was 34 when he found out about the name of his birthplace. That was the time he was living in London, had been in England for the past sixteen years and was on his ninth book – writing a human history of Trinidad, trying to recreate people and their stories. He would go to the British Museum to read the Spanish documents about the region. Recovered from the Spanish archives, these documents – beginning in 1530 and ending with the disappearance of the Spanish Empire – were copied out for

The Politics of Historical Reconstruction   95

the British government in the 1890s at the time of a boundary dispute with Venezuela.

Recalling those days of his meticulous research, Naipaul says:

> I was reading about the foolish search for El Dorado, and the murderous interloping of the English hero, Sir Walter Raleigh. In 1595 he raided Trinidad, killed all the Spaniards he could, and went up the Orinoco looking for El Dorado. He found nothing, but when he went back to England he said he had... He then published a book to prove his point, and for four centuries people have believed that Raleigh had found something.
>
> And then, as sometimes happens with confident men, Raleigh was caught by his own fantasies. Twenty-one years later, old and ill, he was let out of his London prison to go to Guiana and find the gold mines he said he had found. In this fraudulent venture his son died....And then Raleigh, full of grief, with nothing left to live for, went back to London to be executed.[2]

The story should have ended there. It didn't, providing Naipaul with a cue to begin his-story. Spanish memories, he discovered, were long because their imperial correspondence was slow: it could take up to two years for a letter from Trinidad to be read in Spain. In 1625, eight years after Raleigh's attempt to find the 'gold-mines' of Guiana, Naipaul discovered that the Spaniards of Trinidad and Guiana were still exchanging letters about the consequences and settling their scores with the Gulf Indians. And then one day, he chanced upon a letter dated October 12, 1625 from the king of Spain to the governor of Trinidad. Naipaul mentions in the foreword to *The Loss of El Dorado*:

> "I asked you," the king of Spain wrote to the Governor of Trinidad, "to give me some information about a certain nation of Indians called Chaguanes, who you say number above one thousand, and are of such bad disposition that it was they who led the English when they captured the town. ... You have decided to give them a punishment. Follow the rules I have given you; and let me know how you get on."[3]

What the governor did wasn't known. Naipaul could find no further reference to the Chaguanas in the documents in the Museum. But it was evident that shortly after, in the place called Chaguanas, the existence of a people called Chaguanes was wiped out. The little tribe of over a thousand – who would have been living on both sides of the Gulf of Paria – disappeared so completely that no one in the town of Chaguanas or Chauhaan knew anything about them. It occurred to Naipaul that he was the first person, since 1625, to whom that letter of the king of Spain had a real meaning. And that letter – after a disappearance, and then the silence of centuries – had been dug out of the archives only in 1896 or 1897.

Few historians recording those events made any attempt to break this silence and shed light on the events leading to the disappearance of the tribe. That obscure colony of the New World seemed part of nobody's story but it had existed nonetheless. Indians from India may have begun to arrive in 1845, but Naipaul sought to establish that the colony was created long before that.

In my paper, I would like to show how this meticulous recording of history suffices to salvage Naipaul's reviled status as a writer who is indifferent to his birthplace and its history and is only too happy to sever ties with it. In fact, a close study of the meticulously documented historical text *The Loss of El Dorado* and the part-fictionalised *A Way in the World* reveal that the past history of the West Indies that Naipaul stubbornly chooses to disavow in most of his writings is paradoxically what he traces and reflects on in the two works.

It is often said, 'Histories are more than voices, but voices contain many histories.' Naipaul's utterances, in that sense, are the speaking of the voices and experiences whose resonance he is. In *The Loss of El Dorado*, we obtain a historian's perspective on the lives of Sir Walter Raleigh and Francisco de Miranda who lived two centuries apart and were known for their efforts to exploit both economically and politically the corner of South America where Trinidad looks across the Bay of Paria to the swampy mainland of Venezuela.

El Dorado had always existed vaguely in the imagination of the Spanish conquerors of America. Their avarice, feeding greedily on the fabulous accounts readily supplied by the natives – who on their part were only too anxious to get rid of their robber-guests – made them dream of richer rewards than those of Mexico and Peru. Many soldiers of fortune perished in the search for gold, many brave troops of adventurers brought but a fraction of their number back before Manoa – the city of gold ruled by the fabled king who, smeared with gold-dust, bathed annually in the golden lake – was reluctantly relegated to the atlas of the poets. While *The Loss of El Dorado* shows how this delusion drew the small island of Trinidad into a vortex of world events, making it the object of Spanish and English designs and a Mecca for treasure-seekers, slave traders and revolutionaries, *A Way in the World* hinges on the interplay between history and fiction in a West Indian context. It uncovers fiction as an ideologically and culturally conditioned way of reading history and history as an ideologically and culturally conditioned artifice.

Walter Raleigh, one such seeker, came twice with dreams of gold fathered by Columbus and is seen in *A Way in the World* on his last voyage about to return to death in the Tower. Francisco de Miranda, a courtly Venezuelan con man who used and was used by the British and Spanish governments as a would-be "liberator" of Latin America in the late eighteenth century, is in Trinidadian exile exchanging thoughtful, chatty letters with his wife in London. In Naipaul's fictional rendering of the two historical personages in *A Way in the World*, they come to find themselves. A certain tenderness, sentimentality and openness imbue every word they speak. Having stepped into their shoes to understand who they were and their true motivations, Naipaul's own voice, moral reckonings and conscience surface to indicate an authorial identification with the characters.

In the Beginning

Born and brought up in Trinidad, Naipaul was evidently more concerned with the history of the island that had lured the Spanish conquistador and Walter Raleigh alike. And, although he does give us his observations on the other islands, it is Trinidad that provides the backdrop for a few of his fictional works based in the West Indies. In *The Loss of El Dorado* – structured from documents in the British Museum, the Public Record Office, London, and the London Library – it is essentially through two stories – the first, that of Sir Walter Raleigh's raid on the Port of Spain which had been founded as the base for El Dorado and the second, that of the torture of Luisa Calderon, a Spanish mulatto girl of 14 or 15, two centuries on and the subsequent trial of the then British governor, Thomas Picton – that Naipaul unfolds the history of his birthplace.

Naipaul's account goes back to the period when the British took over the island from Spain in 1797. But in actuality, Trinidad's history goes further back in time despite Naipaul's overt effort to disclaim this time and again. The 'absence' or negation of history that Naipaul lays emphasis on, points, in effect, to its 'presence' – presence as the effect of a generalised absence – as is evident in all his works; especially those in which he attempts to retrace his steps back to the point when the British cast anchor in the Caribbean isles.

When Naipaul set about writing that 'awful story' on slavery he had chanced upon in the archives, he wrote in the way he did all his other writings. 'I attempted a narrative, I wrote about people, a human story. I wasn't looking to make points about history. I wasn't writing a textbook, I was trying to make everything live...I was concerned with the way men behaved when unbridled, when there is no control.'[4] That, along with the myth of El Dorado, helped him put Trinidad behind him and vindicate his rejection of it.

It is therefore important to outline the history of Trinidad not in half truths but in its totality; especially in view of his works set out there, each of which have been meticulously woven into Naipaul's preconceived notions of the historical and political frameworks of the island.

It must, however, also be pointed out that Naipaul's notion that it is the specific myth of El Dorado that defines Trinidad's identity is misleading. For one, by showing that his two lost stories of imposed foreign fantasies constitute

Trinidad's past, Naipaul denies the very process of decolonisation including the role of Trinidadians in securing their independence. In contrast with what Naipaul asserts as definitive periods, Eric Williams in *History of the People of Trinidad and Tobago* devotes only 39 of its 282 pages to those two episodes. Williams's account incorporates experiences of the colonised peoples including their substantial uprisings and a mushrooming movement for self-rule. In fact, organised around the oil and sugar industries, Trinidad's labour movement, as has been elaborated upon subsequently, had significant social impact since the mid-1930s.

Besides, one of Caribbeans's most celebrated trade unionists and leader of the British Empire Workers and Citizens Home Rule Party, "Buzz" Butler was anything but an El Dorado-style fantasist. In *A Way in the World* Naipaul mentions him in his account of Foster Morris, a literary figure, who wrote a book, *The Shadowed Livery*, in 1930 on the oilfield strike that took place in Trinidad in 1937 and the men who led it, especially their leader Tubal Uriah Buzz Butler. Morris admits that he had regarded Butler and his followers as a 'bunch of racial fanatics' and Butler himself as 'a crazy black preacher'.

Like Naipaul, he too had failed to recognise the complexity inherent in the revolt, though years later Naipaul concludes that the book is part of the recorded history of Trinidad from the Renaissance to the present.

The Land of the Humming Bird

Trinidad's recorded history begins with the island's 'discovery' by Christopher Columbus on July 31, 1498, when he was on his third voyage to the Caribbean islands. He named the island La Trinidad because a view of the three peaks of the southern range of mountains reminded him of his vow to name the next island he sighted in honour of the Blessed Trinity. The Arawak name for the island is believed to be "Iere" – the land of the humming bird. Columbus claimed the island for Spain. But it was only after 30 years that Spain showed any official interest in her new possession.

In 1530, the Spanish king appointed the conquistador Antonio Sedeno as Captain-General of Trinidad for life, with a mandate to subdue the unruly natives. Sedeno struggled to accomplish his mission but failed. Four years later, he returned to Spain and Trinidad was once again left to her own devices.

True colonisation of Trinidad did not begin until the end of the 18th century when the Spanish king, acting on the advice of a French planter named Roume de St Laurent, issued the historic Cedula of Population, designed to attract immigrants to the island. Proclaimed in 1783, the terms of the Cedula offered free grants of land to citizens of any land friendly to Spain, provided they were Roman Catholic. This meant most of the new settlers were French, since England, Spain's other ally at the time, was mostly Protestant. Almost overnight, Trinidad was transformed into a colonised island, with French planters and free persons of colour flocking from the neighbouring islands.

The Spanish governor who made the most significant impression on Trinidad was Don Jose Maria Chacon after whom the island's national flower, the Chaconia, has been named. Arriving in 1784, Chacon, an astute administrator, settled many land disputes, declared Port of Spain the new capital and initiated development in the more remote parts of the island. The colony prospered under his governorship. Chacon's days as governor, however, were numbered. In 1797, the British – no longer allies – attacked Trinidad and the Spanish, greatly outnumbered, offered little resistance. Trinidad thus became a British colony.

With the abolition of slavery in 1834, followed by an 'apprenticeship' period in which the ex-slaves would still be obliged to serve, the 1830s represented a major watershed in Trinidad's history. Having realised that some replacement would have to be found for the soon-to-be defunct system of slave labour, the island's Council of Government, which was made up largely of planters, appointed an agent of immigration – someone responsible for identifying alternative sources of field labour. Various ethnic groups were tried: Portuguese, free Africans from Africa and America but with scant success. Finally, the planters turned to Asia. The first batch of indentured labourers from India arrived aboard the Fatel Razack in 1845 and today East Indians constitute about 45 per cent of the total population, almost exactly the same as Africans.

But the East Indians and Africans failed to bond. The former would rather idolise the British colonisers than befriend the erstwhile 'slaves'. In fact Naipaul's strong disregard for those of black origin is evident in all his works, irrespective of their nature. Take the instance of Lebrun, a pseudonym in all likelihood for C.L.R. James in *A Way in the World*. Lebrun, says Naipaul, had been raised in Panama and roamed the Caribbean basin in the 1930s and '40s as a communist agitator. A charismatic Trinidadian and 'the man of true African or black redemption,'[5] he belonged to 'the first generation of educated black men in the region,'[6] whose business was to travel to Central America, the West Indies and West Africa and talk revolution. But at the end of it, he made it a point to return to his home base in Britain, Canada or America, underlining the hypocrisy of it all.

Despite being the leader of the Back-to-Africa movement who had declared on a radio programme, 'Since the days of slavery, the Caribbean could be considered as black people's territory,' Naipaul remains unconvinced about Lebrun's conviction. Recalling the comments on Lebrun by Foster Morris, a mid-twentieth century English writer Naipaul meets over lunch, it would seem that Morris merely echoes Naipaul's thoughts:

> A strange idea came to me...it was that Lebrun was really a white man, imprisoned in this other [black] body.[7]

Of Slavery and Fantasies

In an interview with Ray Suarez, Naipaul emphasised:

> My place of birth commits me to an understanding of the new world, the Spanish invasion, slavery, revolution in the new world... So from that

starting point, I have looked at the world, or tried to look at the world, and this is the venture I've been engaged in.[8]

Needless to say, in *The Loss of El Dorado*, Naipaul was particularly concerned with the subjects of slavery and revolution. As he says, 'More than I knew or felt when I was growing up in Trinidad, slavery had helped to make my world.'[9] In course of assessing the responsibility of the past for the present West Indian condition, Naipaul turns his attention to the slave plantation past vis-à-vis the trial of Louisa Calderon, a mulatto teenager who, accused of a possible theft, was tortured senselessly in the late 18th century, at the behest of the then British governor Thomas Picton.

With this incident as a focal point, Naipaul shows how the institution of slavery tragically produced yet another contentious issue in the history of the Caribbean and its people. It cut people off from their personal ancestry, reducing them to nonentities. Slaves were forced to sever ties with their ancestral homes in Africa and brought across the sea to North America through a voyage known as the Middle Passage. Once in the colonies, the families disintegrated further and slaves were often renamed according to the master's whims, sometimes several different times if they changed owners. This, coupled with the fact that the rest of the family lived thousands of miles across the ocean and became untraceable due to the name changes and uprooting process, made the development of a personal lineage, of family traditions impossible. Owners discouraged or prohibited slaves from marrying, yet encouraged children to be taken from their parents and sold off in other areas. As a result, rootlessness rather than lineage and tradition characterised the mindset of the Caribbean people. It is this subject of slavery that Naipaul reflects upon in the Epilogue to *The Loss of El Dorado*:

> History was also a fairytale not so much about slavery as about its abolition, the good defeating the bad. It was the only way the tale could be told. Any other version would have ended in ambiguity and alarm. The slave was never real. Like the extinct aboriginal, he had to be

reconstructed from his daily routine. ...In the records the slave is faceless, silent, with an identification rather than a name. He has no story.[10]

Naipaul goes on to relate how when Picton's view of Trinidad as a slave colony conflicted with the British intentions to establish Trinidad as 'a colony of free settlers...the centre of British trade with South America,' complaints regarding Picton's brutality were taken seriously and the British ordered that his powers be limited.

General Picton's plight also signalled the conclusion of the efforts of expatriate South American Francisco Miranda. Son of an immigrant Caracas draper, Miranda was perceived in England as a Latin aristocrat and respected for his political insight. He was a man in love with the idea of British liberty and moved by the ideal of bringing this new, explosive force to bear upon a repressive Spanish tyranny. But when it became clear that the centre of British imperial power would move from America to the East, and that Trinidad would never usefully serve as a springboard for an attack on South America, Miranda accompanied Trinidad in its fall from history.

Both the stories – the first comprising the end of the search for El Dorado and the second on how the British undertook a highly ambiguous operation in the Port of Spain, two hundred years later, to organise revolts against Spain in South America on the principles of liberty and law, at the same time as they were establishing a slave colony in Trinidad – tell of plunder of the New World and the enslavement, torture and murder of its people, the conquistadors for legendary gold, the English for trade but from a metropolitan vantage point. What is noteworthy is that there is an unmistakable sympathetic tone that inflects Naipaul's detailed accounts of the injustices perpetrated. This, despite the objectivity and matter-of-fact approach that so characterises all his writings.

On the other hand, with Port of Spain forming the backdrop of both the stories, *The Loss of El Dorado* can also be seen as the product of Naipaul's personal effort to salvage not only the generally unknown history of the island but within it something of his own roots as well. For, it was here that Naipaul as a boy first observed the ways of the city, a place which having no independent life altered with the people who came to it. It is thus, as Rob Nixon writes in his work, *London Calling*:

> ...more than Naipaul's rendition of the origins and destiny of a "simple society". It stands, too, as an exercise in archival autobiography, an attempt to explain his personal sense of the absurdity of his East Indian-West Indian beginnings by staging a historical argument for the ineluctable absurdity of Trinidad *per se*.[11]

In the process of doing so, Naipaul, as he mentions in *The Enigma of Arrival*, gave himself 'a past, and a romance of the past'[12]. His research evoked late eighteenth-century Trinidad. In the street of Port of Spain where he had spent much of his childhood and that later became the setting of *Miguel Street*, he could now feel the presence of the homes, 'the street life,' the languages of the people no longer obliterated in its long nineteenth-century colonial torpor.[13]

But ironically, this need to equip himself with a past required that that past be counted as an absence too insubstantial to rank as history because only then could it ratify his lifelong sense of being starved of a real society. In that sense *The Loss of El Dorado* can be read, as Nixon points out:

> ... as extending Naipaul's autobiographical fixation with that peculiar sense of loss that follows from dwelling in fantasies as if they offered the security and substance of reality. As a child, he had lost Trinidad by dreaming of England; the dream England of his books, in turn, evaporated on his arrival in London; then his first trip to the subcontinent destroyed his imaginary India.[14]

The myth of El Dorado was both a dream and a fever shaping and infecting the lives of the Spanish and English, of Antonio de Berrio who occupied Trinidad and Walter Raleigh. Naipaul's fluid narrative follows with meticulous fidelity the increasingly frantic line of an action conducted in real historical time on real ground, the purpose of which was grossly unreal. It is the discrepancy between the actual explorations, the savage hunting down of the indigenous people, the treacheries, the miniature wars, the marching and counter marching, the limitless suffering and fatigue on the one hand, and paradoxically the insubstantial fantasy for the sake of which it was all endured, on the other, which Naipaul's lucid disentangling of events forces on the reader.

It must be noted, however, that Naipaul's commitment to the idea of the 'simple' Trinidadian society's historical stasis bars him from presenting blacks and Amerindians as agents in history even in the emergence of their own society. Dismissing Trinidad way back in 1958 he had said, 'Superficially because of the multitude of races, Trinidad may seem complex, but to anyone who knows it, it is a simple, colonial, philistine society.'[15]

But then, he is equally critical in his reconstruction of the roles of the historical individuals from the letters and archival documents of the late sixteenth, seventeenth and eighteenth centuries. What emerges is the disparity between the heroic images they themselves conceived and the images of greed, the lust for fame and power and the deceits their ambitions entailed. Naipaul takes strong exception to the instances of slavery and the consequent brutality perpetrated by these figures, but, as is typical of Naipaul, on the flip side, there is this parallel effort to show the historical stasis in the 'simple' Trinidadian society whose apparently inert people refrained from being an integral part of the ongoing historical process. It is this paradox that Naipaul fails to resolve in his works, one that adds a complex dimension to them.

In 1967, two years before the publication of *The Loss of El Dorado*, reviewing Bjorn Landstrom's *Columbus*, Naipaul wrote a scathing re-evaluation of the legendary discoverer, Columbus.

> He was looking less for America or Asia than for gold. The Indies, the source of his gold, where he thought he had discovered the Terrestrial Paradise, had become, largely through his example, his *anus mundi*.[16]

From Columbus's own words, Naipaul deduces his egotism, his banality and his greed. The brief commentary, as Lillian Feder says in her work *Naipaul's Truth*, 'thus serves as an antidote to the "heroic gloss" on Columbus's reputation... It can also be regarded as a prelude to the first story of *The Loss of El Dorado*.'[17]

Naipaul quotes from his review in depicting the search for El Dorado by the Spaniards, Antonio de Berrio, who occupied Trinidad and Domingo de Vera who took formal possession of the island and of the Indians who were native to it in 1592. Fearful of competition Berrio sent Vera to take possession of the lands on the Orinoco and to look around. When Vera, returning with seventeen golden eagles and jackals, declared that he had discovered El Dorado, the legend grew. But in its wake, shipwreck and starvation ensued. The quest for El Dorado, says Naipaul in his review, became like a recapitulation of the whole New World adventure, a wish to experience it all over again.

In his work, therefore, he demonstrates how Berrio links the two fantasies and shows further how the El Dorado quest had become similar to Columbus's ventures comparable to that of legendary voyages particularly Robinson Crusoe's. The grandiose aims of survival and conquest – a psychological offshoot of political and economic exploitation – propelled the would-be conquerors of the New World who were ignorant of its geography, actual resources and dangers.

This was however by no means the end of Naipaul's concern with the history of Trinidad, or rather its apparent absence, and his need to locate himself further in the consequences of its occupation by conquistadors, revolutionaries and colonisers. In fact, *A Way in the World* places him within that framework uniting history, autobiography and fiction, each genre commenting on the others.

The Inheritance of Loss

In *A Way in the World*, Naipaul converts the archival material he uses in *The Loss of El Dorado* to an exploration of how closely the history of Trinidad from centuries before his birth to the time of his youth is interwoven with his personal history. Both historical persons and fictional characters are involved in his intellectual and artistic autobiography. In that sense, *A Way in the World* marks a return to the lives of men who were products of and participants in historical events that affected more than one individual life. In fact, history and inheritance serve as propositions which Naipaul can imaginatively locate and play off against each other. Thus, irrespective of whether the principal figures are historical personages like Walter Raleigh, imaginative constructions like the narrator in the section, *New Clothes: An Unwritten Story*, or portraits of Naipaul's Caribbean contemporaries like Blair and Lebrun, *A Way in the World's* narratives are each an exercise in exploring relative levels of cultural, historical or political consciousness.

The work shows Naipaul first as a clerk in the municipality of Port of Spain, killing time until he sails off to Oxford. As in *The Loss of El Dorado*, the "History" of the section titled *History: A Smell of Fish Glue* refers to Port of Spain, the first city of the narrator's experience and the focal site of Trinidadian political developments. The chapter charts the developments within the narrator's lifetime, so that the transformation depicted is the gradual political awakening of the black population, through what could be described as the politics of racial redemption.

The politics of race is introduced with the narrator's meeting a lawyer father of one of his school friends. He is shocked, however, when this 'famous' lawyer mistakenly claims that his name Evander can be found in Homer rather than in Virgil. What is discomforting is the kind of error the narrator perceives: 'But this flaw in his character, so casually revealed, was worrying'.[18] This worry is further compounded by the narrator's next recollection of their conversation when the lawyer extends 'his forearm across the table in a gesture for strength and ... with a smile, and as a kind of pledge'[19] says, 'The race! The race, man!'[20]

Writing from a distance of many years and much experience as a traveller and writer, the narrator remarks how unexpected this idea of an association of black people was in the late 1940s. He admits he is 'moved' and 'understood their feelings' but he could not join a 'group'[21]. At seventeen he already seemed to know that to become the writer he envisions, he must 'belong to' himself. What is equally interesting about Naipaul's account of one of his first encounters with a politicised 'race' consciousness is that he implies that it ultimately stems from a flawed consciousness, one that is responsible for the lawyer wrongly attributing his name to Homer not Virgil.

In the next phase, we see Naipaul as a kind of observer-participant in the world of Caribbean exiles in London in the early 1950s when he reflects on the late years of Walter Raleigh and the career of the Venezuelan liberator Francisco de Miranda. And in the final section, he comments as an expatriate academic in Africa. These excursions provide an adequate background to the present-day dilemma of the Caribbean peoples. They can be summarised in one sentence, uttered by Hislop, the British governor of Trinidad, who tells Miranda more than once: 'In this part of the world it always comes down to land and Negroes.'[22] Naipaul's observations of continuous transformations in Trinidad integrate past and present history. He points out that the skills of the extinct aboriginal Indians were passed on to their successors, among them Asian Indians, his own people. 'I had arrived,' he says, 'at a way of looking that contained both the fabulous past and the smaller scale of what I had grown up with.'[23]

In *The Loss of El Dorado*, Naipaul had quoted extensively from archives depicting the interactions of historical figures from various cultures. *A Way in the World,* on its part, records the remembrances of its author and his protagonists, some from tales told before by him and by his predecessors, the invaders and the vanquished. Using dramatic narrative and imagined dialogue, he recreates history as internalised by those who enacted it and those who inherited its ongoing effects.

Accordingly in the work, Raleigh is depicted as a sick old man on his last fruitless voyage to the New World in

1617 aboard a ship, the *Destiny*. His surgeon holds long interviews about his continuous obsession with El Dorado. The 'land, which in his mind and writings existed as a kind of Arcadia,'[24] is now hostile territory, where he is not permitted to disembark. He has staked his survival on his claim to knowledge of the location of the gold of Guiana and his promise to mine it, counterfeit pledges that ignore his earlier history of failure. Raleigh's version of history, quoted and challenged by his surgeon, is Naipaul's own way of reading and appraising the historical records. But these exchanges are also a commentary on the relationship between two men with opposing motives: the one to weave his memories into epic tales, the other to question their intent. When the surgeon arrives to give him his dose of medicine, Raleigh speaks of the pleasures of his voyage in 1595, of balsam and oysters and cassava, remembrances that would negate his present unwelcome return. The surgeon, however, insists on his own view of both the past and the present and it is in his detailed critique of Raleigh's book, *The Discovery of the Large, Rich and Beautiful Empire of Guiana*, that one hears Naipaul's voice as one does in the speech of several of the other historical figures. The surgeon, and through him Naipaul, discovers the disparity between the two parts of the book: Raleigh's descriptions of 'the eastern side, the Trinidad side,' are accurate but those of 'the main Orinoco', the way to El Dorado, are pure fantasy. The surgeon's emphasis is on the contrast between Raleigh's actual role in the continuity 'of blood and revenge' in the Gulf and his depiction of the region as 'an untouched paradise on the rivers'.

The other principal figure is Harry, or Don José, an Amerindian, or part Amerindian, whom Raleigh had taken with him to England but who had returned 14 years later. He is interrogated by an historian, Fray Simon, with the result that the whole chapter looks at the same events from a series of different perspectives. By closing this narrative with Don José, Naipaul also appears to be deliberately trying to invest the Amerindian past of the area with both a voice and a representation usually absent from the literature of the region. Don José's last reply – 'And I think Father, that the difference between us, who are Indian or half Indians, and people like the Spaniards and the English and the Dutch and the French, people who know how to go where they are going, I think that for them the world is a safer place'[25] – resonates with the kind of vulnerability that is indicative of Naipaul's implicit thesis about 'simple societies' and their absence of an intellectual tradition vested in a sense of purpose larger than their immediate concerns.

Naipaul's purpose in animating these historical scenes is an exercise in testing his own powers of reconstruction. Since it is a Naipaulian sensibility that encases the account, the humanness in question highlights the passionately delusional, quixotic and dangerously careless nature of Raleigh's quest. There is then a deliberate attempt made by Naipaul to participate in the history that made his world. His voice joins those of the others who discovered the truth beneath the legends, some, like the surgeon, posing questions in the interests of a version of history that is thoroughly grounded in empirical and verifiable documentation, most notably Spanish records of the same era, and the body of travel literature written by Raleigh's contemporaries and from whom Raleigh appears to have borrowed surreptitiously. Through the surgeon – Naipaul's surrogate – Naipaul suggests that Raleigh's ambition was to discover a land to be conquered and exploited without risk of failure and a denial of all those sacrificed to his ambition: his own followers ravaged by disease and starvation; two English boys left in the forest in exchange for the son of an Indian chief to serve as evidence on Raleigh's return that his voyage was authentic; the Spaniards killed in Port of Spain, whose deaths were avenged fourteen years later when their compatriots retaliated by cutting the throats of 36 English traders.

In her essay, "The Politics and Poetics of Diaspora in V.S. Naipaul's *A Way in the World*," Stephanie Jones contends that the unity of the novel lies in its interrogation of the legitimacy of diaspora as a means of identity formation. *A Way in the World* deconstructs wholeness and homeland by emphasising the fragmentation of a world in which home is wherever one is at that moment. This is true if one is to take Lebrun, 'the Trinidadian-Panamanian communist of the 1930s,'[26] – a character based on C.L.R. James – whom Foster Morris had described as 'one of the most dangerous men around Butler'[27] as a case in point. As Naipaul portrays him, Lebrun is less dangerous than provocative, 'an impresario of revolution,' always on the run. He grows and changes in the countries he visits and moves on to different political positions. In his later years, he relinquishes the role of revolutionary to become 'the man of true African or black redemption'.

As a boy Naipaul had come across Lebrun's first book in the sixth-form library of Queens Royal College, but did not read it until many years later. The book, which Naipaul does not name, deals with 'some of the Spanish-American or Venezuelan revolutionaries before Bolivar, and he had concentrated on those with Trinidad connections.' In writing his own version of history, it is from here that Naipaul takes his cue. However, it would be wrong to conclude, as Jones does, that the fragmentation of the world enables Naipaul to escape from privileging Europe as the Centre and origin of world history. Jones argues that the narrative begins and ends in Trinidad not because the Centre has shifted but because it has disappeared altogether.[28]

I would like to argue that in his bid to justify and privilege Europe as Centre, Naipaul unwittingly pushes it to the periphery, as Trinidad and the West Indies become the focal points of interest and attention. Therein lies the paradox. Both Lebrun and Blair – with whom Naipaul had worked as a clerk in the registrar-general's department in the Red House in Port of Spain before parting ways – had turned into Black Power advocates in their later years. And, it is as if to confirm his thesis about local political awakening in Trinidad that Naipaul focuses on these two important figures both of whom are used to exemplify the seductive and ultimately corrupt power of the politics of 'race'. Naipaul points out:

> The early days of the black movement had given way to the simplest kind of racial politics. In Trinidad that meant anti-Indian politics and constant anti-Indian agitation; it was how the vote of the African majority was to be secured.[29]

Thus both Lebrun and Blair, whose careers are part of the literary and political history in which the narrator is involved, give Naipaul a chance to present a more nuanced, though still highly critical portrait of Black Power advocates. Through Lebrun, Naipaul examines differing perceptual representations of Trinidad and its place in both colonial and postcolonial registers. Naipaul highlights the mileage Lebrun appears to be able to extract from the materialist perspective he espouses: his reputation for being a 'revolutionary'; the romanticism of being 'on the run'; the patronage of a segment of the Euro-American intelligentsia; and the deference of national leaders in Africa. There is also a reference to Lebrun's visit to the Ivory Coast – Naipaul's focus of attention in The Crocodiles of Yamoussoukro – and his advice acknowledged as the source of a new policy of socialisation adopted by the government. It turns out to be a repressive, tyrannical policy, typical of Naipaul's thesis of the postcolonial aftermath. The disappointment Naipaul expresses about the older Lebrun's apparent lapse into a form of racial politics does little to lessen the opportunistic cast Naipaul adopts to characterise his life as a whole.

Blair, on his part, seems less of an opportunist. When at the age of seventeen Naipaul met Blair at the registrar-general's office, he seemed a person 'of ambition and strength'. His government employment became a springboard for advancement in a larger, intellectually challenging world. He was to enter local politics and later 'to have an international career'. But twenty years later, Blair's success in his government position in an independent Uganda – where the narrator meets him for the second time – sees him being betrayed and murdered by agents of some wild men in the government who felt threatened by him.

The final chapter, *Home Again*, then projects the slightly sinister political ambience in Uganda in the mid-sixties, complemented by Naipaul's own discomfort with his status there. The Asian community was being politically besieged, colleagues Naipaul was comfortable with nevertheless discomfort him in their acceptance of the government's new practice of socialism. South African exiles and 'revolutionaries' do not fit his expectations, and students at the university astonish him with their political arrogance. As was the case with his examination of Lebrun's career, his meeting with Blair serves as one of the gauges Naipaul uses to measure the quality and direction of his own life.

Where Lebrun appears to have slipped dangerously back into a racial identification, still in the name of revolution, Blair is depicted as having steered a more pragmatic course. Rather than endorsing a politics of 'racial redemption', Blair's advisory role in Uganda, showed him to have sublimated that aspect of his 'inheritance', allowing him to operate in a political dimension that transcended such narrow concerns. This ability, Naipaul suggests, was also the cause of his brutal murder, by authorities who do not subscribe to Blair's failure to indict Uganda's Asian community as they had hoped.

Naipaul, however, redeems Blair by imagining a literary ending to his life. In an imaginary sequence credited to the inflections of a Poe story, Naipaul rewrites Conrad's Kurtz as he lies dying: 'And I feel that, as if in some Edgar Allan Poe story, at the moment of death, while the brain still sparked, a question could have been lodged in that brain – "Does this betrayal mock your life?" – the answer immediately after death would have been "No! No! No!"'[30] And, in that vehement negation would lie an affirmation of Blair's life, the intensity of his commitment to change, his assertion that the world [he] will be leaving is better than the one he was born into, his satisfaction in knowing that the revolution he had taken part in had succeeded. Naipaul's response insists that even the continuity of betrayal could not invalidate the lives of those who struggle to exceed the limits of their times. With that, his focus on histories of the past centuries in the face of a bitter present complicates the relationship of the New World to the Old, and in the process swaps the Centre with the Margin.

Endnotes

[1] V.S. Naipaul, *The Loss of El Dorado* (1969. rpt. Harmondsworth: Penguin Books Ltd, 1973) p. 13.

[2] http://www.nobel.se/literature/laureates/2001/naipaul-lecture-e.html (V.S. Naipaul, *Two Worlds*, Nobel lecture, December 7, 2001.) Accessed on January 30, 2002.

[3] V.S. Naipaul, *The Loss of El Dorado* (1969. rpt. Harmondsworth: Penguin Books Ltd, 1973) pp. 13-14.

[4] Farrukh Dhondy, "Interview: Farrukh Dhondy talks to V. S. Naipaul", *Literary Review* (London: Issue No. 278, August 2001).

[5] V.S. Naipaul, *A Way in the World: A Sequence* (1994. rpt. London: Minerva Edition, 1995) p. 130.

[6] *Ibid.*, p. 130.

[7] *Ibid.*, p. 131.

[8] http://www.pbs.org/newshour/gergen/jan-june00/naipaul_3-3.html Online Newshour, March 3, 2000. Accessed on May 5, 2000.

[9] V.S. Naipaul cited in Lillian Feder, *Naipaul's Truth: The Making of a Writer* (New Delhi: Indialog Publications Pvt. Ltd., 2001) p. 94.

[10] V.S. Naipaul, *The Loss of El Dorado* (1969. rpt. Harmondsworth: Penguin Books Ltd, 1973) p. 375.

[11] Rob Nixon, *London Calling: V.S. Naipaul, Postcolonial Mandarin* (Oxford: Oxford University Press Inc., 1992) p. 123.

[12] V.S. Naipaul, *The Enigma of Arrival* (Harmondsworth: Penguin Books Ltd, 1987) p. 159.

[13] *Ibid.*, pp. 155-156.

[14] Rob Nixon, *London Calling: V.S. Naipaul, Postcolonial Mandarin* (Oxford: Oxford University Press Inc., 1992) p. 123.

[15] V.S. Naipaul, *The Times Literary Supplement*, cited in Caryl Phillips, 'Reluctant Hero', in Amitava Kumar (ed.). *The Humour and the Pity: Essays on V.S. Naipaul* (New Delhi: Buffalo Books, 2002) p. 133.

[16] V.S. Naipaul, 'Columbus and Crusoe', *The Overcrowded Barracoon and Other Articles* (London: Andre Deutsch Ltd., 1972) p. 204.

[17] Lillian Feder, *Naipaul's Truth: The Making of a Writer* (New Delhi: Indialog Publications Pvt. Ltd., 2001) p. 95.

[18] V.S. Naipaul, *A Way in the World: A Sequence* (1994. rpt. London: Minerva Edition, 1995) p. 15.

[19] *Ibid.*, p. 15.

[20] *Ibid.*, p. 15.

[21] *Ibid.*, p. 18.

22 *Ibid.*, p. 287.
23 *Ibid.*, p. 41.
24 *Ibid.*, p. 171.
25 *Ibid.*, p. 211.
26 *Ibid.*, p. 128.
27 *Ibid.*, p. 98.
28 Stephanie Jones, 'The Politics and Poetics of Diaspora in V.S. Naipaul's *A Way in the World*', *Journal of Commonwealth Literature* 35:1 (Spring 2000) pp. 87-97.
29 V.S. Naipaul, *A Way in the World: A Sequence* (1994. rpt. London: Minerva Edition, 1995) p. 355.
30 *Ibid.*, p. 368.

8

Negotiating V.S. Naipaul
CYRIL DABYDEEN

The Indian presence in Guyana's coastline on the northeastern tip of South America is perhaps like nowhere else in the world; here it is not unnatural to hear Lata Mangeshkar's voice on the radio with other rhythms of India, all stemming from the echoes and memories of Indian forebears; and in the trinity-peaked island of Trinidad about ninety miles away, where V.S. Naipaul was born in Chaguanas (derived from an indigenous tribe Naipaul later came to realise), it is virtually the same: rhythms, cadences, in the midst of a potpourri world of cross-fertilisation of peoples, races. Here in this region I grew up as a writer; and it's inevitable that I would become keenly aware of V.S. Naipaul: he came to me early in my teenage years, with the 'charm' of the early books. There's nothing innately ethnocentric in saying this; it's the way things were, this consciousness no less in a colonial setting in Guyana where life seemed to be unpredictable, with nothing being fixed in a conventional sense. Later in Canada I would reflect on racial self-awareness, even as I would return to the Caribbean to attend a special event to honour poet Kamau Brathwaite at the University of the West Indies in Jamaica, and earnestly listened to Brathwaite talk about 'ancestors,' Africanness indeed. History's indelible markers, with imperial imprints: in a world novelist George Lamming would say, in context, 'every Caribbean writer carries with him the weight of the pressure of history.' And, 'a writer like Vidia Naipaul is always preoccupied with what he sees.'

In Guyana, in my growing up in the 50s and 60s, it was the sense of what I saw and experienced in sometimes marginal, incipient, or just unstructured, ways. Then reading Naipaul somehow enabled me to fashion sensibility in the quest to understand who I was or kept becoming: in the flux of history commingling with races, creeds, all European, African and Asian tinged with the indigenous. Bhajans amidst bacchanal with calypso and reggae no less: all that our indentured legacy made us confront; but as the literary life loomed, I longed for some kind of permanence.

Simultaneously I read Frantz Fanon with internalised notions of 'self-contempt'; and then it became the struggle with 'Indian arrival' and wanting to establish a sense of place and spirit in a new world aligned with the old. Indeed Naipaul's early writings made an immediate impact, his short stories in *Miguel Street* (1959) becoming at once memorable, including the other seminal books: *The Mystic Masseur* (1957) and *The Suffrage of Elvira* (1958). *A House for Mr Biswas* (1961) quickly established Naipaul's genius because of the Caribbean verisimilitude he depicted like no other; and the Indian presence in the Caribbean became authentic, numinously alive for me. (Didn't Naipaul once say that 'being an Indian in the Caribbean is an unknown fact'?) His books brought home to me the power of narrative and the possibilities inherent in things around me; and in this self-realisation, I contemplated Mohun Biswas's personal alienation or existentialism in the Tulsi household: all that he raged at, being indubitably Indian in an island-world. Later a self-reflective Naipaul would put it all in a wider context: 'As a child trying to read, I had felt that two worlds separated me from the books that were offered to me at school and in the libraries; the childhood world of our remembered India, and the more colonial world of our city ... What I didn't know, even after I had written my early books of fiction, concerned only with story and people and getting to the end...these two spheres of darkness had become my subject' ("Reading and Writing: A Personal Account"). This distilled view is juxtaposed with Naipaul's earlier expression in *The Middle Passage* (1962): 'History is built around achievement and creation; and nothing was created in the West Indies.' In *The Enigma of Arrival* (1987) he speaks of 'the colonial smallness [of Trinidad] that didn't consort with the grandeur of my ambition...'

Indeed, I saw in Biswas a small man; but the contemplation of his circumscribed life was potentially liberating, no doubt with the sense of a new spirit of freedom engendered in his being an artist while coming to grips with his unique or individualistic ways. And Naipaul's own sense of personal or spiritual space he would reflect on, almost with foreboding: 'It made for an extraordinary self-centredness. We looked inwards; we lived out our days; the world outside existed in a kind of darkness; we inquired about nothing.'

Naipaul began steering us in the direction of making us not see ourselves as communal, tribal, or parochial; and in faraway Guyana a new stirring of the imagination grew, as I reconstructed Biswas in Hanuman House seeking self-awareness despite his ingrained lethargic ways, or a life lived in a predetermined style governed by fate: all that the narrative and instinct for words suggested. And Naipaul's own liberation or escape from a too-limited world would be echoed again in what he said, in 1979, perhaps too forthrightly: 'I do not write for Indians, who in any case do not read. My work is only possible in a liberal, civilised western country.' Cold-eyed Naipaul's attitude has always been, with his integrity intact, as I cogitated on it as simultaneously confronted reality around me in a dire colonial setting. Much later when criticism of Naipaul became almost hysterical, as I heard some Caribbean scholars call for Naipaul's books to be burnt, I would replay in my mind what that other Trinidadian novelist, Sam Selvon – once London-based like Naipaul himself – later said to me in Canada in his inimitably unaffected way: 'Boy, he's the best thing we have produced.' This somehow endured despite Naipaul's utterance: 'If you are from Trinidad you want to get away,' as he told *Vanity Fair* in 1987; and 'You can't write if you're from the bush.' Naipaul's ironic-cum-satiric stance would be softened by his explanation of what he meant by 'the bush': as trope, it applied to huge swathes of the world, not just Trinidad – but 'the breakdown of institutions, of the contact between man and man. It is theft, corruption, racist incitement.'

II

I dwelled on Naipaul's attitude to the committed literary life and the sense of forging identity with the spirit being bent on seeking out new, if not old, ways of deciphering and decoding meaning or significance in a world riddled with conflicts in the search for belonging and permanence. But everything kept being seen in vulnerable or predictable ways in small states everywhere, I figured, as my own thoughts see-sawed; and I felt a genuine humanity was somewhere possible, even as cosmopolitan London became the yardstick or prism from which Naipaul assessed the world's inexorably changing ways in the flux of time: captured vividly in his travelogues. Not surprisingly, Naipaul began to change the form of fiction itself: his works formulated as a traveller's response to all that his senses apprehended, with everything expressed in his particular style and wit, always with perspicuity, seen especially in the later books: on India mainly; then, too, it was the Muslim world that came to his scrutiny in his unwavering narrative approach, unflinching as he was. Indeed, his intuition of feeling was all. In his further bend in the river, Naipaul kept seeing 'mimic men' in the settings that were banal, or just incongruous. Later, it was seeking out other meanings in a diasporic new world order as he set his gaze on more than imaginary homelands (as Salman Rushdie did), always with troubling enigmas and, on occasion, mutinies: a million or more to be sure, as India beckoned.

Naipaul's books I read and pondered deeply with my own burgeoning and later expanding metropolitan awareness, with Canadian sensibility and Great White North perspective intermingled. Indeed Biswas's sense of destiny lingered in my consciousness, kept subsisting even in the 'echo-chamber of the subconscious' (Nadine Gordimer), as I saw everything nostalgically or, just in cameo, like the character of the failed forlorn poet B. Wordsworth in Naipaul's short story by that name (in *Miguel Street*); or the more engaging character Hat, as I was yet determined to look beyond an island-horizon. Around this time I wrote my own first novel *The Wizard Swami* (1990), with images being distilled in me; and at the time when I wrote an earlier version of this novel I might have unconsciously immersed myself in R.K. Narayan's and Naipaul's books as one and the same, as I crossed boundaries with the sense of numinous or imaginative space widening before me.

I recall, too, reading other writers from a panoply of backgrounds: mainly English and American, while trying in different ways to come to grips with Naipaul's vision. Then, also, during this inchoate or impressionistic period, I had been teaching Chinua Achebe's *Things Fall Apart* to young teacher-trainees in Guyana. Tagore's lyricism also came to me at this time, with worlds continually coming closer. Indeed, India as a mammoth country – a subcontinent truly– dwarfed Trinidad or Guyana, as I saw in perspective my forebears' own life and mind's imprint while grappling with my already internalised sense of Kiplingesque landscapes, as well as other images of Africa and Asia in the ongoing struggle to repudiate or shun imperial vestiges.

I was conscious too of Gandhi and other stalwarts: images of an early period, for sure, as politics seared our beings, as things kept transforming us amidst shifting ideologies, on shifting grounds. And I envisaged Naipaul appearing sardonically aloof in London because of his special sensibility fortifying a defence mechanism, not unlike an Evelyn Waugh in temperament, come to think of it. I self-reflectively questioned myself also, about who I was becoming while confronting my own disappointments as I started striving to carve out my own imaginative space. Much later, like the Indian writer Amitav Ghosh, I imagined 'truths that were too painful to acknowledge; some because they were misanthropic or objectionable.' Indeed, 'it was Naipaul who first made it possible for me to think of myself as a writer,' Ghosh added –and I also believed this about myself as I grew more comfortable with the indwelling life of the mind and longed for clarity of ideas amidst a whirl of other complex and disparate feelings.

Instinctively I reflected on images in Naipaul's *An Area of Darkness* (1964) and *India: A Wounded Civilization* (1977). Oddly I longed to visit India, far beyond going to an exotic land because of residues of Kipling that I needed to, well, exorcise. I also longed for individuation in finding out more about my own self in a wider world while being a serious artist. When I indeed visited India later, and then read Naipaul's revamped India in *A Million Mutinies Now* (1990), everything came together. I began to see narrative as an end in itself (as Naipaul no doubt conceived it). I also came upon a more than nostalgic, but symbolic, yet immediate recognition of the *jamoon* or neem tree in India as familiar emblems in my growing-up childhood in Guyana.

Invariably I read Naipaul critically and sometimes balked at his stance, even if it all stemmed from his prevailing enigma. ('The thing about being an Indian, and it remains true of Indian writing, now, is that it seems to work without history, in a vacuum,' Naipaul said, with his customary irony.) I began to believe too that it was his consciously deliberate way of individual thought about the politics of place and people's evolution as former empires crumbled, with things indeed falling apart and the centre not holding. Did it ever? I asked. Where's Kurtz now reappearing?

The writing life indeed set Naipaul apart, if not alone, though he might have longed for community, but simultaneously disdained it (therein lies an inherent paradox), while ironically he wrote books such as *Mr Stone and His Knights Companion* (1963) authentically depicting British life to demonstrate his uncompromising cosmopolitanism, and earning praise for this achievement.

This then was the true or authentic Naipaul, I kept thinking, as I reflected on my own sense of integrity: of a writer's true vocation, with narrative indeed having its own *raison d'être*. And one's accepted views clashed against Naipaul's unrelenting gaze and scrutiny, if it was his sometimes jaded vision, as I increasingly wrestled more with all that I read and contemplated.

Underlying it all was the recognition of decay and destitution, not without gloominess: Naipaul's 'mimic men' seen with foibles or idiosyncrasies in distinct ways as once-promising new worlds indeed began to fall apart (Rwanda, Congo). Even if one like Derek Walcott would resort to pun: V.S. Naipaul seen as 'V.S. Nightfall,' while acknowledging Naipaul's superb craftsmanship – for the latter was always a master stylist bent on changing the novel's 'bastardised form' (as he called it), yet acknowledged its fundamental importance: 'Fiction, which had once liberated me and enlightened me, now seemed to be pushing me toward being simpler than I really was.'

I kept being constantly aware of history, post-colonial primarily, which Naipaul no doubt has no patience for, but only of the sense of the individual enduring without wanting to maintain obvious allegiances. Thus the Nobel Prize Committee's citation of Naipaul's award would be for his 'incorruptible scrutiny in works that compel us to see the presence of suppressed histories,' and singling out *The Enigma of Arrival* (1987) – for its 'unrelenting image of the placid collapse of the old colonial ruling culture and the demise of European neighbourhoods.' This I introspected on, and internalised as being at the heart of creativity, with the power of narrative shaping vision above all else and sustaining oneself in striving for or simply wanting to endure.

III

I will continue to regard Naipaul as one of the world's great writers despite controversy about his attitudes and his trenchant utterances ('The dot means my head is empty': on the bindi Hindu women wear; or on Pakistan: 'The Pakistani dream is one day there'll be a Muslim resurgence and they will lead the prayers in the mosques in Delhi'; or, on Britain: 'a country of second-rate people – bum politicians, scruffy writers and crooked aristocrats'). Naipaul's pragmatism it also is, as rituals, magic, romanticism of any sort may be perhaps foreign to his sensibility, and by extension – foreign to worlds of the metropolitan centre he has embraced; and maybe in his travelogues objectification will continue to be his norm.

Not unexpectedly the Muslim fundamentalist world comes in for much of his criticism: in *Among the Believers: An Islamic Journey* (1981) and *Beyond Belief: Islamic Excursions Among the Converted Peoples* (1998) Naipaul's oftentimes caustic observation and analysis would prompt one like Edward Said to say: 'In the earlier book, its funny moments are at the expense of Muslims, who are "wogs" after all as seen by Naipaul's British and American readers, potential fanatics and terrorists, who cannot spell, be coherent, sound right to a worldly-wise, somewhat jaded judge from the West.' Yet Said would acknowledge in his Reith Lectures, Naipaul's role to 'challenge routine, assailing mediocrity and cliches...'; and then writing about Naipaul's 'extraordinary antennae as a novelist,' of his 'sifting through the debris of colonialism and post-colonialism, remorselessly judging the illusions and cruelties of independent states and the new true believers ....' Naipaul's 'colonial rage' at both people and the societies they live in: the seeming chaos of India, Africa, the delusion of Islamic fundamentalists, are indeed seen through his unique lens (whether we agree with him or not) ; and no doubt for him freedom implies being at odds with everyone else, especially with those who lament the colonial past (as he did at a conference in India, which irked someone like Salman Rushdie). But above all, it's Naipaul's fully engaging us: making us think deeply about our unconscious or ideological commitments; and as so often occurs, his narrative insights compel us to keep reading him as he presents us with the essentially intuitive dimension of his art, which may be separate from any easily identifiable social predisposition on his part, as he informs us.

In Canada I am always swayed by Naipaul's prose style, as I recognise a bigger world, not least because of my own preoccupation with endless possibilities. And Naipaul's indebtedness to his father, Seepersad Naipaul, does not escape me too, the life of going beyond mere Hindu ways in small-island Trinidad or coastal Guyana that the writing life initially presented to him – as the recent publication of the letters between father and son attest to in remarkable, even poignant, ways, showing an extraordinarily complex sensibility at work.

As has been said, and is worth repeating – Naipaul is his own main character in his books; in his Nobel Prize acceptance speech he would say, 'When I became a writer those areas of darkness around me as a child became my subjects. The land; the aborigines; the New World; the colony; the history; India; the Muslim world, to which I also felt myself related; Africa; and then England, where I was doing my writing. That was what I meant when I said that my books stand one on the other, and that I am the sum of my books.' While he may favour being in the limbo world of a free state, because of his commitment to art he will keep pushing the boundaries of fiction and autobiography, going to the heart of his ideology as he affirms Marcel Proust's axiom: of 'the secretions of one's innermost self, written in solitude and for oneself alone that one gives to the public' as his very own; which I will contemplate in order to keep sustaining me as a writer, also.

Naipaul, however, redeems Blair by imagining a literary ending to his life. In an imaginary sequence credited to the inflections of a Poe story, Naipaul rewrites Conrad's Kurtz as he lies dying: 'And I feel that, as if in some Edgar Allan Poe story, at the moment of death, while the brain still sparked, a question could have been lodged in that brain – "Does this betrayal mock your life?" – the answer immediately after death would have been "No! No! No!"[1] And, in that vehement negation would lie an affirmation of Blair's life, the intensity of his commitment to change, his assertion that the world [he] will be leaving is better than the one he was born into, his satisfaction in knowing that the revolution he had taken part in had succeeded. Naipaul's response insists that even the continuity of betrayal could not invalidate the lives of those who struggle to exceed the limits of their times. With that, his focus on histories of the past centuries in the face of a bitter present complicates the relationship of the New World to the Old, and in the process swaps the Centre with the Margin.

9

Metaphors of Disintegration in Shiva Naipaul's *The Chip Chip Gatherers*

MADHURI CHATTERJEE

Shiva Naipaul's *The Chip Chip Gatherers* (1973) is a complex novel with several themes running parallel to each other. Winner of the Whitbread Award, the novel is placed against the background of colonisation and its resultant fallouts, and the narrative bears an uncanny resemblance to the author's own life. Although not autobiographical, the novel is rooted in his major preoccupations : confrontation with the self and the problems of identity, family history and the fate of immigrant communities caught between two cultures. Shiva Naipaul sees himself as a symbol of double displacement. For him 'remembering' the past becomes a strategy employed to reconstruct, redefine and reshape his past. The pull of the past disorients the immigrant to recreate himself in his adopted culture. Shiva's expatriate sensibility and double identity shapes his writing and the sense of displacement becomes a recurrent reality in the lives of his characters as well.

The sense of displacement and dislocation raises several questions with respect to poetics of exile, expatriate writing, writer's relationship to his culture, the specifics which govern identity construction and the concept of de-centering. Often the creation of a third space by the writer 'destroys the concept of purity of cultures and brings into being a self-reflexive self and a self-reflexive text' (Jain 102). *The Chip Chip Gatherers* as the title indicates, reflects the social and fragmentary realities of the island society and the oppressive weight of colonialism it carries. The central character, Egbert Ramsaran, is an Indian who, through the processes of assimilation and resistance, undergoes several transformations both in his relationships and in his family formation. He lives almost everything twice over and, in this living, experiments with both the socially accepted codes and the ones falling outside the normative structures. Ramsaran neither integrates nor assimilates with the new culture. He has a troubled relationship with his past and is confused about his identity. He seems to be involved in an internal struggle to forget his past. Relocation and acceptance of his past is necessary in order to adapt to a new culture. As long as they do not accept their roots – characters are doomed to a lonely and isolated existence. The novel also reflects his father Seepersad's literary influence of creating sardonic, comic characters related to his Trinidadian experience. It is almost a farcical portrayal of the tragic comic aspects of an illiterate and divided society's transition from colonial to independent nationhood.

Here the dislocation results from a sense of place and displacement results from extraterritoriality. It also draws attention to the Foucauldian definition of heterotopia – whereby time gets interrelated. Heterotopia is a counter-site like a resting place, a sanatorium, a prison or a theatre, a counter-site where 'all the other real sites that can be found within a culture are simultaneously represented, contested and inverted' and where a juxtaposition of the otherwise incompatible can take place (Foucault 24–25).

The third person narration explains the childhood and past of his central protagonist Egbert Ramsaran and in the process builds up his character. Born in a Hindu family as Ashok, he rebels against the colonised structure and refuses to remain happy at the 'bottom of a dung heap' (13). He however carries no political or colonial resentment. He pleads escape from the island with his childhood friend Vishnu Bholai but the latter refuses to accompany him. However he changes his name from Ashok to Egbert and converts to Presbyterianism in the Port of Spain. The experience of movement that is partly self-chosen and partly imposed on him by history has become very important to him. Shiva Naipaul's way of looking at culture and history is reflected in Egbert's attitude. A similar sentiment is echoed in Edward Said's expression 'The whole notion of coming over or moving from one identity to another is extremely important – to me, being as I am – as well as all are, a sort of hybrid' (Said 122).

Change of location is often a traumatic or a defining experience. Ramsaran's return to Victoria and the subsequent death of his parents is a moment of loss balanced equally with his personal success in having become the richest man of the place. This is a kind of see-saw, marking his material success on one hand and his increased withdrawal from the natives on the other. The distancing marks his sense of identity. Egbert Ramsaran lives in a world so tight, so self-contained, so alienated from the mainstream – it is almost a ghetto. There is also his palatial house which stands as a monument of his achievement and his name 'spoken of with wonder and respect if not affection' (25) but the place projects an image of a scrapyard – where everything he has scrupulously gathered is utilised or piled in the pasturage. 'Salvage of any sort was forbidden. Once they (the trucks) had been brought to the field, they were allowed to rust and fall to pieces slowly, ritually one might say in the sun and rain. Their disintegrating skeletons scattered at random over its surface resembled the dried washed out bones of colony of prehistoric monsters' (9-10). The character framing which takes place right at the beginning is a contrast between the person he is and the gradual deterioration and disintegration which reduces him to a mere chip.

Woven with Ramsaran's narrative are several other lives and narratives – his wife Rani, son Wilbert, illegitimate son Singh, friend Vishnu Bholai, his mistress Sushila and the large extended family of his in-laws. The metaphor of the house adds a new dimension to the narration. It is the central unifying symbol associated with cloistered feudal order where only Ramsaran's opinion is respected and there exists the paternalistic structure of the past. The house becomes a castle – strong, impregnable and unapproachable – and Ramsaran as the landlord presides over by depriving and abusing their rights, 'All men are equally strangers to him and he uses his money to torment and humiliate other persons' (29).

Ramsaran's first dislocation is not so pervasive because his withdrawal is more apparent and prolonged. His marriage to Rani is a symbolic ritual he undergoes without much thought. But she is never allowed to be either his wife or his son Wilbert's mother. She remains a marginalised character, an object of compromise and her 'presence is a final and complete expression of the nonsense her life had been' (37). He keeps an irrational master-slave relationship with her and she is denied all social and sexual pleasures.

Rani, his native wife, comes from another extended Hindu family structure. She has a shrewd and manipulative mother Badsai who banks on this marriage and hopes to hold an authority on the Ramsaran empire. The description of this odd assortment of an extended family – brothers- and sisters- in-law – loosely adheres to the traditional structures of sprawling families and projects the migrant reality. After Rani's death, Sushila replaces her and becomes Ramsaran's mistress, to briefly wield her seductive power on him. There is no duality in him when married to Rani but his relationship with Sushila becomes a kind of an allegory developing a strange plurality in him. It is the beginning of a second withdrawal and the collapse of his identity. He breaks away from his habits and loses interest in his habit of accumulating debts. His elaborate exercise equipment is allowed to rust and fall to pieces. He develops a very laid back attitude and does nothing 'but to take things easy' (194). He even expels his illegitimate son, from the house, after Singh threatens to encounter Sushila. In fact the authorial comment states, 'It marked a definite break with the past. The whole tenor of his life was shattering and Egbert Ramsaran was assisting in the process. No enemy, had he heartily wished it, could have contrived his destruction so skillfully, could have reduced him to such a predicament' (160).

Sushila, his mistress, plays a crucial and pivotal part in unhinging and dislocating the Ramsaran empire. Her individualism does not allow her to relate to the confined world of family alliances and myriad taboos. She belongs to the Badsai clan and is reared by Rani's own mother. She cleverly picks the bait placed by Badsai who as Ramsaran's mother-in-law wants to wield control over his empire. Sushila has supreme confidence in her beauty and has long forsaken her traditional family. She has an illegitimate daughter Sita but is not deterred by this and values her uncertain emancipation. Her act of scandalizing the people is a symbolic gesture challenging the paternalistic structure.

Ramsaran and Sushila both struggle to break away from their past. They break away from the community and the centre it provides but are unable to find another centre. They struggle to plant themselves and escape from the confused world of 'lostness'. But they get stuck in a periphery – a dead space and collapse. The temporal space of the present becomes grim, perverse and confused. Sushila, by leaving behind her old ways of rebelliousness, accomplishes nothing. It is a kind of disjunctive temporality that they are faced with. The partitioning off, the reducing life into 'now' and 'then' doesn't make for a featured, structured whole. Their flight and journey re-enact the middle passage theme of displacement. Familiar routines which had borne the stamp of external verities disappear in the presence of Sushila who effortlessly checks all access to Ramsaran and does away with all the cattle. She also suggests to Ramsaran to pull his house down and build a new one. She coaxes him to buy a beach house to revive his deteriorating health. The moving away from self to carve a new identity is a painful process. Sushila's 'stepping out' of her stereotyped role as well as her sense of individual freedom to wield control over Ramsaran recoils on her. She transforms and deactivates Egbert Ramsaran but feels threatened by her own daughter's physicality. Her utterance, 'Two scrawny legs and breasts don't make a woman. To be a woman that is hardest thing in the world. I should have been born a man ...Then I would never have to ...' reveals her painful desire for release (233).

Sushila disappears from Ramsaran's house the way she had come suddenly. But in this process she leaves both him and his house in shambles. Egbert Ramsaran becomes 'veined, segmented, cracked' (247), suffers a massive stroke and is reduced to his wheelchair 'abstracted and motionless' and the passers-by who panicked at his sight earlier 'impassively stare at the emancipated, collapsed figure' (251).

The construction of the self, the loss of identity, the dislocation and disintegration of relationships have all been explored through diverse images and metaphors. The dilapidation of his house adds another mystery to Ramsaran's self. The image of the house works in many different ways-metaphoric, ironic and subversive.. Home is not a quest for spatial identity but a search for roots. It is a search for a self in a world arbitrarily divided into liberated and colonised world. The house is shared by many – Wilbert, Sushila, Sita – but there is no nostalgic emotion or attachment. The characters' wilful homelessness further reinforces the concept of disintegration. The third person narration subjectively builds the lives of the characters associated with Ramsaran personally and professionally and charts their corrosion and fall, the decay in values and their helplessness in the face of modern aspirations. The word 'chip' means a piece which has been broken off or cut off from an object. Most of the characters have isolated and alienated moorings and remain distanced from their parental primary harbour. As chip-chip gatherers they are merely picking up pieces, unable to construct any meaningful pattern. Is the immigrant eternally condemned to this rootlessness? The 'house' here works in an entirely different way from V.S. Naipaul's *A House for Mr Biswas*, the house that Mr Biswas is always, and against enormous odds, trying to build as a symbol of independence, as a kind of 'housing' for his soul but which remains different from Hanuman house where things are divorced from their functions, they are unrelated and fade off into the darkness. The new house, like Ramsaran's 'impressive' mansion represents the Tulsis' name and status in community but behind lies a further sprawling hinterland full of half-broken antiques and toys, a repository of memory, but where the Tulsis can feel at home. Though it is 'temporary and not quite real' (147). The comparison stresses the 'ghosting' of the immigrant, despite the solidity of their establishment.

The dislocations work in a multiple manner. When home becomes a mythic space of desire it becomes also a place of no return. Home takes many different versions in Ramsaran's house - the characters revolt against assimilation, severe their spiritual and symbiotic ties with their clan and community and move towards displacement and uprootedness. The insanity of their lives leads to their decadence.

The narrative also brings in Egbert Ramsaran's brother Cha Cha and his mistress living in the nearby market neighbourhood, a place which seemed 'mutilated, diseased, starving, abounded and where men and women, as decayed as the fruits and vegetables, they were selling' (198). Also Ramsaran's illegitimate son Singh's demeanor suggests a wild and vagabond existence. He is condemned to the outer edges of society, living in wilderness with his wife Myra. He has no share or say in the family fortune but he is an irregular visitor to Ramsaran's house.

Formal education seems to have its own disintegrating influence on the next generation of colonisers. Vishnu Bholai, the most reputable grocer and childhood associate of

Ramsaran, is reduced to a cipher by the condescending attitude of his wife. Mrs Bholai wants her son Julian to leave the island and become a doctor. Education offers a chance for upward social mobility and new identity in society. Sita's segregation from the wall of narrowly defined female identity and escape from notoriety of illegitimacy is because of her essential knowledge and education. Julian Bholai can escape his father's fate through his education, but Ramsaran's son Wilbert is condemned to subjugation as he receives only practical apprenticeship of a mechanic but no degree. Shiva Naipaul also satirises and paradoxes the middle class aspiration of martyrdom, the parents undergo to ensure that their children acquire educational degrees.

Alienation from the indigenous way of life and the vehemence of its impact is captured through the intense imaging of predatoriness, pollution, decay, disorder. Space is used in a variety of ways in the novel. First there are enclosures which are created – Rani's drab and barren room, Ramsaran's disorganised house, Vishnu Bholai's bright and stuffy house. As contrasted with this are the images of destruction and wilderness outside. Ramsaran's house loses all inmates and stands barren, after Sushila's disappearance, Ramsaran goes into a rage and destroys Sita's books and belongings by putting them in a fire, which is a universal symbol of destruction and violence. Ramsaran Transport Company loses trusted employees like Mr Wilkinson and finally collapses. Julian leaves the island and his sister Shanti finally marries Wilbert and becomes the new inmate of the Ramsaran house. Jasbir Jain in her essay "Identity, Home and Culture Through Dislocations" has observed that the narrative of migrancy is a linear one and 'there is no possibility of belonging once again even as the past controls the present' (Jain 231), also there is no fixed origin to which they can make some final and absolute return. It further hints at the politics of identity and the politics of position. Only memory becomes a reason for continuity because 'without memory, without a certain will to mythologize life for many…will become intolerable…and lose its ethical edge' (Mishra 46).

The novel opens and closes with sprawling chaos and ramshackle waste, vagrancy and vacuum. The concluding paragraph of *The Chip Chip Gatherers* sums it up as: 'The incoming tide inundated the Chip Chip beds and brought with it fresh litter of debris – chunks of seaweed and coconut shell and driftwood'. The tide washes every thing and like the characters stands isolated. 'It suggested totemic splendor, a sacrificial offering to the Gods of fertility and plentiful harvest ... divorced ... and continued to rot slowly on this wind swept shimmering beach of swooping vultures, staring dogs and Chip Chip Gatherers and (Wilbert) himself' (320).

The Chip Chip Gatherers is a narrative of dislocation and also a kind of an bildungsroman, charting the growth and regression marking the life of an individual. It spawns the phenomenon of cultural colonisation and its imprecations in an aesthetically humorous manner. The story of Egbert Ramsaran's life is irrevocably intertwined with the facts of migration, cultural displacement and critical appraisal of the relationship between self and society. Ramsaran's feeling of debilitating despair accruing from a state of spiritual, emotional, non cognition and physical isolation may be considered a pertinent reflection of the predicament of colonisation.

References

Foucault, Michel. "Texts/Contexts: Of Other Spaces", *Diacritics*. Spring, 1986.

Jain, Jasbir. "Geographical Dislocations and the Poetics of Exile : Ashis Gupta and Michael Ondaatje", *Writers of the Indian Diaspora*. Ed. Jasbir Jain. Jaipur : Rawat Publication, 1998.

Jain, Jasbir. ed., *Dislocation and Multiculturalism*. Jaipur, Rawat Publication, 2004.

Mishra, Vijay. "Diasporas and the Art of Impossible Mourning" *In Diaspora*. Ed. Makarand Paranjape. New Delhi: Indialog Publications Pvt Ltd, 2001.

Naipaul, Shiva. *The Chip Chip Gatherers*. Penguin Books, 1973.

Naipaul, V.S. *A House for Mr Biswas*. London: Andre Deutsch, 1961.

Said, Edward. *The Politics of Dispossession*. London: Vintage, 1995.

10

Rites of Passage: George Lamming's *In the Castle of My Skin*

NIDHI SINGH

The presence of the autobiographical element in the monumental first novel by George Lamming *In the Castle of My Skin* published in 1953, has been repeatedly referred to by critics. A close reading of the text reveals that personal experiences in the process of being written get transformed into an act of confronting and redefining the past, imbuing with meaning not only the personal but also the socio-historical scenario of the period. An attempt is made to give meaning to the shared experiences and common past. The work explores the era when British Caribbean was struggling with its ethical, social and political agendas which arose out of domestic strife with its roots in colonial experience. The act of writing becomes an act of redefining the self by confronting the past.

The trope of the rite of passage, of crossing over is skilfully used at individual level as well as to interrogate the dilemma of Caribbean territories as they struggle for post-colonial identity. Ngugi Wa Thiong'O in his article on *In the Castle of My Skin* refers to the three stages in the work: 'a static phase, then a phase of rebellion, ending in a phase of achievement and disillusionment with society poised on the edge of a new struggle ...' (47). Lamming uses this frame to take into account the colonisation of not only geographical landscape but also of the psychic landscape of Caribbean people and expresses their dilemma in his non-fictional work *The Pleasures of Exile*:

> On the political level, we are often without the right kind of information to make argument effective; on the moral level we have to feel our way through problems for which we have no adequate reference of traditional conduct as guide .... We are made to feel a sense of exile by our inadequacy and our irrelevance of function in a society whose past we can't alter, and whose future is always beyond us. (24)

Lamming's *In the Castle of My Skin* projects the need of not only the protagonist but the whole community for a coherent identity. The psychological setback arising from loss of identity caused by unquestioning acceptance of discriminations inherent in colonialism as natural state of affairs is challenged. Asserting the humanity of blacks and connecting with the African diaspora become the stepping stone for interrogation of politics of race and identity.

At one level the novel is about growing up and growing away from the world of childhood. The sense of alienation and isolation experienced by the protagonist ensure his withdrawal and finally his departure from his birthplace. The novel opens with incessant rain marring the celebrations of the ninth birthday of the protagonist. A morose observation sets the tone of the work :

> As if in serious imitation of waters that raced outside, our lives – meaning our fears and their corresponding ideals – seemed to escape down an imaginary drain that was our future. (10)

The sense of frustration and feeling of lack of control over future, though contributed to the nine-year-old protagonist are responses expected from adult sensibility.

The loneliness experienced by George, the protagonist, owing to lack of relatives and family ties, is countered by the presence of strong community life as echoed in the song sung by his mother and in response taken up by women of the neighbourhood '... until the voices seem to be gathered up by a single effort and the whole village shook with song on its foundation of water' (11). The first two chapters reiterate the easy camaraderie that exists among the women and children of the village arising from shared day-to-day experiences. However, the writer emphasises lack of 'consciousness' of the meaning behind their experiences.

The legacy of colonisation can be observed in the social stratification with the landlord at the helm of the power structure and the peasants at the bottom of the hierarchy. It is further strengthened by the servile acceptance of the discrimination colonisation gave birth to within the black community, where the enemy is not the outsider but "My People" (27). Ironically, white supremacy goes unquestioned and unchallenged. On the contrary there is fear of causing offence and a servile acceptance of the stance taken by the whites. School too is used for buttressing the position of the British colonisers. Celebration of the Queen's birthday and predominantly British education system further widen the schism in identity where the students experience a sense of alienation and fragmentation. The dilemma of belonging partly to two worlds but fully to neither is the reason behind the alienation experienced. Irony arises out of the pride taken by the villagers when they refer to Barbados as "Little England". Even religion i.e. Christianity is seen as sanctifying the colonisation of Barbados by the British and future greatness is seen in terms of shared achievements :

> One day before time changed for eternity, Little England and Big England, God's anointed on earth, might hand in hand rule this earth. (37)

The conversation of the students during the Queen's birthday celebrations reveals their perspective. They grope about to give meaning to the world around them with the help of the limited knowledge and half truths available to them. Their curiosity spans not only questions related to interpersonal relationships but also reflects their need to understand the mechanics of not only minting of coins but also with the ambiguous shadow of slavery. Education system as it exists is of no help. Slavery, in the children's opinion is 'too far back for any one to worry about teaching it as history. That's really why it wasn't taught' (58). Filial loyalties, morality, laws regulating their lives, sexuality, violence, British royalty, imperialism, slavery, history, all excite their curiosity and are discussed by them. Though nascent, the process of questioning has already begun which finds fruition in George and Trumper's departure from the village.

It is out of this personal crisis that the leader of the village in the person of Mr Slime, the headmaster, is born. The transition from headmaster of the village school to leader of the people is a successful one. He represents the intelligentsia of the village and is respected for his position which gives him power. The village has faith in his leadership and looks up to him for guidance. The wind of change in the village is initiated by Mr Slime when he gives to the villagers the dream of possessing the land they live on. Ma and Pa, the oldest residents of the village, express their fears and expectations respectively at the steps taken by the headmaster towards the realisation of this dream. Lamming skilfully projects the change that comes over the villagers. The first chapter describes men of the village at evening time gathered around the lamp post '... to throw dice or cut cards or simply to talk' (10), but after the passage of one year the men are presented as '... sitting leisurely round the post talking about the new Friendly Society and the Penny Bank' (81), set up by Mr Slime. For the first time white supremacy is being challenged and Old Man Pa compares Mr Slime to Moses 'come to save his people ...' (78). The reservation that Old Woman Ma expresses about Slime's activities is justified as the novel unfolds and the final betrayal takes the form of dispossession of Pa from his home and the decision to send him to "Alms House" (251). Commenting on leadership, Fanon in *The Wretched of the Earth* holds :

> ... far from embodying in concrete form the needs of the people in what touches bread, land, and the restoration of the country to the sacred hands of the people, the leader will reveal his inner purpose : to become the general president of that company of profiteers impatient for their returns which constitutes the national bourgeoisie. (133)

The strike and the riots that follow undermine the power and position of Creighton, the white landlord. There is a shift of power and prestige from Creighton to Slime. The old world of feudal supremacy is challenged and found wanting. It gives way to the new world where the power is vested in the bourgeoisie class represented by Mr Slime, the contractor and the constable. The emergent scenario further highlights the sharp divide between the bourgeoisie and the peasants. The former become the cause of dispossession of the latter. The cycle of change not only destabilises the landlord's supremacy but also dislodges the poor villagers from the land, from the spot which they were taught to dream of possessing by Slime himself. The position of the peasants in Lamming's novel is reminiscent of that of the animals by the end of George Orwell's *Animal Farm*. Manipulation and exploitation are the key operative words, with peasants being forced to the margins of the emergent society.

The protagonist and his friends Boy Blue, Bob and Trumper grow into awareness of the universe they inhabit influenced by the changes taking place in the community. G's sensitivity to racial discrimination comes through when he fantasises about the shapes of the cloud. He sees one as white man and the other as black, staring at each other trying to understand the predicament they were in and which is not to their liking. Later sitting on the banks of the sea, the boys discuss their perceptions about life at the village. The protagonist realises that 'No black boy wanted to be white, but it was also true that no black boy liked the idea of being black' (127). This attitude problematises the process of identity construction. Irreverence for white settlers gets emphasised when the boys discuss how some people assert that whites who left England were 'scum' and misfits.

Referring to the case of Bambi, Bambina and Bot, they conclude that marriage, a product of British culture leads to 'breakin' up' at the level of human relations, and more important, at the level of cultural value system of the natives.

Change emerges as the leitmotif in the latter half of the work. At the age of eleven, G. joins the High School, the leeway to the 'other world', that of civil service or professions like law and medicine; the world of bourgeoisie. The memory of village life alienates him from life at High School, and he is excluded from the world of village by his friends because they feel his allegiances have shifted. The sense of alienation is two fold and G. expresses it thus :

> It was as though my roots had been snapped from the centre of what I knew best, while I remained impotent to wrest what my fortunes had forced me into. (220)

G. is constantly aware of things changing and the change being irreversible be it strictly personal or related to the village. The future that awaits each boy is different. Trumper emigrates to America, Bob and Boy Blue join the Police Force and G. joins High School. Three years pass and G. decides to go to Trinidad to teach English in a boarding school. Trumper's letters reveal the change that has come over him due to exposure to new world-view, Bob and Boy Blue are part of the police force.

The world outside too was changing with the outbreak of war in Europe. It appears finally the bastion of the British empire was shaken. The effect of war was felt in the village as well. The trains are discontinued and finally even the tracks are removed. The trees are felled. Old woman Ma has passed away and her passing is symbolic of the passing of the old world value system based on faith and acceptance. The landlord's power and prestige have given way to Mr Slime's. The shoemaker and Mr Foster, like many others in the village are forced to vacate the piece of land they live on, the land they had 'rooted themselves into' (24). Emigration to America is now the pattern. Lamming introduces the concept of 'negritude', which is Pan African through the experiences of Trumper. America emerges as the place where African identity is reaffirmed by acknowledging allegiance to 'negro race' (295). Reconnecting with African cultural roots through American experience is highlighted.

The protagonist observes the changes and becomes more aware of the schism within him. Protected within the "Castle" of his skin he hopes to make himself whole surrounded by people who have no knowledge of him and so cannot undermine him: 'When I reach Trinidad where no one knows me I may be able to strike identity with the other person' (261). The protagonist accepts the land of his birth and experiences as his home and hence the pain experienced at the thought of seeing everything he was familiar with for the "last time", but he must travel outside this loved but alienating space in order to find himself.

References

Fanon, Frantz. *The Wretched of the Earth*. Trans Constance Farrington. Harmondsworth: Penguin Books, 1967.

Lamming, George. *In the Castle of My Skin*. (1953). Harlow, Essex: Longman Drumbeat, 1979.

———. *The Pleasures of Exile*. London : Michael Joseph Ltd., 1960.

Orwell, George. *Animal Farm*. New Delhi : Indialog Publications Pvt. Ltd., 2003.

Thiong'O, Ngugi Wa. "George Lamming's *In the Castle of My Skin*". *Critics on Caribbean Literature : Readings in Literary Criticism*. Ed. Edward Baugh. London: George Allen & Unwin, 1978.

11

Race of Races in Sam Selvon's *Those Who Eat the Cascadura*

M. ROSARY ROYAR

> Writing will never be simple Voice Painting (Voltaire). It creates meaning by enregistering it, by entrusting it to an engraving, a groove, a relief, to a surface whose essential characteristic is to be infinitely transmissible.
>
> Derrida qtd. in Bill Ashcroft, 2001,63.

Condemning apartheid, Derrida expounds that it 'sets separation itself apart: "apartitionality" and like all racisms, it passes segregation off as natural'. He, in an exegetical method, underscores 'racism always betrays the perversion of a man, the "talking animal". It institutes, declares, writes, inscribes, prescribes. A system of marks, it outlines space in order to assign forced residence or to close off borders. It does not discern, it discriminates' (263). As a political ideology racism, with its unimaginable and unflinching sway, has marred the histories of people and violated the right of the indigeneity. The white minority's irremediable destruction and inexpressible torture in the name of racism has pervaded extensively and for too long. It has entailed poverty, suffering and oppression.

Reading Sam Selvon's *Those Who Eat the Cascadura* (1972) in the perspective of race, it engraves a world that apparently paints a harmonious existence of people. But beyond the veil, various races make vignettes of their lives. Set in Sans Souci, Trinidad and revolving around cocoa plantation, the text transmits the racial drama in the postcolonial stage of the Caribbean islands.

Roger Franklin is the estate owner and a widower whose domestic affairs have been run by Eloisa. Abdul R. JanMohamed argues that the Europeans have replaced the use-value with the exchange-value (60). He differentiates between the covert and overt aspects of colonialism. 'The covert purpose is to exploit the colony's natural resources thoroughly and ruthlessly through the various imperialist material practices'. The overt aim is to 'civilize the savage' (62). Roger Franklin primarily plunders the exchange value of cocoa. He has not gone into farming for the upliftment of the poor. He comes to Trinidad to get away from dreary burden of living with someone he does not love. When Gladys dies, the estate is in 'shambles and fast going to rain' (13) and he toils mightily to recover it and that is his only possession.

The colonial world has two zones and Frantz Fanon remarks 'the zone where the natives live is not complementary to the zone inhabited by the settlers' and they both follow the 'principle of reciprocal exclusivity' (32). The Africans and the Indians mostly occupy the huts in Sans Souci. The hurricane Jenny with titanic force rushes at a speed of eighty miles an hour and blows off the huts of the indentured labourers and the black community. The temple goes down with no protest before the gale and the worshippers are dry leaves for it. The houses of Roger and Devertie set on hills stand against the weather and the fury of the hurricane. The wealthy white men can easily rectify the minor damages. The workers are just stocked in schools. These people encamp in a locale far away from the colonisers. The site of inhabitation even stands apart and speaks eloquently of affluence and poverty, high and low status literally and metaphorically. The mansions and the huts are the chiaroscuro of royalty and pauperism in the beautiful island in its independent state.

The encounter between Kamalla and Roger, the colonised and the coloniser is more portentous than being dramatic. Her jeering makes him frown. Her 'wild appearance and the glitter in her eye' make him look askance if she has gone mad. Roger uses the weapon of authority and asks her to get out for he is 'too civilised to cope with a primitive situation like this'. He understands her 'veiled threat' and its insinuation that she may bear his child. Before he loses his dignity completely he wants to get rid of her for she taunts him and her mockery enrages him. Doubtless that he has been generous to her 'to ensure the utmost secrecy about the liaison'. When she threatens that as the mark busts, the whole world will know about the white man, he descends from his civility and refinement and becomes wild, strikes her and slaps her that she almost stumbles on the steps. He is 'terrified of a dreadful scene' but secretly ruminates that his 'prestige and standing would not be harmed'. It means notoriety for her. He sees himself 'disgraced as master of Sans Souci by this ignorant woman'. As he repeats that Sarojini does not live there she wants him to settle the business of giving her the right to live in his house. He trembles with a 'compulsion to strangle her' (175-177). She leaves the place and he gulps down a heavy drink.

His desire for the other, a woman of inferior race and his midnight liaison with her do not corrode his heart to be heavy laden with remorse and regret. He is afraid of the stain on his authority. As a man, he ponders that if the village comes to know of his act the other women may envy Kamalla and want to be his consort. As a master, he fears disgrace. In the neocolonial situation Claramma Jose posits that power relationships are recentred and the white man becomes a 'faceless and nameless representative of the dominating power' (25). These shreds of Roger's character show his inability to sever himself from the moorings of authority. To save his face, he controls his surging fury.

Kamalla, on the other hand, dares to defy him, demands her right and she must have her footing in the chaos.

Contradistinguishing Eloisa with Manko, Eloisa's world has become so much circumscribed that potency for rich living seems to have been obliterated. But Manko as the obeah man stands as a stalwart unobtrusively challenging the white men. Eloisa and Manko are silhouetted against slave trade. Both put up a show of indifference to each other but 'It was like a game they had been playing all their lives' (14). Eloisa represents the colonised Christian and Manko the colonised native. Each is staunchly committed to one's belief. At times, Eloisa warns him to give up his dealings with spirits and turn unto God. They travel in different tracks. Ethnicity, to cite Radhakrishnan's premise, is a 'socio-political construct caught up in the connectedness of its own history to prehistories and other histories' (65). It is ostensible that past history of crossing Middle Passage, looms silently but forcefully in the present history of Caribbean, interconnected with the dominant culture of the coloniser and the alienated indentured labourers, Indians. The European, the African and the Indian races commingle in the soil of Trinidad only to practice their separateness.

Manko possesses powers and even Rover, the dog with its animal instincts, understands it. When people with their woes and ailments approach him, he invokes the very spirits they are frightened of and he 'costume[s] his gifts with a certain amount of ritual, knowing the dearth of faith in his fellow men. Instead of taking a bit of logical advice, they preferred him to burn some *veteeveh* bush over a smoking fire and chant incantation' (16). He comes and goes as the spirits direct him. He never tries to convince disbelievers for he knows 'you mustn't play with the spirits' (20). He forewarns that Prekash is going to have a hard time but Sarojini is to be happier than she ever was and with Garry Johnson's arrival at Sans Souci, things are not going to be the same. He assures Sarojini that Garry is a good man but puts it emphatically 'though good is good with white people and is a different thing with black people' (230).

Sarojini reacts and as an act of rejecting her being classified as black says 'I is Indian!' But Manko, as the whites consider the rest to be black people, holds on 'you still black'. Disregarding her insistence that she is different by pointing out to her skin colour, he in a foresighted manner without any wavering in his heart declares, 'Black and white will mix until black is white' (23) meaning that everything would equate. He never retraces his path to his forefathers but he is in a class by himself. He is ostensibly Afro-centric in his own world that he has constructed in Sans Souci.

The negro's superior smile disconcerts Prekash, the overseer of Sans Souci, who is young and inexperienced. In arguments about running the estate, Manko always wins. Prekash thinks that Manko fools the superstitious villagers but is also aware that Manko laughs at his inadequacy. He admits to himself that Manko is an experienced cacao man and in fact 'the most knowledgeable of them all' (29) Prekash, with his shallowness, cannot be compatible with his fellow worker, Manko and never tries to improve their relationship.

A 'sudden change of mood' and 'some strange dimension' (45) encircle the spot with Manko's presence. Entering the scene, Manko surprises Roger, Garry and Prekash by stating what only Garry knows that seven days after he has left England the ship has a fire on board and if the crew has not moved faster it could have been serious. Garry acknowledging it ejaculates 'it's incredible by any yardstick' (46). While Garry is unable to recover from the shock, Manko sketches Garry's future that he does not have many more journeys to make and time flies faster for him than it does for anybody else. Sensing Garry's disquietude, Roger interrupts the discourse 'Enough of your devilish forecast' (47) and asks him to entertain them with his stories. Manko casually explains that *soucouyant* is an old woman who goes at night to suck human blood especially of babies. She sheds skin like a snake and, turns into a ball of fire. On the very same day Roger meets it, the people rub the skin with pepper and salt and she screams unable to wear it. They push her into a barrel, nail it up and throw into the river. Making a critique of ethnic reality, Radhakrishnan posits that it has a name, which is forced on by the oppressor. It achieves a revolution against the oppressor through a process of inverse displacement and it represents itself from within its own point of view (69). Roger categorises Manko's account as devilish forecasts but Garry cannot refute its veracity. Roger wavers in his esteem of Manko who steadfastly holds on and what he has stated he never tries to revert. His assertion cannot be waved off. The master of Sans Souci violates not the truth of *Soucouyant* for he himself has experienced it and is almost thrown off the horse. Reason vies with superstition.

His personal experience in his youth with *La diablesse*, the devil woman with two big eyes, a twist-up nose, the teeth pushing out of mouth and a hoof for foot is a pretty girl when the dance party begins. She becomes fresh and lively while the others get tired. Manko accompanies her in the forest she changes into an ugly woman and he pulls his shirt to show the marks where the picker scratched him. It is incredible for Prekash to realise that 'the white men accept all the talk of obeah and spirits' and they never 'ridicule' (50) him. Manko has shaken Garry and his 'uncanny glimpses into the past and future' [are] threads which [weave] a pattern about him' (51). He doubts if he has quickly fallen under the 'spell of the tropics, embroidering casual incidence with mystery and speculation'. In his 'bafflement' he does not arrive at any conclusion. Bruce King remarks 'ethnicity is a form of cultural assertion which reflects conflict' and it may be a struggle for power. It results also from fear of domination and fear of extinction through acculturation and assimilation (1). These cultural encounters represent a conflict between myth and essentialism, spirits and enlightenment, and supernatural and natural.

The dominant culture imposes an image on the Other in defining its identity. C.L. Innes distinguishes that the dismissal of native culture by the coloniser leads to the assertion of a culture, which is an antithesis of the colonial one (123).

Manko's narration serves as a discourse that opposes the dominant culture. At the same time Radhakrishnan specifies about 'ethnic violence' caused by the dominant ideology and it posits the other as something 'alien, dangerous, criminal and spontaneously and instinctually terroristic' (90). Prekash's instruction to the workers is a corollary to this established notion. Prekash warns them to deport themselves and show good manners to Garry who has been given the privilege of having anything he wants in the estate. He does not want any disrespect towards him. Above all comes the caveat that they think the whole set of them to be 'just ignorant and backward. These people from England have some funny ideas when they come here. They think we live like cannibals in Africa' (67). Radhakrishnan's argument is that as the dominant culture suffers from paranoia it refuses to look into the subaltern culture and maintains it as 'eternally illicit, transgressive and lawless' (90). Abdul R. JanMohamed strengthens the same proposition that the European's narcissistic self-recognition depends on subjugating the native and maintaining his position as a master whereby he succeeds in getting the recognition of the other. In fetishising the native, the self becomes a prisoner of the projected image (66-67). The fetishisation emerges in classifying terms 'ignorant', 'backward' and 'cannibals'.

The central trope designs itself as Manko thinks of challenging the spirits to 'put a spoke in the wheel' of Garry's life. He has to do 'some consultation and cogitations'. He gives donkey-eye to Sarojini to protect her.

> A chinky little bit of thing stick up in a man head, and all the big professors and inventors in the world couldn't do nothing! They sending men to the moon, they inventing babies, they making bombs what could wipe up the whole world, and a chinky bit of thing stick in a man head and causing panic and pandemonium! Any kiss-me-arse bush doctor could do that! (93)

Manko knows that the 'small cactus, with oval-shaped fleshy protuberances' (94) the aloe can draw out the chink and lift the burden of sudden and unexpected death off his wearied heart. It is just a simple remedy but the condition is that it requires Garry's faith.

Against the bush medicine and chanting, Garry after meeting Manko becomes restless, begins to imbricate his background, the nation's history where nothing but knowledge has directed them. He visualises thus: 'Centuries of accepted precepts and concepts, dogmas and proven convictions' have governed him so far. Knowledge in its different contours be it *a priori* or *a posteriori* has been the concrete setting for his nation and a man like him. From a contraposition, he looks upon Manko as 'an old black man, untutored and uncivilized' and how can he bring himself to believe and hope for a cure from him when the 'best medical resources' in his country have failed. Nevertheless, he extends further that the medical science also accepts the value of primitive remedies, 'some root in the depths of the Amazon, some herb from darkest Africa' (99).

Primitivism and rationality collide in the above setting. The conflict between the white and the black reaches a critical point. None yields or merges but maintains its own separate identity that has its trace in the origin. Discussing Manichean opposition between 'the putative superiority of the European and the supposed inferiority of the native', Abdul R. JanMohamed elucidates that the 'oppositions between white and black, good and evil, superiority and inferiority, civilization and savagery, intelligence and emotion, rationality and sensuality, self and other, subject and object' (63) serve as a framework. Manko and Garry authenticate the 'prevailing racial and cultural preconceptions' (63). Garry is at heart unable to accept and digest the cold superiority of Manko who retains his power in an unassuming poise.

Critiquing the return of the subaltern, Radhakrishnan denotes that in the postcolonial state one lives in a state of alienation from one's true being, history and heritage. In the process of self-recovery the subaltern goes through histories of negative identification and he adds its alienation from its self comes to an end when it succeeds in articulating its own hegemonic identity (166-167). Ramdeen's past history erupts with its indentured labour system and its accompanying tropes of alienation from the cultural heritage. He is clear headed when he converses with Roger regarding Sarojini. For Selwyn Cudjoe, 'resistance is an act or complex of acts designed to get rid a people of its oppressors be they slave-masters or multinational corporation' (qtd. by Ashcroft 28). Ramdeen expresses his opposition to Roger in a straightforward manner and thereby it is an act of liberation. Ramdeen asserts 'East is east, and west is west, and never the Twain shall meet' (98). To Roger, he adds another dimension that the 'other coloured races might feel great to be touched with white skin' but it is not so with the Indians and emphasizes that Sarojini must 'marry into her own race' (131).

But Prekash, though raised to a state of an overseer, has not freed himself totally from the chains of former life. Roger desires to maintain his superiority, but at the same time he hates Prekash's servile attitude. He always tries to make Prekash feel at ease, to soothe the transition from colony to independent country (28). The master and the worker find it hard to come out of the vested and imposed images. The path to self-recovery, the return, whether it be through the dominant or subaltern route, seems not to be highly effective with the master and overseer.

The inter-racial romance between Sarojini and Garry dispels Garry's fatal life for a brief period and pure elation comes over him. Abdul R. JanMohamed presents 'the most significant manifestation of the manichean allegory is the racial romance' (71). Garry, the white, is in a flux and arranges with Roger for her safe custody before his departure. Manko warns Sarojini to be cautious of her new phase of life but Sarojini indulges in it and vows that she will not marry any one but wait for him to come back. The idyllic racial romance is a vibrant episode that does not render the expected neat completion. In the midst of hurricane – caused confusion and divulging on Roger's love affair with Sarojini's mother, Kayshee, he confesses that Sarojini may be his daughter. Garry suggests a blood test to (dis) prove the inter-racial mixture. 'Those who eat the cascadura will, the native legend says, wheresoever they may wander end in Trinidad their days' (163). Will the colonialist 'return' to Sarojini, who leaves complex matters in the laps of Gods?

Roger and Garry are in opposition to Manko and the Indians. Myths and spirits rise in strange shapes, which the white may refute but it is Manko who predicts the hurricane and works to protect the young plants and the life of Sarojini. As W.E.B.Du Bois conceives each race contends towards attaining the ideals of life, despite being structured in oppositions. Races are indeed in a race in coursing through their lives down the chronology.

References

Appiah, Anthony. "The Uncompleted Argument: Du Bois and the Illusion of Race", *Critical Inquiry*, 12.1, Autumn, 1985. pp 21-37.

Ashcroft, Bill. *Post-colonial Transformation*. London: Routledge, 2001.

Derrida, Jacques. "Racism's Last Word". *Critical Inquiry*, 12.1, Autumn, 1985. pp. 290-299.

Fanon, Frantz. *The Wretched of the Earth*. Trans Constance Farrington. New York: Grove Press Inc., 1963.

Innes, C.L. "Forging the Conscience of Their Race-Nationalist Writers". *New National and Post-colonial Literature: An Introduction*. Ed. Bruce King. Oxford: Clarendon Press. 1996. pp. 120-139.

JanMohamed, Abdul R. "The Economy of Manichean Allegory: The Function of Racial Difference in Colonialist Literature", *Critical Inquiry*, 12.1, Autumn, 1985. pp. 59-87.

Jose, Claramma. "Talking Back, Writing Forward: Postcolonial Assimilation". *Voices of the Voiceless: Perspectives on Subaltern Literature*. Ed. Francis Peters, J. Chennai: An Ace Loyola Publication, 2003. pp. 16-26.

King, Bruce. "Ethnicity as Response: Richler, Achebe and Naipaul". *Commonwealth Literature: Themes and Techniques*. Eds. P.K. Rajan, K.M George, Jameela Begum, A.K. Radha. Delhi: Ajanta. 1993. pp.1-13.

Radhakrishnan, R. *Diasporic Mediations: Between Home and Location*. Minneapolis: University of Minnesota Press, 1996.

Selvon, Sam. *Those Who Eat the Cascadura* (1972). Toronto : Tsar, 1994.

12

Conflict and Resolution: Selvon's *The Plains of Caroni*

SUPRIYA AGARWAL

Selvon's work is markedly different from the works of other Caribbean writers. Even when we look at his better-known contemporary V.S. Naipaul who also shares an Indian origin and a Trinidadian childhood, it is obvious that colonialism comes in for an altogether different treatment in several of Selvon's novels. He does not dismiss the Caribbean as a place without a history. Instead, he is deeply involved with the problems of economic development and nation construction. His own life course of early education followed by a trip to England follows an almost similar pattern as adopted by the protagonist of the *The Plains of Caroni* but Romesh, unlike several Naipaulian heroes, does not treat his sojourn in England as a permanent severance from his country. Instead, he feels that his homeland needs to be nurtured with love and knowledge. The novel works as a conflict between the claims of tradition on one hand and modernisation on the other.

Trinidadian population, like that of the rest of the Caribbean islands is constituted by immigrant populations brought there, three or more generations earlier – the blacks through slave trade and the Indians through indentureship. On the island there was a mixing of the people of European, African and Asian origin together in an odd division of power. The situation prevalent in Trinidad has been voiced by several writers. Naipaul in his work *The Middle Passage* writes, 'Everyone was an individual, fighting for his place in the community. We were of various races, religious sects and cliques; and we had somehow found ourselves on the same small island. Nothing bound us together except this common residence' (79). The Caribbean economy, which had flourished on the physical labour of slaves and indentured workers, was now in search of its own development faced with the need to use technology.

Selvon in *The Plains of Caroni* portrays a picture of the life of Trinidadians after its independence and dwells on the problems of the new environment and the issues of development. He has traced the various changes that had infiltrated all levels of social, economic and political life. The Yankees had retreated from the island and foreign investment had opened new and better job opportunities in the industry for the people. The infrastructure and civil amenities had improved the quality of life for the moneyed class. Hopes and ambitions of individuals ran high as it appeared to be a land of opportunities, although development also brought with it displacement. Old ways were being displaced; old customs, technologies and ways of harvesting were also undergoing a change. The issue of economic development is a double-edged weapon, the division is not only amongst the people in power and those without it, between the whites and the coloured races or between the rural and the urban but it works in more complex ways. It divides people and it cuts through families.

Nature and men, both, had undergone a change. The river Caroni sang a different song when Sir Walter Raleigh had used it but if it sings at all today it would learn new songs of modern civilisation from the farmers and cane workers who live along its banks. The river sources were beautiful, cool and clear but once it flowed into populated areas it became muddy, sickly brown, sluggish and filthy. Similar was the condition of society. The country had gained independence but its people were not sure how to use their newly-gained freedom. All they looked for was comfort and money. Many thought that once they were sufficiently educated their services were bound to be used by the government. A weaning away from land to the machine was taking place just as migration to England or Canada was. On the one hand is the Company managed by the white people, and on the other is the Wilderness. The Company is a symbol of knowledge, new technology, innovation, discipline, sophistication and prosperity while Wilderness is heralded with birdsong and the village community gathering at the standpipe in the road with workers rising early to work on their fields with cutlass and dry calabash shell filled with drinking water. Outside the small mud houses and huts, children swept the yards with cocoyea brooms, made from the stems of coconut leaves or washed their faces noisily in buckets of water.

My concern in this paper is primarily with the conflict between the past and the present, old and the new, not only in terms of technology but also in terms of human relationships and moral values. There are two powerful images in the novel around which the whole plot revolves. The first is the image of the harvester and its destruction, the second is the figure of Romesh. Both these images work with their own internal opposition: man versus machinery and socially accepted morality versus personal desire. At one level the people are unable to step out of the historical context; on the other there is a deep unconscious need to step out of it and to formulate a new self. Thus the pull is in two different directions. Romesh and Seeta (son and mother) are the epitomes of the movement towards progress and power while Balgobin, Teeka and the local laborers of the cane fields want to preserve the rural ways and reject technology and development.

Conflict and Resolution 155

Most agrarian societies, as one finds even in the novels of the late nineteenth century England, were resistant to new innovations and introduction of machines. This goes on to become both a symbol as well as a centre of the debate centred on development. The Company helped the workers to build their own houses and some of them who came into money (after selling their cane land), like Harrilal in Wilderness, owned large houses. Harrilal was doubly pleased when the Company employed him to continue to run the estate and set about his first job gladly, which was to prepare and cultivate a certain amount of acreage for experimental purposes with a new harvester. But the arrival of the harvester was not welcome to many of the workers; it looms large both literally and metaphorically, as a threat to their livelihood.

Plumbing the depths of Indo-Caribbean psyche Selvon has revealed the trauma that speaks of pain and privation caused by the struggle for finding roots. Balgobin, Harrilal's brother, is an old veteran who had planted and reaped more cane than any other man in Trinidad. He is suspicious of the Company and the new technology coming with modernisation and industrial development. While some people are attracted by the material gains which progress is making available, Balgobin points out the erosion of culture, which nobody was concerned about. Harrilal points out to his brother the benefits, 'Was things ever so good for us? We getting more pay, we getting pension scheme' (13) but Balgobin argues that hard work kills nobody and that 'All these things what happening in Trinidad making you forget you is an Indian and all we customs and religion. You noticed how people is right here in this village? They don't beat drum no more. They want to play saxophone and guitar!' (13).

Balgobin wants the cane workers to remain attached to the land and field work and when his brother tries to convince him that change is for the best, he cynically remarks, 'best for sugar and white people but it ain't best for fellar like we' (12). For the people of Wilderness the harvester represented a space machine, a trip to the moon, a glimpse of the world outside Wilderness and Trinidad. They see the harvester doing the work instead of men and drift back to the village in little gloomy clusters of argument and gesture, leaving a silence in the field. Energised by his intake of rum and instigated by his hatred for machine, Balgobin puts up a fight with the enemy, like a warrior.

Selvon has very dramatically presented the fight between man and machine, Balgobin in the silence of the night challenges the machine which is supposed to do the work of eighty-eight men at a time. 'All right!' he shouted, 'Come on out! one by one the whole eighty-eight of you at one time! I don't care how you come. I will chop every manjack down like how you chop the cane!' (73). For Balgobin who has spent all his life in seclusion and without a family of his own, his instrument, the cutlass has taken the entity of a living person. He calls it Poya, the Indian word for cutlass, carries it with him always and often talks to it when alone. He along with Poya attacked the eighty-eight coward vagabonds whom he thought lived in the machine. In wild fury, all his pent up rage and frustration went into the fight and in frenzy he attacks both the shadow and reality of the enemy. Trampling and kicking the slain bodies he circles the harvester, hits out at it and cuts through its pipe line as if hacking his way out of a jungle of lianas and in the end sets it on fire. The harvester is destroyed beyond repair, reduced to a wreck of twisted metal.

It is this image, which governs the structure of the novel and concretises the struggle between development and resistance to development, between machine and man. The destruction of the harvester caused a sensation that spread much further than the plains of Caroni. It rocketed Wilderness into fame overnight. Newspapermen with notebooks and flash cameras and television and radio reporters from all over descended on the little village on the banks of the river. Communication media played the age old romance of man against machine and the unionists rallied with a vengeance to the cause of the workers. Whatever benefits the island had gained since the inception of the Company were quickly forgotten. The general consensus of public opinion weighed heavily in sympathy with the poor struggling masses. 'Strikes were threatened left, right and centre, every man felt it was his duty to come to the support of the sugar worker' (89).

Selvon, through his literary discourse, explores how the personal and political get entangled with each other in a society. After the harvester is destroyed all the cane farmers in Wilderness went on an unofficial strike and a restless uneasiness settled down on the village. Supporting strikes were threatened on all the sugar estates in the island and other industries were equally eager, sympathetic to the cause, to jump on to the bandwagon. Committees and subcommittees were quickly organised everywhere and lengthy meetings held in order to discuss the future course of action. Even a new political party, the Commu-Demo-Afro-Indo-Trini workers was created with a wide variety of aims embracing every possible aspect of commerce, industry and economics and labour. Very soon the people were divided and it took the form of an agitation against the company. Balgobin, who was seriously ill, passes into a state of coma after the strain of the fight but just before death he becomes a hero. People from all over the island collect at Wilderness to protect him from persecution. Even university students and unionists joined hands, demanding that the Company withdraw all charges against the one ailing poor old man at death's door who had the courage to fight single-handed against the disaster of mechanisation.

Balgobin has a counter claimant to his fame in Pusher, the village butt, who gets free drinks from the younger men but still holds on to the shreds of his dignity in his own way. He always wears his long rubber boots, reaching up to his thighs and the red cap, which was the badge of his office during the colonial period. Although that office had long ceased, Pusher made his rounds in the village regularly morning and evening. He is even ready to take the blame of destroying the harvester on himself, so as to become a hero and bemoans Balgobin's fame and glory when he hears the loudspeaker car announcing his death with the music of a dirge. Pusher's character helps to define Balgobin's heroism by creating a halo around it through his undisguised jealousy.

Samuel Selvon has made use of psychoanalytical concepts to diagnose the ills of the psyche of the colonised. In the persons of Balgobin and Pusher he helps us to read the specificities of history and culture. 'Boots' and 'cutlass' become the symbols of their power to which they cling. Though the main cause of alienation may be political there are psychological, social and cultural conflicts and aspirations, inherent in different individuals. Seeta, Harrilal's wife and Romesh's mother, is also a social aspirant. She has established a position of dominance in the family and controls all financial transactions. She goes ahead to carve a different life for her eldest son Romesh by sending him to the University of Saint Augustine at Trinidad. Seeta nurtures high hopes for her son and wants him to work towards a superior civil status amongst the white as well as to acquire a political office. She reflects:

> People rose to power in Trinidad by all manner of means, no matter how ignorant or stupid they were. And Romesh had education. He was a scholarship winner today - tomorrow he might be the new Prime Minister ... Get him on the right road, and who could tell how far he would go? If it cost her her life, she would see that he got every opportunity. The Company was a good start – in fact, it was the best one. Sugarcane had been their burden, she would turn it into the means of success. (28)

Seeta's psychology is well articulated by Homi Bhabha in his essay "Interrogating Identity", when he reflects on the problem of colonial cultural alienation and the psychoanalytic language of 'demand and desire' (*Location* 43). Seeta believes in the power of white skin and the moment she sets her eyes on Romesh's friend Petra Wharton, she wants to use that relationship to the advantage of her son. Seeta's superior intelligence had cowed Harrilal into submission and it was she who was in charge of the household. This was so unlike the traditional image of the obedient and servile Indian wife that Harrilal did not dare to let anybody know about the true state of affairs in his house. It was a bitter thing for Harrilal to bear but the most he could do was quarrel and grumble constantly at her and blame it on the new type of Trinidadian who was evolving since independence. She was an enigma to Harrilal and his bewilderment started from the day they were married. A mystery is built around her. When the first child Romesh was born she would not let Harrilal go near the baby and from that day her care and affection was all for her son. She spent more time going to visit Romesh at the university than at home and when he came to Wilderness, she kept him to herself. Sometimes as a form of self-protection and to shield himself from Seeta's superiority, Harrilal used to imagine that she was going mad, that the money had gone to her head. Rebuffed and ridiculed by Seeta, Harrilal was afraid of talking unless she spoke to him and it was only in his drunkenness that he could lull himself into some self-respect. Sometimes he took it out on his youngest son Popo, either by thrashing him or by bribing him with a bag of sweets in order to have a silent listener.

Seeta's life is a complex one. In love with Balgobin, she had to leave him to marry his brother. All that they could do was to defy their destinies and capture some unforgettable togetherness in one brief moment of union to last them the rest of their lives. Seeta had decided that the only way she could live would be to turn her great love into great hate. Her love for Balgobin never died and in her relationship with her husband Harrilal she had not tried to transfer her affection. Even after two decades when she is confronted with Balgobin after he had destroyed the harvester, she is like a bewildered panic-stricken girl. Although for long she had lived with a different face and manner and attitude to face the world with.

There are relationships in the novel in which there is an oppositional pull. Seeta, even as she cares for Balgobin abuses and accuses him, Romesh hates his mother but is afraid to let her know that. Romesh's inability to oppose Seeta and Petra's accusation of his having Oedipal complex makes him review his relationship. Seeta practically tries to plan and run the life of her son. Her touch drains Romesh of all hatred and opposition that sometimes overwhelms him. At the moment when he wanted to resist her dominance, she held his hand, squeezed it and at the physical contact he went limp, 'as if he were a baby and she had given him the nipple of her breast. She kept her hand on his, "you, know all these things I doing, I doing for you, Romesh. You not going to kiss me before I go?" "In front of all these people?" He laughed, making a joke of it. 'Why not? Ain't I is your mother?'" (35).

One is reminded of Sigmund Freud and the various stages of cognitive development traced by him in the formation of a personality, in relation to the mother-son relationship. Freud points out that 'the human individual has to devote himself to the great task of detaching himself from his parents and not until that task is achieved can he cease to be a child and become a member of the social community' (*Lectures on Psychoanalysis* 380). No doubt, individual psychological development is interwoven with the networks of social roles, traditional values, caste, customs and kinship regulations but the basic pattern of the human psychology cannot be denied. Romesh also takes time to detach himself from the dictates of his mother and defending his attitude he tells Petra, his girl friend, that he belongs to a different race where they have an unreasonable respect for parents. He takes it as an inherent quality of character which will take time to disappear but Petra refuses to believe that he is so weakwilled and Indianised.

There is a conflict of old and new values in Romesh's character. He himself is not sure about his own self and searches his mind thoroughly wondering about Petra's mention of Oedipus. He reflects, 'Could it be true? Was all the hate he felt for Seeta a way of hiding his love?' (86). He could remember not one single instance in his lifetime, not one fleeting thought, which made him doubtful and yet in an overall pattern of time, it seemed indeed that 'she was a circle and whatever direction he turned he was bound to her' (87). Instigated by Petra, Romesh decides to be his natural self with Seeta and leaving all pretensions he tells her that he is tired of her. Relieved of the burden, he gives a laugh, which even Seeta could analyse as having a ring of freedom in it and a quality of defiance, which evoked a past memory in Seeta.

Romesh symbolises the gradual merging of the traditional with the modern. He is intelligent, confident and wants to live by his own values. Unlike his mother he does not think that he needs the support of the white skinned friend to take him to the top. When questioned by Seeta, 'How else you going to climb up the ladder?' He says 'In my own way, in my own time' (25). Romesh has his roots in the Wilderness but because of education he is able to analyse the situation in a more critical way. He was attached to the landscape and recalled his childhood days, which he had spent amongst mango and cedar trees. He had the habit of rising with the sun and enjoyed the pleasure of seeing something blooming in the street, some attraction like the gigantic samaan tree spreading its umbrella of greenery. But his education and work with the company had distanced him from the people of Wilderness who had held him in awe and were jealous of him.

The crisis occurs when Balgobin dies and just before that his fatherhood is declared and Romesh is owned as the son. It is then that Seeta discloses that she dominated Romesh because she loved his father so much that it was like having him with her and having the chance to be doing things for him. But unlike Seeta, even in the face of emotion and relationship, Romesh has the courage to be truthful. Seeta wants him to conceal Balgobin's role in the destruction of the harvester but he refuses to go along with her and wants the administration to do what is required. The local crowd along with his half brother, Teeka, accuse him of being a white Indian. They call him "Company cocksucker!" but Romesh tries to argue it out with them. 'you have to face it : mechanization in this industry is here to stay. There is nothing you can do about it. Making trouble now will only make things worse for you' (133).

Selvon brings home to the reader the issue of happiness and progress in a developing nation. An individual's happiness need not necessarily coincide with collective happiness. The trend for specific ethnic self-identification is a complex one as the modern man needs to have multiple belongings. Romesh wants to establish his identity but does not want to belong to Wilderness. He does not go to the cremation of his father nor does he want to stay with his mother. He leaves home to proceed to England for research to modernise the sugar industry. Working on the basis of his merit in a neutral environment he contributes to the progress of the community and to the long term act of nation building.

The descriptions of open landscape – mango trees, cedar trees, plots of land planted with paddy, pepper and corn, the tonka-beans, the birds, butterflies and scurrying lizards, open a subtext to be interpreted. Romesh and Petra decide to go to the Maracas Bay to spend some time together but they did not talk much on the trip. 'It was a beautiful drive over the hills with superb views of the valleys and the city' (36). Nature forms the backdrop of several activities, communicating through its silence. *The Plains of Caroni* leaves behind it a sense of the land, and brings alive the struggle of the colourful people as they try to adapt their cultural values to their changed circumstances and play out the roles assigned to them in this drama of progress and development.

Ironically, the two lovers, Seeta and Balgobin (another name of Krishna, referring to the child God), represent the two polarities of their life – ambition and individual desire; progress and a passion for the old way of life. Civilisation is at crossroads and the choice, as always, is a difficult one to make. Balgobin's death also symbolises the death of the old world, but Romesh's own burden of sonhood suddenly forces him into a confrontation with his own circumstances. And as he picks up the courage to accept his mother's relationship with Balgobin he also develops the strength to say no to her dominant ambition. The ending of the novel is a crucial turning point not only in the lives of the individuals but also for the larger collectivity.

References

Bhabha, Homi K. "Interrogating Identity", *The Location of Culture*. New York: Routledge, 1994.

Freud, Sigmund. *Introductory Lectures on Psychoanalysis*. The Pelican Freud Library Volume I. London: Penguin Books, 1963.

Naipaul, V.S. *The Middle Passage*. London: Andre Deutsch, 1962.

Selvon, Samuel. *The Plains of Caroni* (1970). Toronto: William Wallace Publishers, 1985.

13

Creating an Independent Reality: Sam Selvon's *An Island Is a World*

CHARU MATHUR

Sam Selvon, like many other writers of his generation, grew up in Trinidad in the politically turbulent decade of the 1930s and spent his formative years in the era surrounding the Second World War and the subsequent period of decline in colonial power. It was a time when identities of West Indians were undermined by European political, economic and cultural domination. The long history of slavery effectively alienated the West Indian psyche from its roots by promoting a legacy of cultural and racial amnesia and a strong disenchantment with society as a whole. The youth represent the development of a generation that was absorbed into a process of expanding self-consciousness and racial awareness. They began to look towards a more individualistic society with fewer restraints and increased social, political and economic freedom. The colonial order of the dominant coloniser and the subjugated colonised identities represented the unchanging and unfaltering society that they began to question. Emigration to Britain, Canada or the United States was an attempt towards the liberation of the Caribbean consciousness. London was the chief attraction for West Indian immigrants in the 1950s because as British citizens West Indians did not need visas to enter England. Economic hardships and political alienation also had a tremendous impact on the liberation of the colonial consciousness of the youth. Values that had previously held society together became suspect. Social fragmentation and divisiveness that have been the legacy of colonialism resulted in a crumbling of the old faith, giving rise to a need to search for a new one. At such a time politics and religion offered a variety of possibilities that needed to be explored. Besides, the creed of creolisation, which was trumped up to assimilate ethnic and racial differences into one grand all-embracing culture, saw the emergence of a new national identity. By attempting to 'rediscover' the past while emphasising the changes in the present, the West Indians succeeded in moulding the historical influences of Caribbean culture into a new reality.

Sam Selvon's second novel *An Island Is a World* (1955) is about such a personal and intellectual quest in the post-war Caribbean colony of Trinidad. As an earlier generation thinks of returning to India, Foster, a young man goes to England and Rufus, his brother leaves for the United States, each in search of himself and his worth. The novel depicts the great changes in the world and in Trinidad society after the Second World War (1939-45) that occasioned much soul-searching and a desperate feeling about the 'modern' condition where the middle-class outlook, attitudes and lifestyle indicate a considerable creolisation. The philosophical probings of the characters reveal them as rootless, struggling, suffering yet not beings without hope. Each creates his own space depending upon his understanding and response to the situation he finds himself in.

Foster, the protagonist of the novel, is introduced in the Prologue as a man who wakes up each morning with the world spinning in his brain. The Prologue is actually more of an epilogue because now, though the marriage has taken place and domesticity has set in, Foster's mind is still not settled, the phrase 'the spinning world' is repeatedly used in the novel connoting his confused response to the activity going on outside of and beyond himself in the world. It reflects his own sense of rootless and aimless movement in an order in which he does not have a place. Second-generation immigrants from India, he and his brother Rufus have no ties that bind them. They lack any sense of belonging to a community or commitment to persons, place or work. Unable to restore a link with their root culture they create a new one, giving shape and coherence to the life pressing down on them. As stated by Ramchand in the introduction to the novel:

> Foster is interested in a number of spheres: the world of his immediate social relations; the larger world understood in the phrase the brotherhood of men and nations; the inner world of the individuals and the nebulous universe whose eternity and space man's life seem so slight. These four spheres are not separate from one another, and Foster does not want them to be. He is looking for nothing less than a meaning that will reconcile all these worlds and integrate all the levels of his existence. (xi-xii)

His existential approach to life makes him view human beings as subjects in an indifferent, objective, often ambiguous and 'absurd' universe in which meaning is not provided by the natural order, but can be created however provisionally and unstably by human beings through actions and interpretations. Foster's Indian origins do not lend meaning to his life and consequently, there is a rejection of this awareness of history. For people of his generation, as Walcott argues, 'history is fiction, subject to a fitful muse, memory. Their philosophy, based on a contempt for historic time, is revolutionary, for what they repeat to the New World is its simultaneity with the Old. Their vision of man is elemental, a being inhabited by presences, not a creature chained to the past' (Baugh 38). For Foster and his brother, Rufus the vision of man in the New World is Adamic. They are totally creolised in Trinidadian experience and therefore do not think of themselves in terms of being Indians or coloured. They reject ethnic ancestry for faith in the elemental man. However, there is no pretence of innocence for the 'apples of its second Eden have the tartness of experience' (Baugh 41).

The brothers seek this New World by moving away from the island. Rufus goes to try his fortune in the United States leaving behind his wife and child without any sense of guilt while Foster explores possibilities in England. There is a doctrinal rejection of the mother country, which marks a decisive shifting of balance. Rufus's aspiration to work and study in the United States reflects the lodging of the nation in the consciousness of English speaking West Indians as a source of fantasy and longing – a desired destination for ambitious migrants. But the complexion of experience and response is different for the two brothers as they move out of their island home. Rufus remains undisturbed by his exiled state - 'When he remembered Trinidad, it seemed so far away as to be harmless' (115). Though not a romantic he is able to find a viable solution in love. After divorcing his wife Rena, he in spite of having been refused a visa to re-enter the United States, passes through Venezuela and enters Mexico, leaving the island for good. 'Whatever the future held he would go through with it together with Sylvia. There was to be no more looking back, no regrets', he decides (201). But the relationship of a colonial man with a white woman hints at intricate intertwined implications.

For Foster, on the other hand, the shift in location marks a shift in perspective. He is conscious of the lack of national feelings that the West Indians have, when he states, 'We never sort of visualized Trinidad as part of the world, a place to build history ...'(106). He always thought of this as a position of advantage. As any ties to a country or race do not bind them, he believed, they would have 'an advantage with this disadvantage' (106). But he soon realises that it is not so, 'When you leave the country of your birth, it isn't like that at all. Other people belong. They are not human beings, they are Englishmen and Frenchmen and

Americans, and you've got to have something to fall back on too ...'(106). Not mindful of belonging to any particular place, he thought, West Indians could approach the world's problems with an open mind but the western world frustrates him. It offers not elation but cynicism. 'There are people in this country', he writes to his friend Andrews, 'who have never heard of our existence, nor know in what hemisphere the West Indies lay' (105). Such an erasure of identity awakens nationalist feelings in him and he returns to Trinidad. While Rufus succumbs to the colonial mindset that trained to deny what they were and shut off the voices they heard at home, these very voices disturb Foster and spur his sense of belonging to the island. However, its not the weight of the past that tortures him but the demands of the present. His act of valorisation lies in the acceptance and announcement of his Caribbean consciousness.

The novel also shows how the reality of these island-born youths differs from that of the first generation immigrants like Johnny. He is the father of Rena and Jennifer, the girls the brothers marry, and is described as an 'Indian, a jeweller and a drunkard'(8). He has a shop in Port of Spain but his secret passion is the "Big Invention"- the great force of Gravity he hopes to harness one day (11). This search for gravity, perhaps translates as his search for roots. He finds meaning in life by supporting the movement of the West Indian peasants for a passage to India. Foster is aware of this difference between Johnny as well as the departing peasants and himself and therefore admits:

> He was one of them, and yet he couldn't feel the way they did, nor share in the kinship they knew. They were going back home. They had a home. It was far away, but they hadn't forgotten. When they had come to Trinidad they kept some of India hidden in their hearts. They had tried to live in Trinidad as they had lived in India, with their own customs and religion, shutting out the influences of the West. They had built their temples and taught their children the language of the motherland. They had something to return to, they had a country. He had nothing. He had been brought up as a Trinidadian – a member of a cosmopolitan community who recognized no creed or race, a creature born of all the races in the world, in a small island that no one knew anything about. (211)

This dismantling of the shrine of belonging is not a denial of possibility and desirability of belief but an evolution from within. The Indo-Trinidadian experiences a liminal form of cultural identification. The specific history of cultural displacement makes culture as a strategy of survival that is both 'transnational' and 'translational' (Bhabha 172). What seems to be a loss of tradition is a renewal and what seems a death of faith is its rebirth.

A similar development can be seen in Rena and Jennifer who have assimilated the creolised culture of Trinidad. Living in Port of Spain, they are 'modern young women who have no intention of being as deprived of life as their mother has been' (Ramchand ix). Rena was a law unto herself, making the rounds of the dance hall and the good time places, and ended up living with an American in Venezuela. She had no qualms about divorcing her husband or abandoning her child, something her mother could not have conceived of. The younger sister, Jennifer 'would go with any sort of man, just to live in New York or London' (24). The girls' attitude reflects the continued peripheralisation of colonies and how these countries pursued the western ideals of progress without cultivating self-knowledge and self-respect. The creolisation process is, according to Rohlehr, 'partly an exercise in colonial self-contempt, even when one is in the act of claiming one's rights as a full citizen' (Baugh 154). The westernised names of all the Indo-Trinidadian characters in the novel are indicative of the process of acculturation that induces a rejection of Indian names. It was upon a demeaning sense of self-worth that the foundations of individual lives were built and post-colonial reality constructed. Therefore, severing connections with their Indian roots the Indo-Trinidadians throw themselves wholly into the white world.

The culturally hybrid location and the consequent creolisation can also be seen as a strategy of subversion. Bhabha claims: 'Hybridity is a problematic of colonial representation and individuation that reverses the effects of the colonialist disavowal so that other 'denied' knowledges enter upon the dominant discourse and estrange the basis of authority – its rules of recognition' (114). Since the colonised now resembles the coloniser, difference that was the very justification of colonial authority gets diluted and creates a counter discourse.

The young Indo-Trinidadian, now twice removed, is unable to draw upon his genealogical and cultural links with the ancestral country. Snapping of the continuity with that past results in a defiant denial of a pre-colonial past. The dominant influence of the West crystallises to form a creolised culture that places great emphasis on individualism, freedom and consumption and lacks strong kinship obligations and is generally stereotyped as being morally and culturally opportunistic. This emerging way is also reflected in the manner in which male and female relationships are formed within Caribbean society in which bonds between men and women tended to lack emotional depth – an aspect that is evident in almost all such relationships in *An Island Is a World*. The concept of idealistic romantic love, to some extent was missing and instrumentality rather than affection appears to be the primary motivation in forming relationships. Men want sexual gratification and attention to their domestic needs while women are primarily motivated by the need to find a man who can offer economic support. The prologue of the novel depicts such an arrangement of convenience between Foster and Jennifer.

Part of the problem of adjusting to the changed environment and dealing with the quest for significance is one of creating a language supple enough to deal with the growing complexities which accompany displacement. In this connection, Bakhtin states:

> at any given moment of its historical existence, language is heteroglot from top to bottom: it represents the co-existence of socio-ideological contradictions between the present and the past, between differing epochs of the past, between differing socio-ideological groups in the present, between tendencies, schools, circles and so forth, all given a bodily form. These 'languages' of heteroglossia intersect each other in a variety of ways, forming new socially typifying "languages". (291)

The characters in *An Island Is a World* employ such an evolved linguistic continuum that parallels with their sociocultural reality. They speak the language of Port-of-Spain, the Trinidad dialect characteristic of the urban Creole that represents an authentic variety of English. It is laden with the idiosyncrasies of Trinidad speech and behaviour. They speak, what Austin Clark calls, 'commercial English' which is a combination of standard English as is taught in schools together with the 'psychological language', the one in which they express thoughts, ideas and feelings. He further states that: 'In some of its usages it might be a shorthand means of conveying something that would be much more convoluted in standard English. But more often it is more than a shorthand means of expression that hits directly at the heart of the matter' (qtd. in Birbalsingh 260). Take for example, the Indo-Trinidadian Foster meets in London, precisely and pointedly conveys his feelings when he says: 'You know in this country they don't care what you is, as long as you not white, you black. Boy, I is a Indian, and the people does call me a black man' (153). The address "Boy" itself is a loaded one as Selvon uses it to refer to the innocents abroad. As Rohlehr states: 'it indicates not only the strange pre-moral innocence which Selvon's people seem to preserve wherever they are, but a certain immaturity, which persists because these calypsonians refuse to awaken to responsibility, even under the weight of metropolitan pressures' (Baugh 160). It is through an evolved language that the West Indians recreate a world of words in which they move and through which they grope for clarity in the midst of experience.

The displacements, migration and mixing makes the creole identity fluid and open so that the culture evolved lives, changes, innovates and is in a process of continuous construction. For the older generation it could mean preserving and reproducing, as was the case with Johnny and his wife Mary. For the island-born youngsters like Foster, Rufus, Rena and Jennifer, it often means selection. While the behavioural patterns of the earlier generation mirrored the attempted acculturation of colonialism, the young endorsed transculturation. Both live in a world of composite cultures but their choices and degree of adaptation varies, each lending the adopted land the identity of their presence. As a consequence, it marks a shift of the Indo-Trinidadian from the periphery to the centre within Trinidad with creolisation claiming some success in transforming the outsider status of the Indians. As Bhabha points out, 'identity', in such a case, 'is claimed either from a position of marginality or in an attempt at gaining the centre: in both senses ex-centric' (177). The inclination was towards an ostensibly 'Trinidadian culture' seeing ancestral cultures (Indian, African and others) as alien. So things Indian (and African) were treated with certain contempt. Therefore Trinidadians of their generation became obsessed with being 'modern'. Rena's refusal to leave the 'modern' city of Port of Spain, after marriage, shows such an inclination. The modernist cry of despair is, however, replaced by a New World exploration.

It is this dynamic process of creolisation that represents the very nature of Caribbean space. One of the ways of coming to terms with colonialism was the development of Creole nationalism. Foster's friend, Andrews who is a painter and art education officer finds that his engagement with the human situation draws him into politics. His zeal for the West Indian Federation represents the currents of colonialism and resistance locked in counter dialectic struggle. The expressed intention of the Federation was to create a political unit that would become independent from Britain as a single state. But the distortions and delusions of colonialism continued to disfigure this Caribbean endeavour of generating a genuine sense of belonging to a national community. Therefore, the Federation (1958-62) turned out to be 'an artificial edifice constructed on sand and manipulated to appease the outward, nationalist craving of a subject population rather than to satisfy the inner feelings, the core expectations and fundamental needs of an emerging nation' (Birbalsingh 6). In the 1950s, however, it flagged the hope of a united independent Caribbean state. Andrews too revels in a political philosophy rooted in elation. Coupled with this optimism is also an interrogation of the whole political process. As Ramchand points out, 'it saw the beauty and the danger of an elation that could overlook the basic truth that for the individual as for the nation - to find the true self is still arduous' (xx). A lack of self-knowledge and commitment frustrates the Federal programme. Andrews is aware of this when he observes, 'there is no honour here, no ideal, no great sincerity or desire to make conditions any better ... the conditions that exist offer excuse for all our failings, so why should we bother to make things better?' (147-148). Devotion towards a recreation of an entire order is the reality Andrews weaves though he is not quite sure about the success of its realisation.

The shaky political faith of Andrews is replaced by spiritual faith in the priest, Father Hope. He acts as a hinge around whom Foster and Andrews try out their beliefs. Father Hope's faith in God is the reality he creates around himself in order to explain life. 'No man' he says, 'formulates a theory of life to which he could adhere all the time. But in God you have a lasting belief. A remote Goodness, an almost forlorn hope that there's purpose behind it all' (218). Father Hope's idea of truth is subjective where human beings can be understood only from the inside in terms of their lived and experienced reality and dilemmas not from the outside, as Foster was trying to do, in terms of biological, psychological or other scientific theory of human nature. 'If even religion proves imperfect you will find it the least imperfect of all beliefs in the world and the only one from which you could get any lasting consolation,' Father argues (76). But, Foster's understanding that it is only by default that man opts for God motivates his rejection of the priest's view. 'God is forced upon man' he feels, 'making a mock of all his efforts to attain happiness' (220). He thinks that it is because human beings are not given a long enough life span to work out their beliefs; they play safe towards the end of the normal span and take up religion. Foster's perception of reality resists that of the priest because commitment to religious belief would end his search for other possible beliefs. Religious belief privileges the spirit over the flesh though, he feels, in life both are equally important (76). Besides, Father Hope's persuasion that an island is a sufficient world is quite opposed to Foster's view that an island limits one's horizon (65, 73-74). Perhaps ultimately dwindling of faith in the reality he believed in, drove Father to suicide while Foster continues his dialogue with multiple yet plausible realities in his quest to arrive at one that satisfyingly preserves the spirit of emancipation.

Each of the characters in the novel relate to a reality where they are caught in a bewildering web of relations in a semi-plural, multiracial world and are a part of the process of creolisation which goes beyond a despairing sense of violation or loss. They learn some bitter truths about the political nature of the world and do not nurture any sentimental notion of the Island as being one big happy melting pot, which can teach the world how to celebrate life. A Trinidadian person, mixing with so many nationalities, belongs to the whole world, not to just the island was an innocent belief imbibed by their colonial upbringing but life teaches them a different lesson - an island is not like a world because people are not the same all over. However, boundaries of colonial order have begun to disintegrate and a societal transformation is set into motion. The Indo-Trinidadian realises he is neither a rootless being devoid of identity, nor a lost son of India but a man made and shaped by the island now. The island is his world and this is the new reality he accepts and relates to.

References

Bakhtin, M. M. *The Dialogic Imagination: Four Essays*. Ed. Michael Holquist. Trans. Caryl Emerson and Michael Holquist. Austin: University of Texas Press, 1981.

Baugh, Edward., ed. *Critics On Caribbean Literature*. London: George Allen and Unwin, 1978.

Bhabha, Homi K. *The Location of Culture*. London, New York: Routledge, 1994.

Birbalsingh, Frank. *Guyana and the Caribbean: Reviews, Essays and Interviews*. U.K.: Dido Press, 2004.

Ramchand, Kenneth. "Introduction". *An Island Is a World* by Sam Selvon. Toronto: Tsar, 1993. v-xxv.

Selvon, Sam. *An Island Is a World* (1955). Toronto: Tsar, 1993.

14

Diverse Cultural Icons and Codes in Paule Marshall's *Praisesong for the Widow*

ASMA SHAMAIL

> We [as people of African descent] must accept the task of "reinventing" our own images and the role which Africa will play in this process will be essential.
>
> Paule Marshall.

From Langston Hughes's "The Negro Speaks of Rivers" to Alex Haley's *Roots*, black American writers have presented Africa as the foundation of a diasporic identity that provides subjects with a sense of rootedness and belonging. Among many contemporary black authors and intellectuals, it has become commonplace to invoke African cultural traditions as a means to both forge cohesive politically empowering forms of subjectivity and counter the logic of white supremacy. Contemporary black women writers in the United States have interrogated issues of history, culture, and literature related to the Americans. The connections drawn in their fiction between the United States, the Caribbean, and Latin America, introduce a new cosmopolitanism and internationalism to the literature of the United States. By thinking of America as one continent with a common history and by challenging dominant hierarchies of race, class, and gender, black women writers pose important challenges. They have made significant contributions to their own nation's literature and culture by bringing inside its borders sensibilities and concerns familiar to the "Third World" below the southern borders of the United States. The history of the African diaspora and its reconstruction within a black framework necessarily embrace the whole area of 'the extended Caribbean.' The diaspora underwent related processes and left a similar heritage all along the Atlantic shores of America.

The visibility of black women in literature is a very recent phenomenon in the literary history of the United States. During the 1970s and 1980s, fiction by African American women achieved critical prominence. Novels and plays by Toni Morrison, Alice Walker, Gloria Naylor, Ntozake Shange – to name a few – directed a generation of readers to the diversity of black women's creativity and the richness of their vision. In spite of these writer's differences in style and perspective, the history of the African diaspora in the *New World* binds together the imaginative worlds they have created in fiction. The fiction of these black women writers in the United States attempts to recapture and reorganise the fragments of collective history into a new type of narrative. The originality of this narrative lies in the way it emphasises the popular roots of contemporary culture, in the use of creative folk rituals, and in the interconnection between myth and imagination, all alongside the starkest representations of racial, sexual, economic, and cultural abuse. Rooted in culture and community, this narrative is an attempt to counter the versions of facts and truth presented by the coloniser of yesterday and today with the view from the dominated.

Clearly, African American and African Caribbean cultures, like all cultures are modified and will continue to modify one another, particularly in the hybridising space of the city in which the two communities are still concentrated. With each new wave of immigration, the dramas of association and disassociation that began during the first stage of contact continue to shape and be shaped by the historically specific complexities of racial, ethnic, and national identity formation in the United States. Working within this different alliance, the achievement of Paule Marshall is unique.

Marshall, a second-generation immigrant, identifies equally with the US and the Caribbean cultures, creates characters who feel intimately linked to and move freely between two worlds. These contrasting portrayals of dislocation and dual location raise important questions about the role that differences in generation and gender might play in shaping black immigrant reaction to the United States. Her novels focus on the relationship between Africa and a larger America that embraces the Caribbean, the United States, and Brazil, characterised by a diversity of colours and cultures. What sets Marshall's vision apart is her perception of the consequences of cultural displacement for people of African descent, consequences that may significantly exacerbate the oppressions of gender, race, and class. Other black women writer's imaginations in general embrace survival and chronicle defeat in a racist society. Marshall adds considerations of gender and class to what happens to her characters and moreover, she contrasts physical and material survival in Eurocentric spaces with spiritual affirmation that can be acquired through cultural embrace and connection.

The islands of the Caribbean which mark the birth of America linking North and South, are a continuing symbol for the meeting of different 'cultural tributaries,' as well as the initial place of displacement and domination of native peoples and Africans in the New World. When discussing the migration of multiple distinct national groups, attention should be addressed not simply to the specificities of cultural frameworks, national identities, and historical contexts from which these migrations have stemmed, but, perhaps even more importantly, to the fundamentally recreative process of nationhood that occurs upon arrival in new, and in most cases more modern, environments. As Homi Bhabha argues in his analysis of the process of "DissemiNation," upon migration, issues of national identity shift from 'the "selfhood" of the nation as opposed to the otherness of other nations' toward 'the nation split within itself, articulating the heterogeneity of its population.' This 'barred Nation *It/Self*,' Bhabha asserts, 'alienated from its external self-generation, becomes a liminal signifying space that is *internally* marked by the discourses of minorities, the heterogeneous histories of contending peoples, antagonistic authorities and tense locations of cultural difference' (148). A place of intersection for many cultures and languages, the Caribbean was the first geographical space in the recorded history of the countless encounters and clashes that have made up America. As one-generation-removed daughter of the Caribbean island of Barbados, Paule Marshall reads that history with mixed anger and love. Like the Caribbean, her work contains a busy plurality of peoples, races, and colours in a continuous recreation of culture. The many voices and stories in her novels reveal the contradictions and the complexity of the legacy of colonialism at the heart of America. Marshall's ethnographic narratives not only retell America in past but also create their own possibilities of transforming the present and constructing a new future. Marshall's version of the Caribbean, with roots spreading far into eastern United States and across the Atlantic – crisscrossing the routes of colonisers and colonised – is actually present in all her novels and shorter works.

Both Michel Foucault and Frantz Fanon have elaborated on the complexity of the relationship between coloniser and colonised, the illusion of creating myths of a homogeneous (Pan-African) Third World and some privileged grasp of 'truth,' and the deceptive security of a frozen, immutable past. Decades before Gayatri Spivak and postmodernist visions of ethnicity and literature, Fanon warned against black-white simplifications and emphasised the continuous reinvention of culture. Like Fanon, Jose Marti, the Cuban poet and revolutionary hero believed that the tensions and contradictions of the past had to be re-evaluated and rewritten if change was to occur in the present. As historical and cultural texts, the works of Marshall are in dialogue with the already classic texts on the struggle of nationalism and resistance, the works of Frantz Fanon and Jose Marti, and the traditions of Pan-Africanism and Pan-Americanism that they represent.

Marshall is perhaps best known in academic circles for her work on the experiences of West Indians within African-American culture in the United States. In her fiction as a whole she is concerned with the experience of African people throughout the diaspora. Her fiction represents an attempt to identify, analyse, and resolve the conflict between cultural loss/displacement and cultural domination/hegemony. The cultural space surrounding Marshall's characters also include her imaginative reconstruction of African history and culture to establish an underlying unity that links all people of African descent. Indeed, the chronology of Marshall's publications suggests her intentional design to reverse the 'middle passage.' She brilliantly examines the experience of blacks not in transit from Africa to the New World but from the New World back toward Africa. For Marshall, stories are ways to express 'the necessity of reversing the present order' ("Shaping" 111). Simultaneously, she combines forms of written narrative that are western in origin with the style and function of traditional African oral narrative. She thus revitalises an ancient aesthetic within a modern construct and develops a unique literary voice.

In Marshall's reconstruction of black American and Afro-Caribbean culture, women's discourse becomes layered with meaning and significance. Marshall's personal synthesis of Afro-Caribbean and African American heritage is thus crucial to her vantage point of interconnecting yet disparate cultures. To be sure, her cultural identity as both African American and African Caribbean allows her to understand how the two cultures alternately diverge and coalesce. Furthermore, she is aware that both cultures reflect a distinct reality that has no direct equivalent in the Anglo-American way of life. Marshall's vision, with liberty to transcend black culture within the United States, thus enriches and distinguishes her fiction. By overstepping conventional closures of nationality, race, and gender, Marshall rewrites the boundaries between the American hemispheres on the basis of shared cultural, social, and economic relationships and common cultural roots in Africa. Her intimacy with these cultures and her imaginative visioning authenticated her to question them too. Marshall compromises neither her African American nor her African Caribbean identity, rather, she brings both back to their original source in traditional African culture. However, Marshall's imaginative return to traditional African culture is certainly critical to her uncovering of 'hidden continuities' between peoples of African descent. She clearly acknowledges what Stuart Hall describes as 'critical points of deep and significant difference,' which constitutes black cultural identities in the New World. Given the displacement and dispersal of African peoples, cultural identities cannot remain static.

> Cultural identities come from somewhere, have histories. But, like everything which is historical, they undergo constant transformation. Far from being eternally fixed in some essentialist past, they are subject to the continuous 'play' of history, culture, and power. Far from being grounded in mere 'recovery' of the past, which is waiting to be found and which, when found, will secure our sense of ourselves into eternity, identities are the names we give to the different ways we are positioned by, and position ourselves within, the narratives of the past. (112)

In her fiction, Marshall 'positions' herself in an 'imagined community,' and that community, though undergoing transformation, privileges and allegorises a history and culture that stems from a single source.

For Marshall, the identity and well-being of black people today depend on reconciliation with the past. A meaningful self and culture must therefore be sought and reconstructed in the fragments of history and in the reinvention of culture.

Marshall in her interview with Maryse Conde places a strong emphasis on the need for a 'spiritual return' to Africa for 'the reintegration of that which was lost in collective historical past' (qtd. in *Sage* 53). Marshall's distinctive creative imagination introduced pan-Americanism to literature that focuses on the empowerment of the voiceless and those subalterns all over America.

In her provocative essay, "Can the Subaltern Speak?" (271-313), Gayatri Spivak addressed the way the 'subaltern' woman as subject is already positioned, represented, spoken for or constructed as absent or silent or not listened to in a variety of discourses. The question that begs to be asked is: if black women are not credible speakers, what then is the reception of black women's writing, or is it already constructed and specifically located even as it speaks its critique of dominance? Speech, then, is as much an issue of audience receptivity, the fundamentals of listening, as it is of articulation. The subjectivity of black women is one of the ways in which speech is articulated and geography redefined, issues of home and exile are addressed. Black female subjectivity asserts agency as it crosses the borders, journeys, migrates and so reclaims as it reasserts. Historical links to Africa are re-examined and relocated. Significantly, many of the black women writers are critically engaged in an anti-hegemonic discourse with the United States.

Marshall's embracing of cultural continuity and of a spiritual return to Africa speaks of a significant bond among black American women's texts. Marshall's novel *Praisesong for the Widow* (1983) presents a strikingly divergent, fresh meditation on the black America's relationship to Africa as homeland. In this novel Marshall emphasises African cultural similarities, not to minimise obvious distinctions between black people of the diaspora but to encourage a spiritual return to African roots.

In Marshall's novel it is the cultural unity which joins the black people of the Sea Islands of the Southern US to the black people of the Caribbean and, by implication, to all diaspora people, a unity resulting from a common ancestor, one or other of the kingdoms of the African continent, from which the black populations were taken. The heroine is an aging black American widow. The story turns on the life crisis which confronts her after a dream experience aboard ship on her annual Caribbean cruise with two female travelling companions. The experience is so powerful that she is visibly upset, quits the cruise, to the horror and disgust of her friends, and moves into what the blurb describes as a 'harrowing Odyssey' which brings her finally to an understanding of what she has lost and found. The effectiveness of Marshall's novel as a tribute to the cultural connection between people of the diaspora is largely the result of her understanding both the cultures.

Paule Marshall has incorporated and appropriated (and even rejected) both African and Euro-American iconography and mythology to create a new ritual most suitable for her protagonist: a middle-class, African American widow Avey Johnson. The novel explores the cultural continuity of people of African descent, from South to North America, as a stance from which to delineate the values of the New World. Marshall's entire opus focuses on the consciousness of black people as they remember, retain, develop their sense of spiritual/sensual integrity and individual selves, against the materialism that characterises American societies. The journey, the widow undertakes is littered with the cultural signs of a past. The crucial factor about *Praisesong* is that it is a novel about the dispossession of the scattered African people from their past and their original homeland and, in the present, from their communities and from each other. The boldness of Marshall's project here is to analyse a private history of material acquisition and cultural dispossession, which becomes a metaphor for history of the African in the New World.

The text is full of diverse cultural icons and codes responding differently and thereby reflecting the experience of the widow. These gestures of significance begin with the title. The title of the novel, itself suggests the author's incorporation of cultural practice. "*Praisesong*" refers to a traditional heroic poem recited or sung at various celebrations in Africa and also to a religious song commonly used by African American congregations. The widow's narrative becomes a map, with music, song, dance, dress, and ritual as cultural registers to follow her across the terrain to journey's end.

The novel's four sections, titled "Runagate," "Sleeper's Wake," "Lave Tete," and "The Beg Pardon," trace the gradual purging, cleansing, and immersion of Avey in African rituals and also reflect a change in Avey Johnson's character and context. In the first section she escapes her bondage to her white middle-class ethos as she leaves the cruise ship and heads for Grenada. In the second section, she is like a sleeper, awakening spiritually as she reassesses her past, especially her marriage to Jay. She finally mourns the transformation of the ethnic, erotic, fun-loving Jay into the "sanitised," ambitious Jerome. The third section marks Avey's ritual cleansing and purging in preparation for her excursion to Carriacou. And that movement toward Avey's restoration is guided and facilitated by Lebert Joseph, an old man. Her actual boat trip to Carriacou provides the ultimate purgation: the terrible seasickness that Marshall describes unsparingly suggests Avey is dislodging and expelling the sick values of her North White Plains existence. Afterwards, she is bathed as if she were a baby, ritually cleansed by Lebert's daughter, Rosalie Parvay. Finally, in the fourth section, after all this psychic and physical preparation, Avey is able to undergo the ritualistic music and dance ceremony that links her securely to her ancestry.

Marshall underscores the need to understand one's African heritage for an integrated African-American life, especially for relatively successful, assimilated middle-class blacks; moreover, her novels attest to the view that this return to an African consciousness is more easily visualised in the Caribbean where, she feels, stronger ties to one's ancestors have remained. In each of her novels, her main female character takes a spiritual 'middle passage back' to rediscover as well as pass on the history and stories of her people, whether it be Selina's trip to the Caribbean at the end of

Brown Girl, Brown Stones, Merle's voyage to Africa in *The Chosen Place, the Timeless People*, or Avey's jumping ship and finding herself in the Caribbean in *Praisesong*. Moreover, this search for one's heritage – in this case, to remember one's tribe – is seen as a woman's search. In describing the advantages the larger society grants to white women, Marshall exposes the painful limitations that black women face. But she also reveals how black women forge ahead – not always to transcend the barriers but most often to resist them. Thus, Marshall shows that black women have gained from their heritage the flexibility and resiliency to reshape their worlds and that of their immediate families and communities to survive with dignity, with purpose, and with pride.

The novel in which Avey Johnson recovers her heritage and accepts her mission to pass this tale on to the children is indeed a praisesong to this widow: Avey not only learns to sing the praises of the ancestors but she, too, is remembered. The central myth/ legend of *Praisesong* is that of the Africans who escaped slavery through supernatural powers. In this novel, the folk tale is not about 'flying Africans' – the most prevalent form of this tale of freedom told throughout the New World – but about the Ibos who walked on water and walked on back to Africa told to Avey by her Great-aunt Cuney. But whether they walked or flew, the tale has been passed down through generations with a similar meaning, freedom from oppression and the passage back to Africa.

Avey's presence in the Caribbean seems to trigger personal as well as racial memories, and it is in this environment that Avey begins her Middle Passage back. There are historical as well as personal reasons for Marshall to place Avey's awakening in the West Indies. The different historical circumstances of the Colonies in the New World affected dominant views towards the enslaved Africans. For the most part, slavery in the Caribbean was not as devastating to African cultural traditions as it was in North America. Slave owners in the United States, whether for fear of uprisings, domestication, or a misguided sense of Christianity, attempted to destroy all vestiges of African culture. This history, compounded by a melting pot desire for assimilation helped to alienate African-Americans from their heritage in a way which was not evident in the Caribbean. In the midst of this collective historical past, Avey's personal historicity stirs up connecting memories.

For the characters Avey and Jay, Marshall illustrates the problem inherent in accepting Euro-American values that displace those of traditional African culture. Avey's assimilation of the values of Western culture and modern capitalism coincide with her distancing from her African roots. For the sake of social acceptance in a white world, the couple hid away their Africanness and stifled their spontaneity and love. They attained the dream America promises, but lost the sacramental protections of the praisesongs and the little private rituals. The novel does not, however, present material well being as synonymous with cultural disinheritance. It does not offer a critic of material advancement in itself, but rather when it exists at the expense of cultural identity. The novel stresses the grinding desperation of poverty and the rejection, by the white establishment, of black efforts for improvement that contribute to determined efforts to achieve and acquire at the cost of all else.

The infusion of ritual in the narrative through the ancestors marks a distinctive feature of the text which comes in the third section with Avey's ritual of cleansing and purging in preparation for her excursion to Carriacou. The title of this section refers to the Haitian voodoo ceremony in which one is washed clean. Velma Pollard remarks that Marshall 'avoids the hackneyed Christian/ Western symbol of cleansing by baptism (water and blood). The rituals that are really important in parent African societies are birth and death' (296). Keeping with her objective to reclaim African cultural traditions, Marshall clearly prioritises the rituals of birth and death' Marshall includes in Book IV the 'laying on of hands,' a religious ritual common in African American and other cultural practices that combines the sensual with the process of spiritual rebirth. The laying on of hands reflects a cultural tradition of black women. Joanne V.Gabbin recognises such contact as a 'symbolic act of blessing, healing, and ordination... that bestow[s] some gift' (qtd. in Pettis 128). This practice is particularly evident in the recent fiction of black women as a tactic for reclaiming the spiritual dimension of a character. In the novel this ritual is performed by Lebert Joseph's daughter, Rosalie Parvey. Mrs Parvey bathes and anoints the weakened woman in a slow, methodic fashion, periodically punctuating the silence with 'what sounded like a plainsong or a chant' (*Praisesong* 220). The entire process suggests a merging of the physical with the spiritual in order to create a new being.

The dramatic climax of the novel arrives when Marshall vividly details the rituals of the "Beg Pardon" and the "Dance of the Nations." The final section of the novel called "The Beg Pardon" is named for the ritual of ancestor worship, part of the predominant religious systems in West Africa, which has been retained, on both a symbolic and literal level, in the New World. In traditional West African cultures, the ancestors 'act as official guardians of the social and moral order' (Ray 146). The ceremony brings together spiritual, literal, and social links between black West Indians and their African ancestors. Avey's presence joins blacks from the United States with their West Indian brothers and sisters. In African belief systems, earth anchors humankind, and it predominates in African myths, and legends. Therefore, the climax of Avey's regenerative enterprise occurs in its proper setting, for the activities performed on this bare earth restore her cultural properties. The ceremony – a curious blend of half-remembered names and West African practices such as the libation to appease the ancestors, the call-and-response songs to honour family names, and the circular dance accompanied by rum keg drums (replicas of African drums) – reaffirms the participants' honouring, retention, and transmission of their cultural origins. The ceremony is a reminder, as well, of cultural practices lost in the maelstrom of history. The ceremony brings together spiritual, literal, and social links between black West Indians and their

African ancestors. Avey's presence joins blacks from the United States with their West Indian brothers and sisters.

Music becomes the crossroads where America meets Africa and Europe, memory blends with the present, and identity is recreated. Western culture has typically seen dance as an empowering activity, offering a forum for individual self-expression, or acting like a religious ritual that binds the community and spiritually renews the individual. African cultures also recognise dance's affective and spiritual powers giving dance a central place in their communal events, both secular and religious. Marshall had been attracted to dance as a thematic icon for self-proclamation, self-development as well as for literary sisterhood. Avey's participation in the circular dance of ancestral reverence therefore resounds with connective significance both for her personally and for the meaning of the novel. In the circle, a geometric formation that signifies continuity, black West Indians and black Americans symbolically join black Africans. Dance and music as cultural relics fit this ceremony of cultural reconciliation because of their centrality in the lives of African peoples. Frantz Fanon sees dance in the colonial world as the place where 'the most acute aggressivity and the most impelling violence are canalized, transformed, and conjured away. The circle of the dance is a permissive circle: it protects and permits.... [It reflects] the huge effort of a community to exorcise itself, to liberate itself, to explain itself' (*The Wretched of the Earth* 45).

The themes of a dance composition – *Praisesongs*, Ring Shouts, Beg Pardons, Big Drums – converge, representing the richly woven fabric of African-American culture. As Christian points out, the final ceremony 'combines rituals from several black societies: the Ring Dances of Tatem, the Bojangles of New York, the voodoo drums of Haiti, the rhythms of various African peoples... also specifically the embodiment of the history and culture of New World blacks... [in the notes that distinguish] Afro-American blues, spirituals and jazz, Afro-Caribbean calypso and Reggae, Brazilian music'

(*Black Feminist Criticism* 157). Avey is especially moved by one 'dark, plangent note' of music at the Big Drum, a note that comes from 'the bruised still-bleeding innermost chamber of the collective heart' (*Praisesong* 244-45). She relearns the history of her people through such music, then expresses and extends that history through her dancing.

Dancing enables Avey thus to think through her body, to grasp mentally and viscerally her collective and individual history. Her active embrace of her collective and individual ethnic history will change her own life after this journey, inspiring her to the role of extending to other Americans these African and African American cultural myths (qtd. in McCluskey 333), teaching her children, grandchildren, and her wider New York community about the richness of their heritage. Marshall calls this dance 'the shuffle designed to stay the course of history' (250), designed to subvert the drift of historical events that have prevented African-Americans and Afro-Caribbeans from maintaining contact with their ancestral African cultures. Similarly, Marshall's novel, with its Caribbean linguistic play, its blend of mythopoesis and fictionalised African-American history, and its synthesis of literary, musical, and dance elements, creates a hybrid genre that arrests the course of American including African American literary history and expands the perimeters of the 'universal' themes and forms present in canonical twentieth-century American fiction.

In this novel, Africa becomes not only a place to which one may return, but an 'imaginative' space which one may create. In representing, recreating Africa, Marshall reformulates the notions of 'home' of 'mother' culture, and of art. In so doing, she repositions herself and her aesthetic presence. As a writer, she emphasises the presence of Africa and reconciliation with the past and the culture. In this novel, history is enlarged beyond its socio-political and economic aspects to include not only joys and anxieties, dances, celebrations, and people's daily lives (which already enter Marshall's earlier works); but also the spiritual and mythical legacies of African ancestors.

The African connection has been treated before in the fiction, written by black writers in America especially since the decade of the sixties. But the connection has been a two-way, Africa-US, US-Africa. Paule Marshall, by including the Caribbean, Anglophone and Francophone, in her consideration has extended this connection to show a pervasive and tenacious cultural substrate with its origins on the African continent.

References

Barthold, Bonnie J. *Black Time: Fiction of Africa, the Caribbean and the United States*. New Haven: Yale UP, 1981.

Bhabha, Homi K. "Dissemination: Time, Narrative, and the Margins of the Modern Nation," *The Location of Culture*. New York: Routledge, 1994.

Busia, Abena P.A. "What is Your Nation? Reconnecting Africa and Her Diaspora through Paule Marshall's *Praisesong for the Widow*." In *Changing Our Own Words: Essays on Criticism, Theory and Writing by Black Women*. Ed. Cheryl A. Wall. London: Rutgers University Press, 1989, 196-211.

Christian, Barbara. "Paule Marshall," in *Dictionary of Literary Biography: Afro-American Fiction Writers after 1955*, Eds. Thadious M. Davis and Trudier Harris. Detroit: Gale Research Co., 1984, 33: 161-170.

___. "Ritualistic Process and the Structure of Paule Marshall's *Praisesong for the Widow*," *Black Feminist Criticism: Perspectives on Black Women Writers*. New York: Pergamon Press, 1985.

Collier, Eugenia. "The Closing of the Circle: Movement from Division to Wholeness in Paule Marshall's Fiction," *Black Women Writers*. Ed. Mari Evans. New York: Doubleday, 1984.

Fanon, Frantz. *The Wretched of the Earth*. Trans. Constance Farrington. New York: Grove, 1963.

Hall, Stuart. "Cultural Identity and Diaspora," *Contemporary Postcolonial Theory* Ed. Padmini Mongia. Delhi: Oxford University Press, 1997.

Haley, Alex. *Roots*. New York: Doubleday, 1976.

Marshall, Paule. "Shaping the World of My Art" *New Letters*. 1973, 40, 97-112.

___. *Praisesong for the Widow*. E.P. Dutton: New York, 1983.

Marshall, Paule and Maryse Conde. " Return of a Native Daughter: An Interview with Paule Marshall and Maryse Conde," Trans. John Williams, *Sage: A Scholarly Journal on Black Women*, 3.2 (Fall 1986): 52-53

McCluskey, John Jr. "And Called Every Generation Blessed: Theme, Setting, and Ritual in the works of Paule Marshall." *Black Women Writers 1950-1980*. Ed. Mari Evans. Garden City, NJ: Anchor/Doubleday, 1984, 316-34.

Pettis, Joyce. *Toward a Wholeness in Paule Marshall's Fiction*. Charlottesville: UP of Virginia, 1996.

Pollard, Velma "Cultural Connections in Paule Marshall's *Praisesong for the Widow,*" *World Literatures Written in English,* 1985, Vol. 25:2

Ray, Benjamin. *African Religions: Symbol, Ritual and Community.* Englewood Cliffs, NY: Prentice Hall, 1976.

Spivak, Gayatri. "Can the Subaltern Speak?" *Marxism and the Interpretation of Culture.* Eds. Nelson, Cary and Lawrence Grossberg. Urbana: University of Illinois Press, 1988, 271-313.

Waxman, Barbara Frey. "Dancing Out of Form, Dancing into Self: Genre and Metaphor in Marshall, Shange, and Walker." *Melus.* Los Angeles: Fall 1994, Vol. 19: 3, 91. Online article www.proquest.com.

Willis, Susan. *Specifying: Black Women Writing the American Experience.* Madison: University of Wisconsin Press, 1987.

15

Negotiating Interstitial Spaces: Itwaru's *Shanti* and *The Unreturning*

MINI NANDA

> Always and ever differently the bridge escorts the lingering and hastening ways of men to and fro, so that they may get to other banks.... The bridge gathers as a passage that crosses.[1]

The overseas passage of the east Indian emigrants to other parts of the world occurred in three phases, of these the first is from the seventh to the early fourteenth century, the second from the fifteenth to the early nineteenth century and the third phase began in mid-nineteenth century. The migration in the second phase primarily was undertaken as the indentured laborers were lured by the demand for labour arising out of the abolition of slavery in 1838 in Spanish, Portuguese, Dutch and British possessions. They were enthused by the much-hyped opportunities. Many migrated to escape the dismal socio-economic and political conditions in India.

The east Indians were beckoned to try their luck abroad, so that they could return to India 'renewed in wealth and status, fit for an honourable retirement with their long awaiting families' (Lyman 1971:4). Their contribution to the economy of these countries has been significant. In Hawaii, the Caribbean and Latin American, they were responsible for saving the sugar industry, the economic mainstay of these places, from complete collapse.

They had come to these societies on contractual terms for five years, after which they were free to return to their mother country. After serving their indenture contracts, most east Indians traded their return tickets for small plots of land. Over the years they acquired more land. Today their stronghold on land is impressive, in these societies they are regarded as rural and agricultural people. Their contribution to the humanisation of the Caribbean landscape, through back-breaking labour is widely acknowledged.

"The Indian is the soul of the estate – nay – he's the soul of the sugar industry itself". Arthur Martial the Mauritian author (1899-1951)[2] has observed in *The Hindu,* coolies were the pillars on which the modern economies of several countries have been built. They had come to earn an honest living, but were forced to endure corporal punishment, wage arrears, the double cut system (two days wages were cut for one day missed).

The long history of their journey and their labour which is almost 200 years old now is truly amazing and humbling. Frank Birbalsingh gives a moving account of their voyage. They were herded like cattle on the "Coolie Ships," treated like merchandise as were their forbears, the African slaves who crossed the Atlantic on the infamous Middle Passage of three long months. Birbalsingh writes that the passage was more arduous and longer for the east Indian, from the east coast of India, Westward around the Cape of Good Hope and across the Atlantic. It severed them not only from their land and families which they had cherished, but also from their caste, custom and their cuisine (*Jahaji,* Intro. xi). Their women were subjected to the lustful advances of the European crew, condemned to live amidst their own waste and unceremoniously thrown overbroad when they died.

This after they had given up their deeply cherished religious beliefs against crossing the vast ocean, the *Kala Paani*.

> 'Coolie' was the humiliating term which was applied to the east Indians, even after the *Girmitya* - a corruption for the word 'agreement' - had served his five years of bondage, to emerge with different careers as business people, financial entrepreneurs and land owners. The white plantation owners were on the top rung in the social hierarchy, followed by the blacks who saw the east Indians as the ones who sabotaged their demands for better wages. (*Jahaji*, Intro. xii)

Dr. Eric Williams, historian and politician described the situation in Trinidad around 1911 as extremely prejudiced against the east Indians, they were on the lowest rung and were the scorned and ostracised coolies. The same humiliating attitude is confirmed by Edgar Mittleholzer, the Guyanese novelist, who belonged to the coloured middle class. Lucretia Stewart an unbiased traveller from Britain to Trinidad after 1970 observed that the Indians were dismissively called coolies behind their back (*Jahaji*, Intro. xii).

In an alien country, where the working day was unduly long, the idea of a rest day inconceivable, the labourers found their movement severely curtailed and hemmed in. The anguish of the loss of one's motherland becomes more acute, a memory which is captured very movingly by Vijay Mishra in his essay, "Diaspora and the Art of Impossible Mourning", of how 'the individual experience of long period of indenture gets transformed into a collective trauma'[3] (34). Mishra writes that in Itwaru the deep sense of loss erupts through his works, as in the poem by Arnold Itwaru dedicated to the more liberal and accommodating Cyril Dabydeen (1987:14):

> You want to know how I'm doing
> and, courteous, we now measure words
> from the bamboo corrida coconut sunset walks
> I am looking well, you say,
> flights journeys woundings not withstanding
> you touched bruised limbs, and despite the pain
> in this machine reality
> we have to, we do, we grow.

In this miasma of despair, the memories of the past are kept alive materially through religious books, photographs, diaries, objects, even a handful of dust of the motherland. V.S. Naipaul who has written on this sense of loss in *A House for Mr Biswas* (1969) later noted in *Finding the Centre* (1984) that the indentured labourer, journeying almost to the end of the world, ready to meet the wilderness, brought holy books and sandalwood, images, various religious shrines, plates and jars... as if they carried India with them and wished to recreate something of their world (V.S. Naipaul. Archive 1:1.3). For the world that they came to was foreign in landscape, language and its social hierarchy. The Caribbean was an artificially constructed multicultural society, where the racial conflict was among the whites, blacks and browns. The east Indian workers were seen as 'trouble', for they did not understand the language nor the order or rules of the white plantation owners. A set of unjust rules governed the interaction (or the lack of it) between the whites and the brown.

The two novellas *Shanti* and *The Unreturning*[5] deal with this conflictual situation, they also present two oppositional narratives of Shanti, as insider of the colony and of Dev (*The Unreturning*) who lives in Canada, as the outsider. Both have spent their childhood in Guyana and studied there. Shanti is a student, a girl who has suffered because of her girlhood and the other, a man who has been humiliated for being subversive to the rigid colonial order and has left for Canada. Moreover Itwaru's novella has been published under two different titles, *The Unreturning* (1988) and *Home and Back* (2001). Both the titles express the deep anguish of alienation from the cherished space home, and again underline the conflict. As expressed in the epigraph to *Home and Back* :

> Memory now, memory, my memory, my memory of you... This living, this life we life here - it is also a way of forgetting, even as we try to remember, as we the still living do, and must do, even when it hurts to do so?

For Shanti and Deo memory of the past is a mixed one, happy as well as sad. It hurts, for both Shanti and Deo occupy the in-between space. This interstitial space is constrictive, disjunctive and leads to subversion. There is a relentless questioning of the hierarchies. It can be very personal and at times it can relate to community. The interstitial space is also very vulnerable for it is open to imperial attack – physical, legislative and also educational – out of this vulnerability sometimes something positive emerges.

As Frank Birbalsingh writes in his finely researched work that the term "Jahaji bhai", Hindustani or Urdu for ship brother, was used as an address for the new relationship, forged by the immigrants with other shipmates in an attempt to attenuate the loss of family and friends (*Jahaji*, Intro. xi). The sense of community emerges from the interstices of a rigid social structure, which gives a certain meaning to life. Partha Chatterjee writes that the narrative of community substantialises cultural difference, and constitutes a 'split and double' of group identification. Where the colonised refuse to accept a cultural domain marked by the distinctions of the material and the spiritual, the outer and the inner (quoted by Bhabha p.6). Bhabha writes that by moving away from organised categories of class and gender and the focus turns to those moments and processes, where there is the articulation of cultural differences. The articulation occurs in these interstitial spaces which become the site for the articulation of the self. The in-between space also initiates new signs of identity, there is collaboration and contestation in defining idea of society itself (Bhabha: 1994, 1).

There are problems of identity and gender which the two novellas deal with, the discrimination against almost all the women labourers, the play of economic and political power weighs heavily against all the indentured workers and the problem is compounded by race and colour. Religion is used as a weapon of empowerment. Sookraj the school headmaster in *Shanti* had converted to Christianity for his personal benefits. Frank Birbalsingh names Sookraj as an 'embodiment of colonial toadyism and sycophancy' (1995:159).

For Sookraj lacked Christian values of compassion and mercy, he terrorized his young students. He gloated over his power over his pupils, his proud credo of "Ever Onward", limned on his office wall, was his personal goal of carrying the flag of British glory onward, through corporal punishment. He saw his students as 'bad seed, a curse, my people...' (64).

In his lyrical narrative style, Itwaru underlines the irony of Sookraj's misplaced mission – to educate the children whom he despises and beats up – and the comfort he tries to draw from the Bible. 'The Lord is my Shepherd; I shall not want ... He leadeth me beside the still waters... and I will dwell in the house of the Lord forever' (65). Religious resolve fails to help Sookraj overcome his deep lust for Shanti. 'Her evil worked its insidious presence in the doomed hours of his dreaming to torture him in an agony of desire no prayer of his could relieve' (84). Religion creates dilemma, when there is lack of faith or conviction and Sookraj who had read the Bible several times after his conversion, would silently realise that nowhere was there such beauty as in the Hindi texts and would wonder if abandoning of the Hinduism of his birth has been a mistake? (25).

The religion of the labourers is held against them, they are considered brutes and pagans, grinding economic disparity and deprivation also marks their lives. Through east Indians outnumber their white masters, but they are marginalised on multiple grounds, gender, labour, colour and lack of material holding. Their language – Creole – is considered 'vernacular' and is unintelligible to the masters. Their staple food *dal* and *roti* is deliberately mispronounced as *rooti* and *doll* to malign the eaters and to abuse the meaning and sacredness of their food. Which constitutes their bare sustenance. Food is sacred to them, because it is ancestral, it is their history and gives them a sense of sharing and of community. This space is very personal and it is their life.

In the life of Shanti, the eponymous protagonist of the novella *Shanti*, there are confluences with many such unknown and unsung people and their small histories. The pressing issue of home and homelessness, of location / relocation and dislocation, of the silence that surrounds and the memories that crowd, all come together. Her family is relocated in the sugar plantation for over forty years, and their lives form a palimpsest of yet another history of oppression. What is salutary in these conditions is the presence of the frail old woman (Shanti's mother) demanding a pension, weeping and shouting to be heard. Crying out that since both she and her husband had worked all their lives on the estate and were now old with no money for sustenance and medicine, she is claiming her right to pension. Shanti's infirm mother, through her individual effort against the pervading imperial powers, is negotiating the interstices, which Bhabha writes are continually and contingently 'opening out,' which dismantle fixed boundaries and hierarchies, where the present is not just 'a simple transitory,' but stretches to an 'interstitial future'. This opening out of marginal space, provides an agency to the minority identities (219). And the site becomes pregnant with exciting possibilities, the old woman demands a hearing, Shanti questions the corrupt system and Deo refuses to obey discriminatory orders.

It is a ground where the dividing lines are imperial, brutal and unfair, marked by lustful devouring. Booker tells Gladys, his east Indian victim, 'stop whimpering you fuckable bitch! You won't die, It'll do you good to have a white man. You should be happy' (*Shanti* 16). What we encounter is a site covered with mines as it were, where negotiation is difficult and could be fatal. But the tentative step is nevertheless taken.

The Biblical image of Ruth amidst the alien corn reverberates in *Shanti*. Her reality shamed her, her poverty and her inadequate clothes, which barely covered her, made her wish to be 'invisible'. From such a dire condition, Mr Sookraj rescues her, he endeavours to sublimate his lust for her and takes her into his house as family. The makeover from a hungry, deprived child, to a co-opted member of the family is completely overwhelming for her. She is a quick learner and excels in her studies. She fervently places all hope on education, which would open the doors to a better life.

Itwaru writes that Shanti now existed on three realms – one of school, second, the headmaster's largesse is his house and thirdly, her own home and her ailing mother. She felt that she would grow under the guidance of the headmaster and his wife Eve, she completely absorbs herself in the world of books. Shanti's memories were not of India, a country she had never known, but of her childhood when despite poverty and want she had felt loved and cared for. She has some happy recollections of the festival of Diwali, when her father was able-bodied, and would bring her the sweetest mangoes. Her mother would decorate their mud house with *diyas* and sing a mysterious *mantra*. From early childhood Shanti had a questioning mind and wondered at the justice of God and at the relevance of a faith that made her parents slog, without any hope of reward. She wondered what kind of a God was Ram who could be unmoved by all the injustice in the world? Her individual angst gets translated into the insecurity and anxiety of the community at large. Her own world was unintelligible to her where workers were 'local' and 'creole' in the eyes of the masters and their language reduced to a mere dialect.

Deo, the protagonist of Itwaru's other novella *The Unreturning*, remembers his own childhood where he had grown up with a lot of animosity. He resented being 'ordered to do things'. He rebelled against humiliating procedures and was whipped for his recalcitrance. The teachers generated a sense of fear in the classrooms. Both rebel at an individual level, the interstitial space becomes a site of contestation, of questioning the educational system as well.

Shanti studied a curriculum designed in England, which expected one to know the language, the history and geography, the flora and fauna of England. The contents of the syllabus were foreign: hygiene as promulgated by the westerners, arithmetic of pounds and shillings when her own currency was in dollars and cents.

The binaries that Itwaru creates are gut wrenching. In *Shanti* there is a single, gargantuan overseer – Booker – an imperial presence, on one side, and the helpless attenuated triad of Shanti's family on the other side. Her frail, rickety old father, wailing mother and a shell-shocked Shanti herself. They are no match for the superior brutal strength of Booker and his 'conquering empire lust,' that violates the daughter in the presence of the horrified parents. Bhabha writes that the recesses of the domestic space become site for history's most intricate invasions (p.9). Both the personal space (body) and the domestic space are violated, its sacredness defiled by the invader. The body becomes the site for aggression. But the moment also leads to a process of initiating new signs of selfhood and rebuilding and redefining it, through inner conviction, support of friends and enabling power of education.

The palimpsest of history of oppression binds Shanti, Rosa and Gladys together. They relate to each other with a deep sense of bonding. Rosa, herself a mother of twelve, realises that Shanti is a special child, while her own children are bitter, unruly and disgruntled. Shanti on the other hand, is the brilliant one, with the sun in her eyes. Nature works as a healing agent. Shanti gradually emerges out of the shadows of darkness and despair. Booker meets his nemesis in his brutal murder, when he is dismembered. No white man had ever been murdered before, the murder sends shivers through the colonial power structures. Shanti's nightmares of burning and falling are over. There rises in her a new vigour and a growing desire to change the shape of her life. Her friends are her source of inspiration and strength, contrary to the pressures of the male world. bell hooks in *Feminist Theory* has dwelt on this hesitant bondedness that comes into play hesitatingly in opposition to oppressive structures:

> Women are the group most victimised by sexist opposition. Male supremacist ideology encourages women to believe we are valueless and obtain value only by relating to or bonding with men. We are taught that our relationships with one another diminish rather than enrich our experience. We are taught that ... we should not, and do not bond with one another. We have learnt these lessons well. We must unlearn then. We must learn the true meaning and value of sisterhood. (p.43)

Shanti realises that the pious proclamations of the pastor in the church and the headmaster in the school were false. Both gender constructs and imperial hegemonic structures come in for questioning. It was the British who had ruined her parents and her family, robbed her of everything and violated her. 'Why must she be the British Queen's loyal subject? What had the Queen done for her?' (p.56).

In the crepuscular hour, Shanti is homeward bound. She recounts her 'litany', her sad past to her dear friend Latchman, the telling empties her of all her tears and she begins a new life with him. She fails to get a job, even though she had qualified. But she stands by her convictions of not surrendering to the demands of a corrupt system. She asserts her selfhood by her personal integrity and outspokenness.

Deo, in *The Unreturning*, finds the gates of the past locked as he returns home from Canada to visit his old ailing mother. For Deo there is a split in the memory of the past. As the epigraph in *Home and Back* had poignantly outlined memory which hurts, one goes back to Vijay Mishra's evocative essay, where he quotes from Derrida's *Memoires for Paul de Man* (pp. 29-30 quoted by Mishra).

> What is impossible mourning? What does it tell us ... about the essence of memory [of amnesia, of remembrance]? ... the idol, or ideal of the other who is dead and lives only in us?

Mishra writes that true mourning then becomes a tendency to accept 'incomprehension', which means leaving it as an 'absence' (p.30). The absence of the healthy mother, his house, his room, the deep vacuum in place of the past sense of belonging, swept by confusion in/of the present. The grey, frail, wasted and weeping woman 'was' and 'was not' his mother, who had lived in the bone and marrow of his being. The room he had lived in was never so small, bare and harsh, it had never smelt of death and sickness. Outside, the once familiar tree was now dismembered like him, his home and his memory, its branches cut. Homi Bhabha sums up the process of memory and remembering very accurately, when he writes, 'Remembering is never a quiet act of introspection or retrospection. It is a painful remembering, a putting together of the dismembered past to make sense of the trauma of the present' (63). Deo is confronted by a present which is totally bewildering, for his mother and the land of his birth have become painfully unknown, it was like a personal betrayal.

'There' in Canada he is considered just another immigrant, the sense of self-representation is denied to diasporic people, and 'here' the place he had always known as home, he now stands like an outsider. He is as much a stranger here as he is in the steel and concrete world of Canada. Mishra writes in his essay that Arnold Itwaru perceives Canada as a nation state 'created and upheld in the ethos of imperialism' (1994:7) where self representation is denied to diasporic people. To his own community, Deo remembers that he had symbolized whiteness, for 'abroad was success' (p.108), it was progress in Guyana. The east Indians who were facing the rule of the black people for twenty-five years, the white's regime was regarded as 'fair'. The blacks had stripped them of their dignity. The east Indians were now clubbed under the rubric of 'Foragners' in the land of their birth.

Deo remembers his past as a teacher in the Guyana school, where he has witnessed the strange, weird twist of situation, where both teachers and parents had become the agency of terror. 'These parents who do the same to their children. Parents who do not tolerate questioning. Parents who flog their children into obedience' (p.135). As a teacher Deo had believed that respect had to be earned and not forced out of fear, his classes were full of interactions with the students who were encouraged to ask questions, to debate an issue with him. His liberal approach was an anathema to the administration. He had never used a whip and had encouraged the students to think for themselves. Between the dictatorial regime and brutal school administration, Deo managed to make his work exciting for himself and his students. Deo's non-compliance with the dress code – he refused to wear a tie – and his liberal approach does not go down well with the school administration. His defiance was both an assertion of identity and a subversion of the colonial imposition especially at the secondary level, that was, as a matter of course, based largely on foreign materials that bore no relation to the daily lives of the pupils or their environment. (1984:460). He does not get his teaching certificate, but years later the government discarded the jacket and tie, and adopted the simple shirt as the preferred national garb for men, which Deo had always worn.

Education did not percolate to the grass roots level, it was static not dynamic and did not knit society together. The racial lines between the black and the east Indians were sharply drawn. On his return, Deo sadly realises that his dying mother symbolises his dying nation, what confronts him is 'an impossible dream, an absent future' (141). The brutality of the past colonial regime had reaped a new crop of dictatorship. There was no sanctity even for the common man's grave and the founder dictator - Forbes Burnham's body was taken all the way to Russia to be embalmed (148). The writer informs us:

> The return was over, but perhaps had never begun. He had thought he was returning home and he had come upon this .... He had left with cumin, ... and turmeric on his tongue, not this bitter sorrow he was now leaving with. (158-159)

Both Shanti and Deo are unhappy and discontented with the plight of their community. But both possess the spark that could ignite a process of restructuring, the confronting situation. There is the sense of deep mourning for their people, both Deo and Shanti suffer the loss of their parents, as well as the comfort of care and nature. There is a bitter sweetness in the remembering by both of them, the hope kindled by the Diwali diyas, the sweetness of the manages and the flavour of spices. Through this reworking of the past they struggle to make sense of their 'traumatic present' (Bhabha 63). The borderlines become the place from where something begins its presenting (Bhabha 5). In the interstitial space they seek to create a new meaning for their lives and their community.

In the angst of the present, we can draw hope from Bhabha who writes that one should constantly remind oneself that the real leap consists in introducing invention into existence (p.18). This creative invention, emerging from the cultural interstices, also breaks the time barrier of a culturally collusive 'present'. The invention is fraught with possibilities of humanism, of mutual dialogue and understanding. For as Bhabha emphasises the fact that the colonised intellectual has a unique position, one in which he/she is empowered to help his community.

The borderline culture demands an encounter with 'newness', that breaks with the past and the present to gesture to a new beginning. The moment is fraught with possibilities, it becomes the bridge to reach an innovative site of collaboration and of defining the idea of society. The interstitial space which is one of experience, one of lived reality, leads to an agency which is empowered to act, not to fall into despair or in the trap of unattainable utopias, but a lived reality of survival, of negotiation and resistance.

Endnotes

[1] M. Heidegger. "Building, dwelling, thinking", in *Poetry, Language, Thought* (New York : Harper & Row, 1971), pp. 152-3. As quoted by Homi K. Bhabha in The *Location of Culture* (New York: Routledge, 1994), p. 5.

[2] *The Hindu. Literary Magazine*. Sunday, April 29, 2007. Ramya Sivaraj, writes in the article "A necessary exile", that at Moka in Mauritius, the Indian Folk Museum of the Mahatma Gandhi Institute is dedicated to keeping alive immigrant history. Some 2,00,000 photographs and half a million coolie records including birth, death and marriage registers, dating from 1842 to 1920 are part of the impressive archives, which makes it the largest on indentured labour anywhere in the world. On display are some implements used by the workers, temple relics, antique jewellery once work by early women arrivals. In the same article Dr. Marina Carter, who has authored several acclaimed books on Indian emigration, says that it is important for the descendents of Indian labourers to not make the mistake of freezing their life histories into perpetual victimhood, but also as a story of remarkable human endeavour. The metaphorical expression, 'coolitude', coined by Mauritian poet Khal Torabully, where the pejorative term is turned into an intricate neologism, where the travel of the labourer, becomes a process of meeting of cultures, languages... a process whereby the mosaic

of India with its cultural diversity is engaged with alternity and otherness.
[3] Vijay Mishra. "Diaspora and the Art of Impossible Mourning," in *In Diaspora* Ed. Makarand Paranjape, (Delhi : Indialog Publications Pvt. Ltd., 2001), p. 34. Mishra adds that the women torn by the trauma of *Watno dur sang - din cale kudari rat nind nahi awe-* in the fields. The song is a kind of mourning for the lost homeland and the ordeal in an alien place.
[4] Arnold Harrichand Itwaru. *Entombed Survivals*. (Toronto : Williams - Wallace Publishers, 1987) p. 14, quoted by Mishra p. 46.
[5] Arnold Harrichand Itwaru. *Shanti* and *The Unreturning* (London : Peepul Tree Press, 1988. New Delhi : Penguin Books, 1992). References are to the Penguin edition, p. 125. *The Unreturning* is set in Guyana, twenty-seven years after Independence. In his introduction Itwaru writes that majority of the people in Guyana were the descendents of Indians, who came as indentured labourers, they were despised by both the British and the Africans. They were "another people in an elsewhere which sought their labour but despised nearly everything else about them." (Introduction : January 1992). Also see Jasbir Jain's article "Stranger Come Home", in *Perspectives on Diaspora: Indian Fiction in English*. Eds. Tejinder Kaur & N.K. Deo (Jalandhar: Nirmal Publication, 2005), p. 92. Jasbir Jain writes that the epigraph of *The Unreturning* is from *Taittareeya Upanishad*, whereby the blessing of day and night, the seen and heard is evoked.

References

Bhabha, Homi K. *The Location of Culture*. New York : Routledge, 1994.

Birbalsingh, Frank. *Jahaji* : *An Anthology of Indo-Caribbean Fiction* Toronto : Tsar, 2000.

Birbalsingh, Frank. *Novel and the Nation* : *Essays in Canadian Literature* (Toronto : TSAR, 1995).

hooks, bell. *Feminist Theory: From Margin to Centre*. South End Press, 1984.

Itwaru, Arnold Harrichand. *Entombed Survivals*. Toronto : Williams - Wallace Publishers, 1987.

Itwaru, Arnold Harrichand. *Shanti* and *The Unreturning*. (London : Peepul Tree Press, 1988). New Delhi : Penguin Books, 1992. *Home and Back* (Toronto : TSAR publication, 2001).

Itwaru, Arnold Harrichand and Natasha Ksonzek. *Closed Entrances*: *Canadian Culture and Imperialism*. Toronto: TSAR Publication, 1994.

Jain, Jasbir. "Stranger Come Home: Itwaru's *Unreturning* and Karodia's *Daughters of the Twilight*", *Perspectives on Diaspora: Indian Fiction in English*. Eds. Tejinder Kaur & N.K. Deo. Jalandhar: Nirmal Publication, 2005.

Lyman, Stanford. *Chinese American*. New York: Random House, 1974.

Mishra, Vijay. "Diaspora and the Art of Impossible Mourning." In *In Diaspora* ed. Makarand Paranjape. Delhi : Indialog Publications Pvt. Ltd., 2001.

Naipaul, V.S. *A House for Mr Biswas*. London : Penguin Books, 1969.

____. The V.S. Naipaul Archive, Series I, II, III, & IV. A special collection, McFarlin Library. The University of Tuba, 1996.

Sivaraj, Ramya. *The Hindu. Literary Magazine*. Sunday, April 29, 2007.

16

Cultural Transformation in Diaspora: Arnold Harrichand Itwaru's *Shanti*

INDIRA BABBELLAPATI

Arnold Harrichand Itwaru, the writer taken for the present study is placed within the framework of a multicultural society. It is pertinent to consider a writer's point of origin while attempting to analyse him placed in such varied cultural environs. Since Itwaru is of East Indian origin from Guyana, this article attempts to focus on the old Indian Diaspora that shaped Itwaru's sensibility as a writer. Typical of the postcolonial writer of the last decade of the 20th century, Itwaru is a 'cultural traveller,' a term Elleke Boehmer (1995:223) goes on to explain as 'ex-colonial by birth, "third-world" in cultural interest, cosmopolitan in almost every other way, he or she works within the precincts of the western metropolis while at the same time retaining thematic and/or political connection with a national background'.

To Seodial Deena (1995:78) the relationship between Third World literature and multiculturalism is 'reciprocal'. The Third World literature 'enhances multiculturalism while multiculturalism provides a voice for volumes of Third World literatures that have been marginalised and silenced by traditional literary canon...'

Like his protagonist Deo in *The Unreturning*, a sequel to *Shanti* (1992), Itwaru migrates to multicultural Canada with a heavy baggage of bicultural affinities. 'Let us look beyond this glittering façade, this seductive display of appearances which so flatter the imagination' (1996:103), is the writer's clarion call to all those living within the Canadian multiculturalism. The hyphens that characterise Itwaru's identity, Indo-Guyanese-Canadian, signify the 'vibrant social and cultural spaces occupied by the diaspora in nation-states', (Mishra 1996:16) as much as the writer's own proclamation of his identity, his 'otherness'. Typical of diasporic writers, Itwaru has an advantage in having a 'feeling of participating in several cultural groups or traditions without being fully at home' (King 1998 : 16).

Shanti is set within the era of the ending of the formal colonial rule. In Itwaru's words the novel is 'about the people who became another people in an elsewhere which sought their labour but despised nearly everything else about them' (Author's note in *Shanti*). If *Shanti* forms part of the historical legacy of colonialism and indenture, *The Unreturning* weaves Caribbean and Canadian locales in the protagonist's journey in an effort to merge the several fragments of his life in Guyana and Canada. Together the novels are Itwaru's attempt at redefining himself vis-à-vis the social and historical parameters of the Caribbean and the Canadian societies.

In *Shanti,* Itwaru addresses the social, economic, political and cultural oppression East Indians experienced in the Caribbean. In the process, Itwaru tries to relocate himself in the history of the Indian diaspora in Guyana in order to gain a proper perspective of his present reality, the reality of living in Canada's multicultural society.

Shared histories, cultural affinities and common racial memories are integral to diasporic consciousness. The Indian diaspora shares a consciousness 'generated by a complex network of historical connections, spiritual affinities and unifying racial memories' which get manifested in the 'cultural production of the Indian diasporic communities around the world.' [http://into. greenwood.com/ books/0313279/ 0313279047.html]. The Indian diaspora dating back to the eighteenth and nineteenth century indentured labour to the West Indies and Fiji now occupies diverse geographical areas from the South Pacific to South America, from the Indian Ocean islands of Mauritius and Singapore to the cities and suburbs of London, New York, Johannesburg and Toronto. The Government of Trinidad declared May 30th as a permanent national holiday marking it as 'Indian Arrival Day'. The Indian ship with 217 Indians aboard anchored in Port of Spain on that day a century and a half ago. It is a landmark in the history of the Caribbean as well as the Indian diaspora. Very few Indians are aware of the fact that there are several Indians settled in Trinidad, Guyana, Surinam, Mauritius, Fiji and other countries much before the mass migration of the professional elite to the US began.

The national or geographical dislocation of the old Indian diaspora resulting in the cultural estrangement of these Indians is not of their choice (Ramraj 1998:229). Indians were forcibly taken to these far flung places, all British colonies, as cheap labour to fill the English coffers as African slavery formally ended by that time. Repopulating the place for the purpose of plantation slavery has given rise to new forms of culture which are neither native nor extensions of settler culture back home. The result of the juxtaposition of the diverse population is creole culture of which Michael Dash says '[settlers] through a pattern of apparent consent, opposition and overt resistance, manage(d) to create unprecedented cultural transformations from a series of dialectical relations that united oppressor and oppressed' (1998:47).

The sociological clichés that are used to describe the Caribbean society as an 'ethno-cultural melting pot' and a 'multiracial Creole community' do not really describe the indenture society of the Caribbean. It's a turbulent society, exploitative and even destructive. The old Indian diaspora in

Guyana is pitted against hierarchies, struggles and divisions from the Imperial power as well as the Africans. The cultural and emotional dislocation caused by the 'psychic tremors of indenture' was a 'deep, dislocating rupture in the psyche of the people called the helots of empire' (Nandan, 1996:52). The East Indians, aware of their cultural superiority looked down upon the African slave community, though they themselves were dominated by the politics of subversion. They lived an uncertain social life devoid of physical or psychological security.

Though diasporic writing is 'about or by peoples who are linked by common histories of uprooting and dispersal it develops different cultural and historical identities depending on the political particularities of the dominant society' (Ramraj, 1998:229). Itwaru's world view is largely influenced by diasporic culture that is 'filtered and burnished in the crucibles of captivity, displacement and oppression' (Davies, 1995:16). The violence involved in the day to day living in the plantation society causes cultural and emotional dislocation in the lives of the Indian settlers. Besides, the Caribbean history of indenture and colonialism has a 'combined effect of crushing a wealth of cultural meaning' (Boehmer, 1995:197) on these Indians who were forced into accepting a subordinate social and cultural position. Conflicting cultures or cultural conflicts have come to dominate all literatures of postcolonial period. Bruce King (1998:7) points out that the 'international literature of postcolonialism, in all languages is based on the conflict between what is perceived as the traditional culture of the past and incorporation into a global modern culture'. The social identity as defined by the homeland culture of the Indian diaspora is constantly at threat from the African settlers. The Caribbean society of the plantation period had very little scope for cultural interaction minimising the emergence of new cultural forms other than the culture of servitude.

The Indian diaspora that we see in *Shanti* is 'relatively homogenous group set apart from a finite number of politically significant other races' (Nandan, 1996:79). To the Indian diaspora India is 'an enigmatic legacy'. No one had been to that 'magical place' though they all declare themselves Indian and follow customs *said* to be Indian. Some even spoke snatches of Hindi punctured by broken English and heard Hindi film songs over the radio. But none of these is of any consequence in calling themselves Indian for calling themselves Indian has a far reaching purpose beyond time and space – it acts as an emotional fillip for 'in it there was some dignity.' They all strongly believed that there is no dignity in being a Guyanese whom all Indians looked down upon with contempt. These Indians share a common culture in spite of belonging to a caste bound pluralistic ancestry. The diaspora's cultural practices are used as prefixes, derogatorily, to establish the Indian identity. These expressions are mostly aimed at distorting the notion of Indianness which is fundamental to an Indian's very existence in Guyana. They are largely hated for what they cannot help – their Indianness.

In spite of the constant flux of cultures, culture per se remains as 'the sum total of ways of living built up by a group of human beings and transmitted from one generation to another' (Random House Dictionary). Culture is the only area of human living that needs no physical demarcations. Cultural differences are so embedded into our system that everywhere we find undrawn territorial lines based on culture or its differences. Hobsbawm rightly quotes *Revue de Deux Mondes* to state that the 'true national frontiers were not determined by mountains and rivers, but rather by language, the customs, the memories, all that distinguishes one nation from another' (1995:98).

In their manner of speech, the food they eat, religion they practice, inter-racial and gender inequalities they confront in day-to-day life, family and familial relationships, marriages they celebrate, and in their superstitious belief, the factors which set a people apart from other peoples, these Indians retain oneness within the diaspora as following analyses of different cultural components show.

Language: The multilingual Indian here becomes a linguistic homogeneity. The diaspora speaks Creole interspersed at times with a word or two of Hindi. 'In

Caribbean culture,' says New (1998:119), 'Creole speech... spoken by the cane workers...recorded in the eighteenth and nineteenth centuries tells more profoundly of social inequity.' The entire narrative of *Shanti* is in Creole. The plantation workers' speech is redundant with fragmented utterances. Though these utterances are stylistically incomplete they are emotionally packed, reflecting their fragmented lives as well as the social inequities. The 'gunfire accent' of the ruling class is beyond their comprehension. East Indians are only 'local', 'a creole', 'work soiled labourers babbling in a language *they* called a dialect.'

> 'Manja, sah Mista Connel, sahib, one gat fi talk wid yuh, sah! Please, sah,' she pleaded. She did not want to offend. She was here to beg his mercy.' (p.9)

The helplessness reflected while talking to the English overseer is not found when the mother advises the daughter. Though the speech is also in Creole it is full of resolve:

> 'Shanti,' her mother would say, 'lemme tell you dis, me daughta. You mus guh to school - you mus learn, me daughta, Learn. Dis nah life f yuh. Dis nah life, me tell yuh.' (p.5)

When Master Sookraj comes with a proposal that he is willing to educate Shanti for which act of kindness she will have to be his domestic worker, Shanti's mother asks showing all her resentment :

> 'De lass maan who bin ya damage all me life. Wah you want now, Teecha Sookraj.' (p.27)

She is referring to the rape of the daughter in 'empire urgency' by the white overseer vulgarly displaying his authority in return to her plea for a pension. Notice the tone of vehemence when an Indian speaks to an African:

> 'Get out! Get out a yah before me bring me ask pan Yuh, you! Bhoodoor, Gaddaha! Get out o dis-blasted place before me bruck Yuh Mudda-cunt in ...' (p.32)

Cultural Transformation in Diaspora

As we notice even the common Indian words have undergone transformation in the Creole speech. Indian names such as Latchman, Gobnin, Shanti, to name a few are very common Indian names.

Speaking about language in diaspora, Ramraj says that allusions to Indian languages and literature recur more in Indo-Fijian than in Indo-Caribbean writing for a stronger tie with India exists in Fiji when compared to that of Trinidad and Guyana. We also find more references to Indian myths, Gods and goddesses, religious rites and rituals besides Hindi words and phrases in the Indo-Fijian diaspora. (1998:221-22).

Food: Mishra (1996:74) gives a detailed account of the food habits of the old Indian diaspora. We find a uniformity in food habits of the Indian diaspora in Guyana. They eat the same kind of food garnished with the same spices used in the old world – coriander, cumin, black pepper, turmeric, curry powder, etc. Curry, dal and roti dominate their fare. Mishra traces the uniformity in their food habits to the identical ration all the indenture Indians received. Africans who always had an offensive tone of superiority towards Indians abused them for the culture specific food they ate. It is very common to hear expressions such as 'dese fuckin coolie curry-eaters' and 'backward dal-an-rice miserly coolies'. A deliberate distortion of the words 'doll' for 'dal', 'rooti' for 'roti' are aimed at making Indians feel 'inauthentic, 'unimportant', 'inferior'. Terms like 'coolie-doll-rice-eater', 'oily-coolie-curry, rooti-enter' are aimed at degrading the meaning and importance of what the Indian ate. The repronunciation is an act of destruction – 'outbursts of incisive social hatred'.

These derogatives based on food went beyond race. These are meant to violate what food represented to the Indians. It is a reflection of the animosity between the two Diasporas against a hope to 'feel racial and personal dignity'. The African's distortion of the food Indians ate is the tip of an iceberg of a history of hatred that dominated the two diasporas.

Religion: Religion is one of the most fundamental of human identities besides language, dress and food. It is a powerful means and a resource which can establish clearly defined cultural identities in a diaspora. The Indian diaspora in Guyana consists of mainly Hindus though there are some conversions to Christianity. They celebrated Hindus festivals and worshipped Hindu gods. It was a close society as far as Hindu rituals are concerned. The headmaster of the school, a Christian convert, traces the backwardness and rebellion of the Indian diaspora to the religious practices:

> The backwardness and the ungratefulness of the lot ... this madness which kept them in their mudhuts ... this ancestral evil they re-enacted in their barbaric *Kali Mai puja every year*, had certainly grown its demonic seed. (p.83)

Here is what Shanti thinks of *Diwali*, the commemoration of the victorious return of Ram, the Hindu god as practised in some parts of India. Her responses to the religious beliefs of her parents are very typical of the second generation diaspora.

> ... she did not know how a god's name could be such a common one ... where was Ram returning, to where was he returning, and what did that have to do with her or anyone here in this village so far away from Ram's kingdom? ... why was this god-king stupid enough to want people to worship him? ... it was preposterous that Ram was called here where her father and mother worked from dawn to the dusk ... without his aid or presence. (p.77)

But the same Shanti as a child responds differently to the mantras the mother hums:

> ...the mother began to hum the melody and text of an old and mysterious mantra whose un-understood presence brought in the child an arousal of joy. (p.78)

The Hindu way of life the Indian diaspora followed is constantly under threat from the missionaries. If one wants to work in a church school, one has to be a convert. The pastor looked down upon the Hindu religious practices and his attempts to increase the number of converts are always foiled:

The pastor railed against the pandits and mantras and bhajans, the pagan mud and abeer and dantaal and drum and jhall of Paggwah ceremonials as he offered life eternal mashed clean in the blood of Christ, the Lamb of God, [he] could not understand the stubborn resistance of these ignorant crops of sinners whose life he needed to cash in for his everlasting life... (p.96-97)

Inter-racial relationships: Interacting within clearly defined cultural and ethnic identities leads to an intense hatred between the two diasporas – Indian and African – in Guyana. Cross-cultural relations everywhere are often marked by exclusion, exploitation and appropriation. East Indians in Guyana are projected mostly as victims of racism. The Africans and East Indians are historic enemies in the Caribbean. The Indian diaspora is a target of discrimination from the Africans as well as the white masters. Blacks going on rampage, destroying the Indian community are very common. The Indians on their part thought of Blacks as 'these rambunctious, bare faced bullies had no right to live in civil society' (p.31).

As far as the white ruler is concerned any closeness to the 'bloody loud-mouthed coolies' made them uncomfortable because the rulers harboured a subconscious fear for these 'coolie-dawgs', the Indians. If the Blacks referred to Indians as 'coolie-mudda-cunts" reducing Indian mothers to whores, to the English they are 'animals'. The Indians contented themselves that their ancestors were never slaves and never in chains. The reason for their animosity is the Black's claim to the land:

'We de niggroes been here first ... we sweat and blood meck dis country.' (p.22)

Latch, a second generation of the Indian diaspora, never believed in racial fights – two of his mother's half brothers were Afro-Guyanese and his grandmother had had children from an Indo-Guyanese, an Afro-Guyanese and an Anglo-Guyanese – till he was caught unawares by an African woman wearing a Madras handkerchief. Since it is similar to the one his mother wears, Latch takes her to be a friendly soul. On the contrary she complains gathering all the blacks in the vicinity that:

> 'Since dat Jaygan maan get into politics all dese damn coolie people think dey can give we black people rudeness, yuh know!' (p.52)

However, there are also people like Gertrude, a black who goes beyond all the physical limitations to see the oneness of man. When her bosom friend, an Indian, dies she laments:

> ... these Indians would not accept a black woman there [at the cemetery]. Stupid custom she thought sadly, people have so many stupid cruel customs. (p.82)

Social hierarchies do exist within the Indian diaspora too. The clerks who worked for the English overseer, the school teacher, a Christian convert, an Indian doctor married to an English woman, etc. consider themselves superior to the cane-cutters. The school strongly believed in the dictum 'for the cane-cutters and rice-growers the rod was necessary to keep them in order' (p.58). The likes of Babulal who worked for the whites were embarrassed and ashamed of their own people. To Babulal they are dogs. For Teacher Sookraj, a staunch believer of British practice of justice and fair play, the Indian diaspora is of 'a bad seed, a curse.' To him the children of Indian diaspora are 'miserable, misguided, and disorderly. He prefers not to mingle with those loud-mouthed angry dal-an-rice coolies, drunkard' for they do not know how to respect. It was below his dignity to attend the funeral of his ward's mother. But these limitations do not come in the way of his carnal craving for Shanti, his ward.

Gender Inequality: Gender inequality is found at three different levels:

i. In the way the white rulers treated the Indian women.

ii. In what the Africans thought of the Indian women.

iii. What Indian men themselves expect of their women.

The white man always saw the Indian women as 'animals ... vigorous, fuckable female animals at his disposal and pleasure' (p.15). Indian women were targets of repeated sexual abuse in 'empire urgency' by the white man. In their terror these women reconcile to their lot and conclude that it was the lady's luck to be laid by an English man and they should be happy at that. A young Indian daughter was usually an object of blackmail and it was very common for helpless parents to stand witness to the white man raping their daughters. The rape of an Indian girl by a white overseer is central to the narrative of *Shanti*. These women were victims of repeated sexual assaults, both in the cane fields or in their very homes. They even mothered 'light-skinned disconsolate' children conceived out of violation. Yet, the women survived 'nonetheless, in a state of silent and personal resentment' (p.20) that finally culminates in a silent rebellion that butchers an English overseer for the several rapes he committed.

The tone of servility and helplessness turns into repulsion and disgust when these women respond to an African man. The women considered the African man's sex and his race a bestial thing. It was quite spontaneous for a woman to 'curl her haughty coolie lip in disgust whenever she saw [an African]' (p.74). For an African an Indian woman is the target of the long years of hatred. The following lines summarise what these men think of Indian women:

> This was where he wanted the Indian woman, on her back ... screaming, babbling, begging him for mercy... These women thought themselves superior to him ... they were too good for any black man, these women who scorned him, who made him a no-man, who felt violated by even the passing glint of desire...(p.73)

The Indian men generally worked as manual labourers. Women too toiled as much as men. In addition to their daily struggle for survival the women suffered severe malnutrition as well as repeated childbearing. Man considered a woman's flesh his property and the assault on his property by a black drives an Indian man to suicide for 'his dignity as an Indian man was for ever destroyed' (p.95). Fathers always thought it was their sacred duty to get their daughters married to men deserving their honour. Young girls who spoke openly of boys were considered loose and shameless and did not deserve any respect. No decent girl would ever tarnish the family by going about with boys. Mothers too warned their daughters not to be alone in the company of boys. Young Indian boys were trained to expect every Indian girl to be 'decent', a virgin. Otherwise, she was considered filth for 'Indian girls offered their virginity to their husbands.' Latch in *Shanti* feels committed to marry Shanti after an accidental sexual involvement. The 'self-righteous' young man later taunts her by calling her a whore for he suspects her virginity.

Marriage: Marriage, an intrinsic part of the social fabric, has fixed cultural boundaries. In the old Indian diaspora in Guyana, though there are instances of inter-racial marriages, Indians married mostly among their clan. It's very common for a Hindu wedding to be preceded by the singing of village women. Only men and boys danced at weddings. 'Fancy modern jukebox music, vulgar loud shameless Hindi songs to which so many Hindi singers had stooped, and so many East Indians in the district found delight in' was not appreciated when played at the time of marriages. Booming drums, the tassa and the bass drum reverberating about coconut palms considered auspicious by all Hindus is a very common sight in the Hindu marriage celebrations. Marriages celebrated with all the pomp are connecting links between now and a 'time long gone and for ever irretrievable' (p.32). The African dismissed the whole celebration as 'his stupid coolie- babu music'.

Family: Family in the old Indian diaspora is typical of the modern micro-family for obvious reasons. These Indians were forced to scatter to different parts of the country depending on the demand for labour. In a way they were all destitute and lived too far a distance to visit one another often. However, they mostly met either at marriages or funerals. Otherwise they remained as strangers. Shanti sees the family of her parents at her mother's funeral – 'This sister [mother's] was a distant glimmer of a presence somewhere in childhood...' (p.80). In spite of the gender inequality, the women were more vocal than the men in pleading with the white authority for better lives, though in vain. It is in fact the women who raise a silent voice of protest against the white domination. Their long drawn suffering makes them encourage their daughters to pursue 'eddication' as a possible escape from the plantation life. The Indian family in the diaspora too is patriarchal. We do not find extended family relationships. It is mostly death that brings members of a family together while death-like living separates them.

Besides the above mentioned components of culture the Indian diaspora shared common superstitions like 'old ugly bitter black-tongued emaciated evil women' turning into vampires to feed on the blood of sleeping children and adults; 'ode-higues' the ghosts that could only be kept of the house if they were guarded by X marks on the doors and 'manicole' brooms on the lintels. They believed in witchcraft and frequented witch-doctors to exorcise themselves of the evil spirits that are said to have possessed them.

From the old Indian diaspora in the Caribbean a new culture of surveillance has been born, a new ancestry of servitude as well that weighs heavily on the generations to follow. Shanti openly rebels against the system and lashes out at the distorted version of history thrust upon them by imperial watch-dogs in the name of education. When Latch is very keen on becoming a school teacher, she tells him:

> ...you must be neat and clean and tidy and obedient and without a mind of your own... all the rest...will shit in your mouth. And to this you must obediently say, Thank you, Sir...

> 'and you're talking to me about fairness? What will you do in fairness... when they hire you? Will you teach that Britain and the British are better than you and me? Will you teach the murders committed on your foreparents and mine by the British as the acts of heroism? Will you teach that when enslaved people resisted they were called rebels whose attempts were promptly out done by the authorities? Will you teach your pupils that the sugar estate's willing of people through overwork is right? Will you? Will you?'

It is fitting to conclude with the following lines summarising the plight of the second generation of the Indian diaspora in Guyana:

> ... (Latch) would often enter into a brooding reflection and desire for the riddance of the burden of his brutal and frightening ancestry, one which had made him and all the people around him, (not the headmaster, the school teachers, the catechist or the church pastor) the people, his people - insecure, afraid, humble even in their suffering, like his parents and all his friends' parents, like Shanti's, like old sickly Gertrude, like most of the people in his dusty one-road village and country, so quickly turned into the ubiquity of cursed mud during the season of rain.' (p.87)

References

Boehmer, E. *Colonial and Postcolonial Literatures: Migrant Metaphors*. New York: Oxford Press, 1995.

Dash, M. "Psychology, Creolization and Hybridization", *National and Postcolonial Literatures*. Ed. Bruce King. Oxford: Clarendon Press, 1998.

Davies, C.B. ed. *Moving Beyond Boundaries: Black Women's Diaspora*. Vol 11. New York: New York University Press.

Deena, S. "Colonial and Canonical Control over Third World Writers". *The Commonwealth Review*. Ed. R.K. Dhawan, VII (2):78-112. 1995.

Hobsbawm, Eric. *Nations and Nationalism since 1780*. Cambridge: Cambridge University Press, 1995.

Itwaru, A. H. *Shanti*. NDL; Penguin, 1992.

Itwaru, A. H. "Visible Invisibility: The Anguished Other and the Canadian Discourse". *Indian Journal of Canadian Studies*, Vol V. 103, 1996.

King, B. "New Centres of Consciousness, New postcolonial and International English Literatures". In *National and Postcolonial Literatures*. Ed. Bruce King. Oxford: Clarendon Press, 1998.

Mishra, V. "New Lamps for Old: Diasporas, Migrancy, Border", *Interrogating Postcolonialism: Theory, Text and Context*. Eds. Harish Trivedi and Meenakshi Mukherjee, IIAS: Shimla, 1996.

Nandan, S. "The Diasporic Consciousness from Biswas to Biswasghat". Interrogating Postcolonialism: Theory, Text and Context. Eds. Harish Trivedi and Meenakshi Mukherjee, IIAS: Shimla, 1996.

New, W.H. "Colonial Literatures". *National and Postcolonial Literatures*. Ed. Bruce King. Oxford: Clarendon Press, 1998.

Ramraj, V. "Diasporas and Multiculturalism". *National and Postcolonial Literatures*. Ed. Bruce King. Oxford: Clarendon Press, 1998.

17

Re-locating Alter(native) Voices of Silence in Lakshmi Persaud's *Raise the Lanterns High*

JAYITA SENGUPTA

The novel *Raise the Lanterns High*[1] by Lakshmi Persaud can cast a network of shadows. And as shadows weave into more shades of flickering images through the mirror of the mind, stories emerge. These stories or narratives in the repository of the atavistic memory of the woman, named Vasti Nadir, jostle for discursive space in her subversive imagination to question the symbolic order of meaning. The novel does not write feminism; rather it mirrors the woman's spurious silence and her sacrifice and self-immolation by accepting the life thrust on her. While it requires courage for the Sati to mount the funeral pyre, it requires more mental strength to accept death-in-life through the enacting of a compulsive ritual of marriage, despite violent eruptions of conscience.

Persaud herself comments on this latest novel of hers as one which foregrounds the theme of 'travelling'. She observes: 'The novel unravels the fabric of several traditions, and feels their very weave'.[2] Unlike the woman protagonist in her earlier novel, *Sastras*, Vasti Nadir, despite her dynamic mental set up cannot challenge the patriarchal stasis and ultimately gags her conscience to yield herself mind and body to patriarchal rape. The writer's objective thus in this novel is to project and criticise the woman's defeatism. The writer intends to point to the tradition of martyrdom that women have acceded to, in the name of duty and loyalty to their family and customs. At the same time she impels the modern Caribbean women of Indian descent to find images of the various selves subject to patriarchal oppression and stories of resistance to the same, to relocate themselves in the past traditions and recreate a new historicity. The novel, thus addresses silence about women and women's silence in Caribbean literature and culture using the subversive strategy of semiotic imaginary in Vasti Nadir, and by creating 'monumental history'.[3]

This paper thus endeavours to take a cursory glance at the history of Indian woman's silence in Caribbean fiction to relocate the novel in its cultural/historical consciousness. Next, it will proceed to analyse the discursive nature of the text itself in its semiotic rendering of women's oppression and resistance in various histories/cultures/ traditions, through the mirror of Vasti's atavistic memory and her consciousness.

The Silence (d) Indian woman in Caribbean literature

The first mention of the Indian woman is probably in the 1930s when the Duke of Normandy sang about his affair with one in a calypso in such lines: "After she gave me parata/ She had me cooraja". [4] In Attilla's *Dookani* (1939), the idea of the Indian woman in calypso associated with the exotic feast is further extended to the 'ideal lovable and unattainable': 'She was exotic, kind and loving too/ All her charms I could never describe to you ....' [5] Executor in *My Indian Love* (1939), names the Indian woman as Dookani, whom he meets at a tent in Caroni during the *Hosein* festival and narrates how she declares her love for him in stereotypical East Indian pidgin thus establishing her identity as an unsophisticated rural maiden, the butt of laughter for Executor's audience. Fighter's *Indian Wedding* and Dictator's *Moonia*, as stereotypical renderings of the Indian women continue to ridicule the Indian woman and her society in more racial overtones with hostility matching humour. While the Indian patriarchy was adamant in maintaining its ethnic purity, their women would be objects of fascination for the Creole men and instances of cuckoldry would flare up a racial conflict between the Creole and the Indian societies. These works thus in their depiction of the Indian woman in calypso project the status of the Indian women in Caribbean society as suffering from double marginalisation and gagged in their self-expression. Hence when male Caribbean writers who use Indian experience as raw material (beginning with V.S. Naipaul, and others such as Sam Selvon, Shiva Naipaul, Ismith Khan, Wilson Harris and Edgar Mittelholzer) and yet continue to ignore the identity of Indian women in fiction as individuals, one is not really surprised. As Ramabai Espinet observes:

> The Indian woman is invisible because no novelist has yet been able to regard her existence in the West Indies and give voice to the peculiarities and perceptions of that particular existence .... We live in a cultural situation where Anglophile and Americanized attitudes and values are thought to be desirable and the movement towards 'creolization' is inevitable. Gradually, repressive Indian attitudes towards women are being jettisoned along with other items of cultural baggage, and are being replaced, predictably enough, by other equally repressive though different attitudes which prevail in the dominant culture of the West. [6]

Espinet further points out that the idea of the Indian women as 'submissive, shy and timid', undercuts history and is a fallacy which needs to be corrected. She narrates that many of these women had crossed the *kala pani*, not because they were always compelled to do so, but they chose to. Even V.S. Naipaul's own great-grandmother, Espinet confirms, was one of these women. Yet, as she critically comments, Naipaul too in his fictions presents the Indian women as stereotypes. Espinet cites the example of Shama in *A House for Mr Biswas*, who is projected in the main as slim, pretty, retiring, dutiful and loyal as fitting of an Indian woman and wife. Mrs Baksh too in *The Suffrage of Elvira*, in her unattractiveness is simply used as a literary device to illustrate the powerlessness of the Indian male. Again the Indian women characters when compared to the delineation of European women characters such as Sandra, Jane and Yvette in Naipaul's fiction appear limited. As Espinet's analyses would suggest, Indian women in Caribbean fiction remain frozen in ritualised, indirect perception. It was absolutely necessary for women writers of Indian origin to rescue the Indian women in fiction from their stereotypical frame. Mahadai Das, Shana Yardan and Rajkumari Singh are among the first Indo-Caribbean women writers to foreground a new Indian historicity in Caribbean culture with regard to women. Works such as "I am a Coolie", an essay as well as a poem of the same name by Singh for example, argues for re-inflection and political mobilisation of 'coolie' as a term of affirmation rather than denigration. When we move ahead to analyse Lakshmi Persaud's work, we have to locate her in this tradition of women writing herself.

Mirrors of Conscience and Alter(native) Voices

Persaud in this novel uses Vasti Nadir's consciousness as a net to mirror the stories of female oppression (Part One) and feminist resistance (Part Two and Part Three). Leitmotifs of binoculars and mirrors signify Vasti's consciousness depicting its capacity for other experiences, other cultures and histories. While the binoculars bring home things which are afar, mirrors can allow for apparitions and visions of faraway impressions or imprints in history. The strength of this text lies on these two leitmotifs, besides those of 'moon' and 'lantern' as motifs of light. These together express the writer's intention to interrogate Patriarchal Law through a patriarchal narrative of rape and silence.

The novel opens with a Lacanian split between the ego and the ideal,[7] causing the child Vasti's entry not into the symbolic order of language but into the various streams of her semiotic consciousness which flicker through the ancient mirror which her great-grandfather had bought. Chapter One of the novel depicts, Vasti's childhood encounter with a scene of rape as she returned from her school on the last day of the term. Striding along with a carefree spirit, the child, Vasti had ventured a shortcut through the sugarcane fields with her new binoculars. She had cooled herself in the oasis that came in the way and enjoyed the solitude of the nature around her, which a Lacanian reading would signify as the 'ego-ideal phase'. It was then a sudden stifled, deep cry of anguish had split her consciousness. Focusing her binoculars in the direction of the sound, Vasti had envisioned the rape of a young girl by a young man. The ringed finger of the man pressing down on the girl's breast was framed in Vasti's memory forever. Engraved on the ring was an eagle with its wings spanned as if in flight and there was scroll attached to its feathered back, which too had wings. The novel in foregrounding Vasti's search of the 'ringed finger' is her search for the man to see if he kept his promise of marriage to the girl he had abused. As Vasti narrates, the powerful impact of the vision of rape through her binoculars has transmuted her 'self' with the girl's:

> I did not know it at that time, but I had mentally adopted this schoolgirl, wishing with all my heart that I could ensure he did not renege on his promise to marry her ... And in fact this did come to pass, but in a manner I had least expected.

The identity of the 'ringed finger' is soon disclosed in Chapter Three, and its symbolic significance too explained as:

> ...an emblem of unadulterated power, an eagle in its flight, wings lifting with the wind, though buffeted, defying the elements – its shadow sailing effortlessly. A bird of prey carrying an open scroll of ancient writ. 'And the word was with God.' (23)

Eagle, the royal bird, is a symbol of patriarchy and is a bird of prey. The shadow of the bird in flight suggests the trailing shadow of history of man's supremacy over women and the scroll of ancient writ suggests the power of the symbolic order of the society or that man's word or law is God. So the text in keeping with the symbolic order writes that Vasti's secret desire to find the rapist and see if his promise of marriage is fulfilled. The ring as an identifying symbol of patriarchal power betrays the owner, Karan Wallis, with whom Vasti's marriage has been fixed. The writer informs the reader of the 'ringed finger's' identity much before Vasti herself learns the truth, to create a sense of anticipation of Vasti's reactions and to confirm her intention of revising the Lacanian model of 'desire'.[8] Persaud intends to replace Lacan's concept of eternal deferral of desire with an enactment of the same. Vasti's desire is not a desire for idyllic love; it is desire for reparation of the split enforced in her virginal consciousness with the scene of rape. And such idea of reparation grasped by the child's mind only reveals how conditioned she is by the social and cultural codes of her society and community. The patriarchy would rather agree to the child Vasti's conditioned consciousness and differ from grown up Vasti's interrogating self and her dialogics of the 'other'. The writer thus interrogates through Vasti the very basis of the 'ego-ideal phase' in Lacanian conception. For Persaud, 'innocence' is 'ignorance of shame'. It is only painful knowledge of the patriarchal control which allows for a dialogical narrative and understanding of women's source of energy and deconstructive powers of a revolutionary language.[9]   In other words, the feminine imaginary is activated after the split, to allow for clearer understanding of the mirrors of history and conscience.

Vasti narrates that the mirror which her great-grandfather had bought at an auction was one with a strange history which titillated her child imagination and continued to haunt her consciousness even later. The mirror had belonged to the rebellious Indian queen who had made her escape from being burnt alive with her dead husband on his funeral pyre. As a child the mirror had fascinated Vasti with the ephemeral realities it would suggest to her with changes of light, colour and shades. The mirrored images so engrossed her child mind that at times she wondered whether she too was an apparition of some sort, or a 'mirrored reflection of some inexplicable reality in the vastness beyond' (11). Such thoughts stayed with her as she grew up as a young woman and her search for a reflection's source or reality became an exciting and challenging game for her to unravel some secret, some lurking truth and it increased her 'awareness of the silent world of living images and their diverse energies' (11). With her ability to absorb other(s) experiences, which included the young girl's rape and her readings from history, Vasti in the novel becomes the symbol of women's negation and mute resistance. Vasti's imagination here could be understood as a set of intentional relations and as a necessary constituent of all acts of knowing as Sartre points out in *Psychology of Emotions*. Her imagination allows for a spontaneous inquiry into the possible and hidden structures of reality, 'an epoch of the existing world which consciousness performs *within* mundane experience.'[10] As she analyses in Chapter Two:

> Thanks to the mirror, I was able to experience other perceptions of life which enabled me to have an imaginative understanding of it though I myself was irretrievably bound, harnessed to the carriage of custom, tradition and community. There was no escape. (14)

The following chapters however sweep over time to talks of Vasti's impending marriage. The writer comments on the Nadir household as one which is more modern than the others in the village locality. The house was 'the only concrete-built'(24) in Pasea village with electric lights as Vasti's father had purchased an electric pole. Vasti, the youngest daughter of the Nadirs, is more like her father in her aspirations. She is progressive minded and wishes to bring about change in the mindset of other mothers in their handling of their daughters. As a school teacher, she wishes for a reformation. In a conversation with Pushpa, her elder sister, Vasti discloses her thoughts to her:

> I want to try and help my young girls at school to begin that crucial questioning, to begin to walk the path that leads to their thinking for themselves, becoming discerning. They cannot do so without the tools to open words apart as if they were oysters, to discover them afresh, taste their true meanings.
>
> I want to meet their parents and discuss the social consequences of the rapid changes taking place all around us in the 1960s. I want to engage their mothers, Pushpa, I want to show that these changes can be approached sensibly. (30)

Yet, ironically enough, Vasti finds herself trapped in the prospect of an impending marriage which she is sure would act as a foil to all her thoughts and aspirations. Her father's sudden demise had made her mother cautious and she had reverted to her traditional 'pathways'. Like any mother of an unmarried young woman, she considered that it was her duty to get Vasti married off to a Brahmin boy, without caring for Vasti's career and her choice of life. The novel unfolds Vasti's conflict as she grapples with her consciousness which rejects the very idea of marriage. Yet, Vasti does not wish to hurt her family and her mother's sentiments. Her deep anguish to yield to a life of 'boxes' than for the 'open skies' (49), exorcises the oppressions of women in the past. Vasti tries to visualise the preparations for her engagement. The ritual of the altar being freshly decorated with coloured rice in 'intricate motifs of life-giving flowers' and offerings of ghee, pitch-pine, marigold and roses, implicated to her an altar of self-sacrifice. To be a life-giver and to yield to the expected norms of marriage and bearing children, she will have to extinguish her own desires and her 'self'. The weight of the traditional ceremony with its implied significance of patriarchal control which reduces women's worth and self-esteem, presses down on Vasti, to allow for her semiotic energies to erupt through her symbolic mind. She finds herself comparing her predicament to those Inca maidens at the juncture of their sacrifice on the crest of the mountains. The songs sung in praise of their courage and honour matched with Vasti's earning of a similar honour in enacting out the ritualistic marriage following the traditional mores of her family and community. As Vasti interrogates her fate: 'How had I got into this situation?' (51) her mind wanders along the streams of cultural history depicting various traditions of Patriarchal control.

In a waking dream, at the hour of the still darkness of the approaching dawn, Vasti's consciousness mirrors the shades of women's oppression. Before sun's rays establish logo-centric control, Vasti's atavistic memory weaves images of pain and horror across history and traditions. She finds herself joining a caravan of silent women, in their long unending journey through time, shuffling and dragging their tired feet, burdened by the weight of their baggage of customs and traditions. Vasti's consciousness is quick to point out that they are 'women' and not beasts of burden and that 'custom-made iron bars keep the women in place' (51). As night falls, 'lanterns' ahead show Vasti the way to glass cubicles, where she finds young women and female infants going in. Vasti is attracted to one such cubicle named "Sweet Rosebuds" and is about to enter when she is stopped by two sturdy women at the gate. So she peers through the clear wide glass to envision a scene of pure horror. As she looks on, she finds a four year old girl's foot being folded like an oblong napkin. The child struggles in pain and her mother too pleads for her child, yet the grandmother is insistent on 'sweet rosebuds' or feet like 'tiny, plump, soft, fine, perfectly formed lotuses' as the wealthy Chinese men of high status preferred to have their wives feet to be so! The feet may have lost their ability to walk but it performed the other function – offering pleasure to her husband in future! Such is man's privilege over women in Chinese tradition. Just as Vasti makes efforts to reconcile her horror and indignation, she envisions another tale of oppression in another cubicle named "The Bondo Sisters". Vasti wishes to go in and be one of their community, where she is once again pushed out as she does not qualify for "bonding". So she peers in despite their efforts to shoo her away with signals and writings such as: "THIS IS OUR CULTURE. GO AWAY. SEEK YOUR OWN" (56). Another woman from Sierra Leone joins her, who explains the tribal ritual of removing the clitoris and stitching up the labia, to her. As Vasti once again struggles with her queries, whether it was a surgery, the woman backfires that it is 'savagery' for it is a man's world which gratifies male pleasure and satisfaction. Vasti witnesses the scene of torture and understands the full implication of savagery as the operation is done without anesthesia. Her yells of protest, draw others attention, and the woman holding the bloody knife moves towards Vasti with a raised hand. Vasti comes to herself from her waking dream, trembling in horror and fear. Her intuitive mind is weary travelling so far back in time and into various cultural traditions of women oppression. But there are some nagging questions which haunt her: *'Had there ever been a time when we women were as worthy as the men?'* (57) Despite such imagination and such questionings and even such understanding of a change as a necessity to reshape the society, Vasti like her sisters in the silent procession, yields to her mother's choice and looks to her for support. She speaks her father's words: 'Education is the best thing we have. It should teach us to observe with care and to change our minds with evidence'(57) and yet enacts her mother's choice knowing the 'enormity of undertaking' (56).

However, Vasti is yet to learn of the reality of the burden that she undertakes, for she is yet to discover the true identity of Karan Wallis, her future husband. When Vasti goes to Singh's shop to fetch her necklace, she comes across the Eagle ring and learns the name of the owner. As she stares at the ring in stunned silence she visualises it as a cobra slowly raising its hood and flicking its tongue to reach her. She remains mesmerised by the dangerous implications of the image of her future. Vasti had thought that her sacrifice was possible without losing the integrity of her inner voice. But the knowledge of Karan Wallis's identity and a future with him pushes her to the edge of her sanity. Vasti imagines slugs in the garden when there are none and her weak nerves take her obsession with mirrors and reflections to an extreme. She asks her elder sister Pushpa to come to her room and demands an explanation for a reflection for an octagonal roof of glass in one of her two windows. Though the source of the reflection is the roof of a conservatory quite further away from theirs, the window appeared to have caught the shadow of it somehow. Vasti insists on seeing the real source of the reflection. Her urge to seek reality beyond reflection grips her mind profoundly. And on the wedding day, which had been wet and windy as if mirroring her restlessness, she is left alone in her chamber. In the evening, the narrative observes that "the raised lantern of the moon showed itself fully and shone directly upon her." Vasti finds herself forcibly pushed backwards by some magical powers and she stumbles before the ancient mirror bathed in moonlight. Persaud's linguistic intentions are quite clear here for the key phrase, 'raising lanterns' occurs in the text, the second time, to suggest deconstructive forces or the disruptive feminine principle in Vasti. If the previous experience in Vasti's waking dream projects images of female oppression, the Part Two of the text, mirrors through Vasti's unconscious, the story of the Indian queen, the original owner of the ancient mirror. The narrative here lyrically expresses the power of imagination bestowed on Vasti by the feminine principle – the moon[11]:

> Then, as if a long traveled light, reflected by the moon, had caught her in its powerful widening gyre, she was pulled by a whirlwind force, sucked into its vortex like a spinning leaf, lifted high, defying the force of gravity, following the light. When its magnetic force shifted, her body dropped. (83)

Vasti falls into a deep unconsciousness as she travels through time to the ancient kingdom of *Jyotika*. She is initiated into an active psychic experience, which Nor Hall refers to as 'a kind of veiling that paradoxically permits seeing. Covering the eyes for a time to the external world permits an inward focusing that tends to draw one's attention "down" and sometimes "backward"'.[12] Vasti thus wakes up to the sound of artillery at Jyotika, a kingdom of Rajputs in India, far back in time and history. As she lifts herself from the cold marble floor, she tries to figure out where she is. The language of the narrative here again is rich with symbolic overtones, suggesting the winding alleys of the deep unconscious. Even as the narrative here signifies the feminine unconscious, it reminds the reader of the Keatsean 'Chamber of Maiden Thought'[13]:

> There was no end to this spacious corridor, where dusk slept. Its high outer wall was perforated with designed clusters. Only through these vents, did sunlight see the inner passage where shadows played as branches waved and wings flapped. Way in the distance, swirling winds howled ... (87)

The quoted passage also closely matches with Hall's description of the sacred cave of initiation. [14] The network of light and shade created by the lantern of conscience allows for the imagination to take rapid strides across the 'vale of tears' or 'howling winds' to a meaningful existence or to the 'vale of soul making' in Keatsean conception and to a sense of rebirth or initiation in Hall's theory of the archetype of rebirth. A strange premonition which sweeps over Vasti as 'a wave on the seashore' tells her that she had been here before. Her semiotic surges impel her to an intuitive journey and the light of a raised lantern or her feminine unconscious shows her the way to her solution. Vasti experiences the 'othernesses' of the other(s) in the story that unfolds before her. Her quest to go back in time when men and women had been equal, prompted by her waking dream earlier, has not been in vain. Vasti is absorbed in the drama inside the Queen's chambers. She recognises Queen Meena, a figure of perfect beauty and grace, who is also accomplished in fine arts and Queen Dayita, the prima classical dancer with her proud carriage and her long, strong hair, Queen Renu, the dusky beauty, who is a thoughtful, reticent scholar from far south. Vasti has a feeling that she is from the future, peering into the past having travelled back in time. Though she is experiencing it all the second time, there is much that has been lost in oblivion. The mist of centuries had blurred the outcome of the drama in her memory. So an intuitive curiosity eggs her on. The narrative unfolds the story of the king's death in the battlefield and the proclamation of the new king, thus compelling the queens to adjust their mind to the changing circumstances and prepare themselves for the ritual of sati. While the elder two queens try to reconcile themselves at first to the custom of sati, the younger one, Renu, the scholar cannot accede to this barbaric custom. She is the one who shows sense to the other two queens suggesting that their beloved king had never wanted his queens to throw away their lives in this manner. Renu suggests that they utilise their talents which till then had the sole purpose of pleasing the king. She thinks of their opening a school for children which would invite its pupils from all sections of society. They take the royal pundit Krishna into confidence penning down their reasons for not performing sati in a scroll. The Pundit is at first terrified and suggests opium to the queens before they approach the pyre, so that they will not sense the agony of the burns. The queens however remain firm in their resolve and the royal pundit devises another means by employing Kala, the slave girl, the mother of Sujata, an illegitimate, yet a royal offspring. The pundit offers good fortune for Sujata should Kala undertake the burden of sati instead of the queens. But this too does not work as the young pundit Baalaaji comes to her rescue, with good advice. The story unfolds this young Pundit's origins too. Baalaaji senior had brought up this young Pundit as his own, though he was actually a son of a very poor lowborn couple who had offered him to the senior pundit for his well-being. The secrets of Baalaaji's birth and the fact that a North Indian Pundit could do such a thing as go against the caste/ class bars takes Krishnajee by total surprise and transforms him. He helps the queens in their escapade and Baalaaji too leaves the kingdom of Jyotika with Kala and her daughter to seek better fortune elsewhere. Pundit Krishnajee braves the common folk during the funeral of the Rajput king. He tells them that there were no sati queens as such was the king's wish. It is only the new king, the younger brother of the previous one, who sees through Krishnajee's cunning and Renu's plans to escape sati. He salutes the queens and the pundit and his elder brother for his choice of both. The story is interesting as it is one fired with feminist resistance to useless customs and the need to bring about a change in society. The motif of the 'moon' as the feminine principle or 'Eros' and the mirror as one which connects past with present and the 'self' with the 'other' continue. Dayita looks at the same mirror which is in Vasti's possession later and asks advice from it. The mirror talks to her: 'We, the reflecting class, see all, but seldom disclose all' (286). The plurality of 'we' and 'class' is very interesting suggesting 'otherness' as a class by itself, which is all knowing. The 'self' can enjoy such 'othernesses' by submitting itself totally to the experience of the other(s) and in completely annihilating its ego. Vasti has this 'negative capability' to enter into others stories through the mirror of her unconscious and find solution to her conflict, travelling through time and space by the light and shade of the 'raised lantern' or her conscience. Fantasy as a mode allows the writer to define her objective of suggesting the reformative powers of the feminine deconstructive principle.

Part Three of the book alternates with chapters on the queens' escapade from satidom and Vasti's slowly coming to consciousness and her acceptance of the wedding. As Vasti looks for support from the queens who advise her from the mirror, Karan, her husband, comes in, and the past makes way for the present. To Vasti who steps in and out of the mirror of the unconscious or from past to present, Jyotika is more of a reality than her life is! She has to be drunk to accept Karan and the moon beams help her as the fertility principle. The novel closes with Vasti's mother hoping that Vasti would prepare her daughters for a change larger than she has experienced and the writer's comment: '...will the three queens come to hold her hands, to guide her? She needs their wisdom to cope with her own time. Will it come, and if it does, will Vasti recognise it?' (351)

As a patriarchal narrative, the text suggests reparation of the split between the ego-ideal with marriage to the man, who was the cause of the split. Yet it does not suggest the 'eternal deferral' of the desire for the unity of ego-ideal.

Rather, the novel focuses on the feminine imaginary which holds immense possibility for a dialogical discourse with self and the other(s) across time and space to create a new historicity. The tense query at the end of the text is more about the preservation of the semiotic powers even when Vasti enacts the customs of the symbolic code. The ritualistic fire of marriage or the fire of consummation cannot solely be an act of self immolation. It can be a creative force, should her semiotic waves and her light of conscience guide her to a 'monumental history' when the time would demand it.

Endnotes

[1] Lakshmi Persaud, *Raise the Lanterns High*, (London: Black Amber Books, 2004).

[2] Lakshmi Persaud, *Caribbean Studies Centre Black History Month Public Lecture* at London Metropolitan University, Oct 22nd 2003.

[3] The history that contemporary language theory leaves out, but semanalysis develops is the history of transformation which Kristeva refers to. For details, see Toril Moi. ed. , "The System and the Speaking Subject", *Kristeva Reader* (New York: Columbia University Press, 1986).

[4] Alison Donnell *et al.*, *The Routledge Reader in Caribbean Literature* (London: Routledge, 1996) pp. 201-202.

[5] *Ibid*

[6] Ramabai Espinet, "The Invisible Woman in West Indian Fiction", *Routledge Reader in Caribbean Literature*, p. 425.

[7] Lacan renames Freud's 'pre-Oedipal phase' as 'the imaginary' or the 'mirror phase' or the 'ego-ideal phase' to emphasise the fantastical nature of the child's relation to its world before it acquires language. For details see Elizabeth Grosz, *Jacques Lacan: A Feminist Introduction* (London & New York: Routledge, 1990).

[8] Identity for Lacan is a series of displacements of desire to reunite with an imaginary narcissistic 'ego-ideal' after the child moves beyond the mirror phase. See *Jacques Lacan: A Feminist Introduction*.

[9] Kristeva refers to the semiotic disposition in language as 'genotext' as opposed to 'phonotext'. The 'genotext' or revolutionary drives are constrained by social codes and yet they show up within those codes as a return of the repressed in language. These repressed unconscious drives according to Kristeva are revolutionary and embody a 'moral gesture' to shake foundations of contemporary society and bring about social change and reformation. See, Kelly Oliver, "Revolutionary Language Rendered Speechless" *Reading Kristeva: Unraveling the Double-bind* (Bloomington & Indianapolis: Indiana University Press, 1993).

[10] Judith Butler, "Sartre: The Imaginary Pursuit of Being", *Subjects of Desire* (New York: Columbia University Press) p. 107.
[11] The idea of the Moon as "Eros" as suggested by Esther Harding, in *Woman's Mysteries, Ancient and Modern* (New York: G.P. Putnam's Sons. 1971)
[12] Nor Hall, "Psyche's Search", *The Moon And the Virgin: A voyage Towards Self-Discovery and Healing* (London: The Women's Press, 1980) p.25.
[13] Robert Gittings, *Letters of John Keats* (London: Oxford University Press, 1970)
[14] Nor Hall, The Moon And the Virgin: A voyage Towards Self-Discovery and Healing, p.24.

References

Butler, Judith. "Sartre: The Imaginary Pursuit of Being", *Subjects of Desire*. New York: Columbia University Press.

Donnell, Alison et al. eds. *The Routledge Reader in Caribbean Literature*. London: Routledge, 1996.

Espinet, Ramabai. "The Invisible Woman in West Indian Fiction", *Routledge Reader in Caribbean Literature*. London: Routledge, 1996.

Gittings, Robert. *Letters of John Keats*. London: Oxford University Press, 1970.

Hall, Nor. "Psyche's Search", *The Moon and the Virgin : A Voyage Towards Self-Discovery and Healing*. London: The Women's Press, 1980.

Harding, Esther. *Woman's Mysteries, Ancient and Modern*. New York: G.P. Putnam's Sons, 1975.

Lacan, Jacques. *A Feminist Introduction*. London & New York: Routledge, 1990.

Moi, Toril, ed., "The System and the Speaking Subject", *Kristeva Reader*. New York: Columbia University Press, 1986.

Oliver, Kelly. "Revolutionary Language Rendered Speechless", *Reading Kristeva: Unraveling the Double-bind*. Bloomington & Indianapolis: Indiana University Press, 1993.

Persaud, Lakshmi. *Raise the Lanterns High*. London: Black Amber Books, 2004.

———. *Caribbean Studies Centre: Black History Month Public Lecture* at London Metropolitan University, Oct. 22nd 2003.

18

'I Cannot Always Be a Little You': Daughter-Mother (Country) Relationship in Jamaica Kincaid's *Annie John*

PUNAM GUPTA

When Jamaica Kincaid wrote the short story "Girl" in a single afternoon in New York in 1978, she says that she knew she had found her voice as a writer. The voice that this immigrant-Antiguan writer had found was that of a mother, instructing and berating her young daughter: 'Wash the white clothes on Monday and put them on the stone heap; ... don't walk barehead in the hot sun;... walk like a lady and not like the slut you are so bent on becoming...' (3) Kincaid had come to realise, no matter how far from home she might go, no matter what changes she might bring about in her life, she would never leave home and she would never stop hearing her mother's voice. In fact, the freedom of New York and the empowerment she felt she had gained as a successful journalist helped Kincaid to see that her mother is the 'fertile soil' of her creative life (Cudjoe 402) and she finally began to dig into that soil.

Kincaid's muse, however, is not only her personal relationship with her biological mother, but also her relationship with her mother country, England/Colonial Antigua. For Kincaid there is a direct relationship between European dominance and mother-daughter relationship (after it became disharmonious). Moira Ferguson has said '... the relationships between Kincaid's female protagonists and their biological mothers are crucially formative yet always mediated by intimations of life as colonized subjects'(1).

A 1994 interview extract of Jamaica Kincaid by Ferguson would be pertinent here:

> MF : In terms of the autobiographical dimension, does it sometimes happen for you that what you thought you wrote opens up later – so that the unconscious element is even wider than you thought?
>
> JK : Oh, absolutely. Oh, yes. In my first two books, I used to think I was writing about my mother and me. Later I began to see that I was writing about the relationship between the powerful and the powerless. That's become an obsessive theme, and I think it will be a theme for as long as I write. And then it came clear to me when I was writing the essay that became "On Seeing England for the First Time" that I was writing about the mother – that the mother I was writing about was really Mother Country. It's like an egg; it's a perfect whole. It's all fused some way or other. (176-77)

Jamaica Kincaid continually fuses diverse formulations of motherhood, maternity and colonialism. This doubled articulation of motherhood as both colonial and biological explains why the mother-daughter relations in her books seem so harshly rendered - the relationship is always fraught with fear, alienation and ambivalence, is always about separation. Kincaid almost seems to be asking herself how can she be of this woman and yet not be dominated by her. The same mother whom Kincaid's protagonist in *Lucy* (1990) could describe as her only true 'lover', is also the 'Devil', to escape whose clutches Lucy crosses the sea. Almost throughout Kincaid's works, there is a deep sense of anger, born of a sense of loss and betrayal and of her obsession with the question of how domination hinders the formation of an authentic identity. The focus of this paper is to explore

Kincaid's engagement with this question of domination and the relationship of the powerful and the powerless as manifest through the daughter-mother (country) relationship in her coming-of-age novel, *Annie John* (1985).

The book jacket of *Annie John* proclaims it as 'the traditional story of a young girl's passage into adolescence.' But behind the seemingly simple stories of school girl infatuations, first menstruation, forbidden adolescent games and gracefully-clad West-Indian women, looms an overpowering specter of betrayal and death. While Annie wishes to cling to the heavenly world of childhood innocence and of her mother's unvarnished attention, that world is slipping away and Annie is temporarily lost at the degradation that replaces it.

The early chapters of the book describe the 'paradise' of Annie's childhood, which has been created by her mother. The instructing mother of "Girl" is present, but Annie finds joy and beauty in her mother's daily activities and in being allowed to spend 'the day following my mother around and observing the way she did everything' (15). The world belongs to her mother and so does the child, whose life is symbolically contained within her mother's life, just as the mementoes of her childhood, within her mother's trunk. The mother arranges and caresses the items in the trunk, telling stories as she does so, of the girl's infancy. The sessions with the trunk are for the child a feast of love from the mother, for whom Annie was the centre of the universe: 'No small part of my life was so unimportant that she hadn't made a note of it...'(22). There are other instances of love from the doting mother. Annie tells how they used to have herbal baths together, how her mother would wrap Annie in her big skirt at the thought of a curse from a strange woman, how her mother had kissed Annie in all those parts where she had burnt coal marks. 'It was in such a paradise that I lived' says Annie(25).

But with Annie's reaching puberty, this paradise is lost. Annie turns twelve, grows tall, develops a different smell and is suddenly no longer welcome in her mother's world. The mother harshly tells her that they can no longer have dresses made out of the same cloth and can no longer spend time browsing through the trunk of childhood memorabilia. Her mother tells Annie, in a bitter way that rather than 'trailing in her footsteps' she should learn things that will make her into a `young lady'. Annie generally finds her mother cross with her over one thing or the other. 'What a new thing this was for me: my mother's back turned on me in disgust' moans Annie (28). She says when she looked at herself in the mirror she saw a 'strange girl' there and really wished she could 'cut back on [her] growing' (27) to win back her mother's love. Annie feels betrayed: 'All that was finished'.

Returning home from Sunday school one day with a prize for Bible study, Annie hopes to 'reconquer' her mother; instead she walks in upon her parents making love and is transfixed by the sight of her mother's hand 'white and bony, as if it had long been dead.' Annie is sure that she can never let the hand touch her again or let her mother kiss her again. Diane Simmons is right in suggesting that to Annie, the mother seems to be '...hideously duplicitous, both rejecting the daughter, as a result of her imminent maturity and engaging in the activity that is most obviously associated with this killing maturity' (108).

To compensate for a sense of maternal loss, Annie desires membership in the school community: 'My heart just longed for them to say something to me' (34). In an attempt to replace her mother's love, Annie falls in love with one of her classmates, a girl named Gwen. Annie finds herself in a distinguished position when an essay that she writes, wins her the applause of the class. The theme of the essay, of course is related to her personal conflict – the rift with her mother. In the essay Annie describes a scene in which she and her mother are taking a medicinal bath in the sea, naked like two 'sea mammals'. This blissful, amniotic moment is disrupted by 'three ships going by' (43). Loud celebrations are taking place on the ships; they are cruise ships, bringing tourists to the Caribbean. They could also represent the three ships of Columbus's voyage. Their arrival disrupts the blissful scene, and in panic, Annie realises she has lost sight of her mother. The essay ends with the mother spotting the crying child and rushing back to comfort her. Annie tells that but for the ending, the essay was true. (Annie's desire of her mother's returning to her had not been fulfilled).

Annie has succeeded in recreating a new adoring universe for herself, but it proves temporary. After she begins to menstruate and old friends desert her, she becomes rebellious. 'I had to do exactly the opposite of whatever she desired of me' (61). She takes on with the unwashed, unfettered Red Girl, who is everything Annie's mother disapproves of. In her relationship with the Red Girl, Annie does not, as with Gwen, seek a lost ideal. Rather, she repeats a relationship that is similar to the one with her mother, for like the mother, the Red Girl is sure of her own power in her relationship with Annie.

The Red Girl broadens Annie's horizons by taking her out of the controlled sphere of her mother. She teaches Annie to play the unladylike game of marbles and also to climb the heights of the forbidden lighthouse. Annie's mother accuses her of playing marbles and after a futile though furious search for the marbles, she asks, her 'Where are your marbles?' Annie replies treacherously, 'I don't have any marbles. I have never played marbles, you know' (70). Annie's relationship with her mother has been pushed almost to the breaking point.

For Annie, rebellion in the form of Red Girl friendship was only a step along the way of finding a new world. There is, however, one last Red Girl fantasy that Annie experiences – she saves the Red Girl from a shipwreck and they go and live on an island forever. Once again cruise ships pass by their island, to which the two send 'confusing signals' causing their destruction. Simmon's observation is pertinent:

> European conquest and colonial empire, represented by the ships, have confused the signals between Annie and her mother, causing their love to founder, and their 'cries of joy' turn to 'cries of sorrow', like those of people aboard the ships. (111)

There is yet another arena of power struggle between Annie and her mother i.e. Annie's future and her studies. The study of history at school suggests to Annie that her own relationship with her mother mirrors the relationship between coloniser and colonised. Both Annie's mother and the colonial authorities teach that she should first adore them and then, in the sincerest form of flattery, strive to become them or as nearly like them as possible. Both at home and at school, Annie is expected to empathise with a power that is determined to quash her individuality and make her into a flattering mirror of itself. Annie and other children at the school – all descendants of the slaves – have been so taught to celebrate the British Empire that they become confused: 'Sometimes it was hard for us to tell on which side we really now belonged – with the masters or the slaves–'(76).

As Annie's conflict with her mother intensifies, she gains an insight into the workings of manipulative power in other spheres. She begins to see how authority can manipulate the way in which things are perceived. The dunce cap, for instance, which was to be worn as punishment by a girl who had not learnt her lesson and was, therefore, a badge of shame, was made to appear '...all aglitter, almost as if you were being tricked into thinking it was a desirable thing to wear' (75). Similarly the picture of 'Columbus in Chains' which is meant to evoke pity among students induces in Annie quite different feelings. To her he is not a superhuman historical figure, as she has been taught to believe, but an inhuman tyrant. Connecting the picture of the chained Columbus to her incapacitated grandfather (She had heard her mother talking thus of her own father), Annie captions the photograph, 'The Great Man Can No Longer Get Up and Go' (78). As punishment for this 'blasphemy', Annie is made to copy out the first two books of Milton's *Paradise Lost*. Milton's work as we know is the story of Lucifer, who had dared to challenge unchallengeable authority and as punishment had been cast out of paradise.[1]

Initially, as one observes, Annie's struggles were aimed at denying and then rebelling against the change she had perceived in her world of the loss of her childhood paradise. Finally, however, denials and rebellions give way to grief. Annie is aggrieved at the way the world around her aims to dupe her at every step. It seems to her that the world is intent on killing all that is authentic within her. Annie and her mother put up a face in front of the world, pretending to be as loving as ever to each other. The reality, however, is quite otherwise, as Annie hears herself chant, 'My mother would kill me if she got the chance. I would kill my mother if I had the courage' (89).

To the spiritually deserted Annie, the world seems to reflect back to her only the image of her own oddness. Standing in front of a store window, she fails to recognise herself, as she sees herself not as a real person, but just one of the things hanging there. Simmons observes:

> If the world sees her as an oddity, it also sees her, as does her mother, as a kind of criminal, and now the reflection in the window reminds Annie of a painting entitled The Young Lucifer, which shows Satan pretending bravado, but really 'lonely and miserable at the way things had turned out'. (114)

Added to this is the misery Annie experiences at the hands of a group of boys standing across the street, who mock her lonely 'oddness' by curtseying to her maliciously. In spite of the fact that Annie recognises one of these boys as her childhood chums, she gets no solace even through the chivalry of men. All this betrayal has such a deep effect on Annie's psyche, that on her way home, she suffers a physical disorientation – she feels herself alternately grow too big and too small.

But this is not all. Insult is added to injury when on reaching home, Annie's mother projects upon her the vision of her criminal puberty. (Annie's mother was shopping in the same store where Annie was gazing at herself in the shop window). Instead of being comforted by her mother for the malicious mocking she has been subject to, Annie is chastised for being a 'slut' who is 'making a spectacle of [herself]' (102). Here, for the first time, Annie strikes a telling blow against her mother. She replies back, 'Well... like mother like daughter' (102). Annie has now almost understood the secret of betrayal by her mother. In the ridiculous accusation, Annie understands that the mother betrays herself, not Annie alone, in criminalising maturity. Annie understands that it is not only her daughter that the mother has seen through the window, but it is her own self, her reflection as cast back to her by a society that sees black women only as sluts. In her study on black mothers and daughters. Gloria I. Joseph had rightly suggested that '... a theory about mother/daughter relationships among Blacks is incomplete without a consideration of racial relations and racism' (80).

Having seen behind the facade of maternal moral nurture and the myth of her own moral culpability, Annie decides that all her life cannot be lived within her mother's shadow. She makes the first move towards her departure. She requests her father to make her a trunk. She no longer wants her things to be stored in her mother's trunk. Now follows a sort of mental–physical collapse for Annie. For three months, she remains bedridden. Her collapse is accompanied by a three-month spell of rain. The deluge figuratively washes away the life that has become too painful, clearing the way for a rebirth. When the rain ends and Annie also recovers, some things have changed forever. One of the big changes that has taken place is that Annie is no longer the 'Little Miss' as her parents and everyone else called her. She assumes her own name. The last chapter of the book, which is also about Annie's last day in Antigua, before she sails off to England, starts with the words 'My name is Annie John' (10). Annie thus claims an independent identity for herself.

The mysterious catastrophe of lost love at the centre of *Annie John* (and Kincaid's fiction in general) can be explained with the help of studies in psychology that explore mother-daughter relationships. In Alice Miller's study of narcissistic mothers, the sudden emotional abandonment of a previously beloved child is common. These mothers suffer from an inadequate sense of self, and need 'someone at their disposal who can be used as an echo, who can be controlled, is completely centred on them, and offers full attention and admiration.' Any move towards maturity or autonomy on the part of the child is experienced by the parent as a hostile act, even as an attack, and the parent responds with a combination of hurt and anger (Miller 33–35).

Thus, in *Annie John*, suddenly one day Annie's request to her mother to enjoy the feast of browsing through the trunk, meets with an absolutely unrecognisable response from mother, 'Absolutely not! You and I don't have time for that anymore' (27). 'Anymore' is the time when the twelve-year-old girl has begun to show signs of impending maturity. In Miller's explanation of Annie's mother's behaviour it is her 'narcissistic rage' on seeing the first signs of the development of a separate identity in her daughter on whom she has counted to reflect her back to herself selflessly and constantly.[2]

Another psychologist, Nancy Chodorow explains the phenomenon of maternal narcissism as occurring particularly in patriarchal Western middle-class cultures in which a woman does not work outside the home, and a woman's only socially valued role is to raise her children. Chodorow suggests that this mother invests a lot of anxious energy and guilty in her concern for her children and looks to them for her self-affirmation. Chodorow also talks of 'boundary confusion' – uncertainty over where they stop and another person begins. A mother is more likely to suffer 'boundary confusion' with a daughter, whom she identifies as herself and hopes to hold in infantile dependence forever. As the mother holds the daughter, so would the daughter hold the mother. (Kincaid's fiction is full of the agony of loss, yearning and rage at a love that has been and never more will be).

Annie John's situation, however, is more complex. Because of her beginning, to mature in a racist society makes Annie the victim of a doubled 'narcissistic rage': one at the hands of her own biological mother and second at the hands of her mother country. Diane Simmons has put it this way: 'In Annie's case, the mother's refusal to accept the girl's pending maturity mirrors the colonial society's refusal to recognize the mature humanity of those descended from slaves'(64).

Like the betraying mother, the mother (land), in pretending to nurture the child, actually steals her from herself. Quoting Craig Trapping, Simmons says that 'the self is faced with extinction by the very processes of acculturation which all who nurture the child commend. Only imitation and blind acquiescence are acceptable, not the questioning gaze of an emerging intelligence' (2). In her 1991 essay "On Seeing England for the First Time", Kincaid wrote:

> I did not know then that the statement "Draw a map of England" was something far worse than a declaration of war... In fact, there was no need for war – I had long ago been conquered. I did not know then that this statement was part of a process that would result in my erasure – not my physical erasure, but my erasure all the same.... (qtd. in Simmons 9)

This design of the colonial education, to 'erase' the reality of the colonial child, was not commonly perceived. In her 1989 interview with Selwyn Cudjoe, Kincaid says that her own mother was an 'Anglophile' who strove to give her daughter a 'middle–class English upbringing'. Everything around Kincaid seemed to accept English domination, and the doctrine that a thing could be 'divine and good only if it was English'. But Kincaid says of herself that even at the age of nine, she 'refused to stand up at the refrain "God save our King." I hated "Rule Britannia"... I never had any idea why. I just thought that there was no sense to it' (Cudjoe 397-400).

As Annie John approaches puberty, the mother increasingly imitates the colonial educational system, which seems bent on erasing all that is native to the child, rewarding only that which imitates the European rulers. Thus, the mother suddenly wishes Annie to join a number of programs to make a young lady out of her. But just as the teachers in Annie's school constantly imply the basic inferiority of their students by holding to them a model they will never be able to imitate, the mother constantly implies that her fundamental nature will always be that of a slut, rather than of a young lady. Both teachers and mother repeat the subtle yet constant colonial theme: ceaseless effort must be made to civilise the child, to turn her into a satisfactory imitation of a European; this effort, though can never be completely successful.

Kincaid is suggesting that Annie's mother is a victim of a colonial and racist system, a woman who had internalised the conflict between two worldviews. This confusion had a direct relationship on Annie's relationship with her mother. Having internalised from the mother (country) the notion that a rampant sensuality is inherent to people of African origin, her mother saw 'any sensuality as just the end'. At the same time, however, the mother does have complete faith in African tribal customs and folk magic and thinks herself confident enough to safeguard her people from any evil forces. This contradictory map of the world that the mother presents to the daughter is impossible for Annie to follow. To survive, the daughter must ignore the mother's internalised contradictions and carve out her own identity in a world that for the most part does not allow her to be herself. Her first step in this direction is to leave her birthplace for a foreign land. I conclude with lines from Saundra Sharp's "Double Exposure", a poem which is addressed to her mother :

> I am not you anymore
> I am my own collection of
> gifts and errors (179).

Endnotes

[1] In Kincaid's novel *Lucy*, which is a sequel to *Annie John*, the protagonist Lucy does identify with Lucifer. This happens especially after Lucy's mother in a fit of rage tells her daughter that she has named her after Lucifer - the Devil himself.

[2] Kincaid has made elaborate references to her mother's narcissism in her works. In the interview with Moira Ferguson, she says in one place that when Rousseau says in his Confessions "Am I not Great?", 'He sounds just like my mother.' In Lucy, Kincaid is equally vocal when she says 'my mother's love for me was designed solely to make me into an echo of her... in her life she had found that her ways were the best ways to have...' (36).

References

Chodorow, Nancy. "Family Structure and Feminine Personality". *Woman Culture, and Society*. Eds. Michelle Z. Rosaldo and Louise Lamphere. Stanford, California: Stanford Univ. Press, 1974.

Cudjoe, Selwyn R. . "Jamaica Kincaid and the Modernist Project : An Interview." *Callaloo* 12. (Spring 1989) : 396–411.

Ferguson, Moira. *Jamaica Kincaid: Where the Land Meets the Body*. Charlottesville : Univ. Press of Virginia, 1994.

―――― "A Lot of Memory : An Interview with Jamaica Kincaid." *The Kenyon Review* XVI. 1. Winter 1994 : 163–188.

Gloria I. Joseph and Jill Lewis. *Common Differences : Conflicts in Black and White Feminist Perspectives*. New York : Anchor Books, 1981.

Kincaid, Jamaica. "Girl". *At the Bottom of the River*. New York: Farrar, Straus and Giroux, 1983.

―――― *Annie John*. New York : Farrar, Straus and Giroux, 1985.

―――― *Lucy*. New York : Farrar, Straus and Giroux, 1990.

Miller, Alice. *The Drama of the Gifted Child : How Narcissistic Parents Form and Deform the Emotional Lives of Their Talented Children*. Trans. Ruth Ward. New York : Basic Books, 1981.

Saundra Sharp. "Double Exposure." *Double Stitch : Black Women Write About Mothers & Daughters*. Eds. Patricia Bell-Scott et al. Boston : Beacon Press, 1991.

Simmons, Diane. *Jamaica Kincaid*. New York : Twayne Publishers, 1994.

19

Identity, Subjectivity and Voice: A Reading of Austin Clarke's *The Polished Hoe*

C. VIJAYSHREE

Discussions of literary writings by the marginalised communities be it women, blacks, dalits or ethnic minorities are often dominated by the vexing question of agency, voice and authenticity. As Gayatri Spivak alerts us, '...the idea of the disenfranchised speaking for themselves, or the radical critics speaking for them; this question of representation, self-representation, representing others is a problem' (61). How subjective location determines the legitimacy within the discursive nexus of identity is an issue that keeps coming up with insistence in these critical discussions. What Adrienne Rich describes as a 'politics of location' (210-231) reacts to a history of exclusionist politics a vortex that has created literary, cultural and historical vacuums that warranted the current eruption of autobiography and personal narratives. It is generally accepted that a story about colonialism or slavery or any other kind of oppression can only be told effectively by those who have lived through it. A narrative about exploitation can only be told by the exploited in their own voice, that too in first person, in some sort of autobiographical form – confession, testimony or a personal narrative. This is what Austin Clarke does in *The Polished Hoe* (2003), which narrates the tale of plantation horror, sexual abuse of black women and exploitation of farm labour.

Set in the West Indian island of Bimshire in the 1950s *The Polished Hoe* is primarily the personal narrative of Mary Mathilda, the central character of the novel, a descendent of slaves, a mulatto child, who becomes the kept woman of the white plantation manager Mr Bellfeels. Having killed Mr Bellfeels her master, tormentor, benefactor and abuser who first rapes her when she was still a child of eight and keeps her his woman and property for the rest of her life, Mary Mathilda calls Percy the local police Sergeant to take down her statement. As she narrates the circumstances of her life, she unwittingly unravels the evils of colonialism and the legacy of slavery and recalls the pathetic experiences of other villagers who too had fallen victims to the power greed and racial arrogance of the white minority of the village.

The most important question relating to the authenticity of the narratorial voice that comes up here is: How does Clarke create a genuine female voice to articulate a black woman's experience of sexual abuse? While he can identify with the narrator in terms of racial identity, he is removed from her experience of reality, as he has no direct access to female experience of colonial and racial exploitation. Clarke manipulates the narratorial framework in such a way that the first person narrator – Mary Mathilda – and the participant auditor Sergeant, both are representatives of the community whose collective history gets represented here. Mary Mathilda's reminiscences of her past of pain, humiliation and sexual abuse are linked with the experiences of many other exploited women like her – her ma, gran, great gran and so on. Percy's memories also take up considerable space in *The Polished Hoe*; his memories of his island upbringing – compromised by fear and subservience – balance Mary-

Identity, Subjectivity and Voice 249

Mathilda's monologues. Through memories of Mary and Percy, Clarke reconstructs not just two lives but the colonial society that contains them. On many issues they share common memory; so they check with each other, confirm, complete and complement the narrative leaving no scope for loose ends or gray areas.

The narrative time is limited to twenty-four hours but covers the lifetime of one woman as well as the collective experience of a whole community marked by slavery, colonial domination and exploitation. The temporal location of the narration too is important since it constitutes the moment of emancipation for the chief narrator Mary who by killing her exploiter ends decisively not only the life of the white plantation manager but the unjust exploitation of the local people by the white landlords. In liberating herself she liberates her people. The narration begins thus:

> My name is Mary. People in this village call me Mary Mathilda. Or, Tilda for short. To my mother I was Mary-girl. My names I am christen with are Mary Gertrude Mathilda, but I don't use Gertrude, because my maid has the same name. My surname that peple 'bout-here uses, is either Paul, or Bellfeels, depending who you speak to ....(3)

The first thing the narrator does is to define her own identity within her family, and within the village community. Once the place of the narrator is thus defined the narrative finds its location easily. Most of what follows is viewed from the perspective of Mary. It is primarily her experience, and she after all has the legitimacy to tell the tale better than anybody else. A few lines later she clearly tells the constable taking down her confession: 'Nevertheless, Bellfeels is not the name I want to attach to this statement that I giving you...'(3). So no confusion remains regarding how she locates herself vis-à-vis the tale she tells.

Mary, as part of her narration, recalls several stories of colonial atrocities the village lived through. The story of Clotelle, her mother's friend, who was found hanging from the mango tree, and who subsequently became the subject of a popular Calypso remains etched in Mary's memory. Her mother had told Mary how Clotelle, a five-month-pregnant was brutally raped in the cane field the night before she hanged herself. Then Golborne with his enlarged testicles is another testimony to colonial horrors. He was not born with this deformity. But some twenty years ago, the plantation Manager found Golborne moving intimately with his daughters' nursemaid and the present deformity 'is the direct result of the venom in the beating administered by Mr Bellfeels on Golborne'(16). Golborne, the fastest body-line fast bowler of Bimshire, now walks around awkwardly, with his two large testicles protruding from his pants, bearing the visible sign of humiliation he and his people lived through. Then there is Pounce, who never troubled a living soul, but was shot at for stealing a couple of potatoes from the farm. Mary's reminiscences of her own childhood in Bimshire are interlinked with the lives of all these victims. The narrator has no plans of recording the history of the island and its people, but there is no way she can talk about herself in isolation from the people with who she has lived. As she herself puts it, 'This is my history in confession, better late than never, which in your police work is a Statement. And I wonder as I sit here this Sunday evening, why I am giving you this history of me personal life, and the history of this island of Bimshire, altogether wrap-up in one?' (20). The why of Mary's question may best be answered recalling Paul Ricoeur's formulation of what he calls tremendum horrendum. To quote Ricoeur, 'Horror attaches to events that must never be forgotten. It constitutes the ultimate ethical motivation for the history of victims' (187). It is this history of victims that Mary narrates in her confession. Mary tells the young constable, 'There is a story-and- a-half I could tell you about the doings and the happenings in this small island of Bimshire! Stories to make your head curl! Stories and skeletons bigger than the square-mile area of this island'(36). These horror stories include the story of her mother who too was raped at the age of sixteen by Mr Bellfeels, that of Clotelle and other women on the plantation who could just be dragged into the cane field to quench the lust of any man 'in the scheme of things, in a more higher position' (104). For Mary, telling her story is important and even imperative because narration becomes an act of liberation, and self-emancipation. As Ella Shohat aptly theorises:

> The denial of aesthetic representation to the subaltern has historically formed a corollary to the literal denial of economic, legal and political representation. The struggle 'to speak for oneself' cannot be separated from a history of being spoken for, from the struggle to speak and be heard. (173)

Mary's narrative goes on unimpeded drawing on her memory, collective history of her community, her family stories, the island's songs and calypsos. She is conscious of the fact that she is digressing, but her narratees – first, the constable and later the Sergeant welcome these digressions because they can see their own past rehearsed in these digressions. In fact it is these digressions, which enlarge the scope of the narrative and convert a personal story into the collective history of the community. Mary is clear about the purpose of her narration. As she puts it, she still has 'to leave the history for Wilberforce, and one to be left back to the people of the village and people coming after me so they would know what happened. And I still have to save my soul' (100). Mary's personal experience of exploitation and humiliation go back to her childhood. On a Sunday morning, when she was eight, Mr Bellfeels spotted her and decided to own her. Mary distinctly remembers her first encounter with the most powerful man of the island... 'he passed the riding-crop down my neck, right down the front of my dress, until it reach my waist. And then he move the riding-crop up back again, as if he was drawing something on my body'(11). It indeed was his way of establishing his rights on Mary's body just as he did on her mother's some years ago. Mary recalls how her mother stood paralysed as 'Mr Bellfeels passed his riding-crop slow-slow, slow over my body, as if he was telling Ma to her face, Old woman, look, I don't need your wrinkle-up body no more. I have Mary-girl, this young delicious piece o' veal, to feast on, at my heart's delight'(59). From that day on Mary's body was monopolised by Mr Bellfeels and she is kept off limits of boys of her own generation with who she has grown up and shared several joyous moments. Her place as Mr Bellfeels' mistress becomes secure when she bears him a male child and she lives in the second greatest house in the island. Her son Wilberforce is light-skinned and intelligent and receives the best education with the monetary support from Mr Bellfeels and becomes a doctor of tropical medicine.

Mary lives with Mr Bellfeels in the Big House which provides shelter to her and her son, but agonises over her seclusion, isolation and loss of freedom. She tells the Sergeant:

> 'This great house is bigger and definitely nicer and prettier than the shack I was born in. Than any in the village. But is it a happier place to live in?
> ...
> 'Your freedom, your life, is taken from you, as a woman in this Island, for the certainty that you will have food, and a roof over your head, and over your children's head. Yes.
> ...
> 'But is this happiness?
> ...
> 'There were always eyes following me. Put there by Mr Bellfeels to follow. He was never sure of my faithfulness. Yes! But the eyes followed me, even when he no longer had any uses for me.'(275)

Living under surveillance and subjection, Mary spends hours polishing her farm hoe though she is not clear about what she would do with it. The polished hoe eventually becomes her weapon of revenge, when she fells Mr Bellfeels with it on a Sunday afternoon, ending her own servitude and the subjugation of the whole island. Mary's narration places the climactic incident of her killing the plantation manager in perspective. Her resort to violence may be explained on the ground that her degradation by the hand of the plantation was irredeemable, even though she has gained some marginal reprieve from heinousness. The gruesome fact that Mr Bellfeels who brutally abused the

Identity, Subjectivity and Voice 253

body of Mary happens to be her own biological father makes him unworthy of any compassion. Mary does what she does because she believes in restitution.

As Mary narrates the entire story of her life weaving into it tragic tales of many other island men and women, Percy, her chief auditor, adds his own stories of island life completing the picture of slavery and colonial regime in the Caribbean island of Bimshire. Clarke reconstructs the history of slavery and plantation life from a gendered Caribbean perspective. The gendered perspective produces tales of personalised tragedies unparalleled in their intensity. The gender-conscious tales are of women like Clotelle whose bodies are abused most brutally, Mary's mother whose agonising humiliation at the surrender of her daughter to her own seducer, Mary who was reduced to a sex object at the age of eight, and of men like Golbourne, Pounce and Naiman who endure the undermining of their manhood and live deprived lives. Hangings, floggings and maimings, or being taken down a secret tunnel beneath the house to be fed to the sharks, was a fate meted out equally to labourers threatening revolt and men presuming on the master's property. The most gruelling histories of domination and resistance, we understand, dwell not in objects and places but bodies and injuries inflicted on bodies.

In reconstructing the history of the island through bodily tales of his protagonist and other characters, Clarke echoes and responds to the literary tradition of slave narratives, first person non-fictional tales of the ordeal of slavery such as Frederick Douglass's *Narrative of the Life of Frederick Douglass, An American Slave* (1845) or Harriet Ann Jacob's *Incidents in the Life of a Slave Girl* (1860), and Afro-American novels about slavery such as William Styron's *The Confessions of Nat Turner* (1967) or Toni Morrison's *Beloved* (1987). One can also see Clarke connecting with the Caribbean tradition of peasant novel popularised by George Lamming, Earl Lovelace and Sam Selvon. In fact, there are intertextual references to Frederick Douglas and Nat Turner within the tales narrated by Mary. When three plantation workers; Pounce's father, Golborne's father and Manny's grandfather ask for more wages they are seen as 'bastards' who 'had pattern their rebellion after Nat Turner, the American Negro' and were flogged until their blood flowed in streams. What happens in Bimshire is nothing different from the horrible history of slavery elsewhere, Africa or America but none of the histories of the island make any mention of slavery. Mary's narrative culled from the oral histories she has heard people of the island narrate offers a corrective to the official records by articulating the ugly reality of slavery silenced in the documented histories. She tells the Sergeant; 'But even if we in this island do not see ourselves as slaves, the treatment that Ma tell me about that she suffered through, and what my great-great-great-gran went through, you would have to invent a new name for it, if not slavery'(356). Mary Mathilda's confession thus turns out to be a serious indictment of the brutalities of plantation managers, which were in no way different from the atrocities of slavery.

The power of Clarke's narration lies in his exploitation of island voices stippled with songs singing games and riddles. The narrative is told in the language of the island, which does not merely express the experience of Mary and other plantation labourers but embodies it. 'The vernacular is the lingua franca of Bimshire, of Barbados,' says Clarke. 'One can no longer deprecate this language by calling it dialect. Because if we West Indians consider ourselves to be a people, then certainly we have got to make a judgment on the language the English colonisers spoke to us – and some of that language is unintelligible... not syntactically unintelligible, but unintelligible when spoken to us by those people.' Every language has its way of thinking, and therefore when Mary speaks we not only hear the language of the island but feel the experience shared by the islanders. In her narrative Mary connects with the blacks elsewhere, in Africa and America. She sees her ancestry linked to Africa through her Great Gran who she often heard mumbling prayers in a strange language, which Mary comes to recognise as an African language by and by. Mary also recalls her only trip to America where she saw coloured people travelling in a segregated compartment along with her and felt one with them at once. As the train passed Atlanta-Georgia, she became at once aware of the racial undertones of the song 'Georgia' she often sang and danced to along with her son Wilberforce for the entertainment of Mr Bellfeels and his friends. She becomes conscious of her racial identity as she discovers that Blacks everywhere share a similar predicament. As Mary puts it, 'It must be something in us, if we people, coloured people, Negroes, whatever you want to call us, that connects us together, no matter which plantation we are to call home-prison, as Ma always referred to her life in this plantation, as.' (367).

Mary in fact finds echoes of her own inner feelings in Spirituals and American Blues. This is the language produced by oppression and cruelty and its central impulse is survival and resistance. In *The Polished Hoe* we have what Gates calls 'a speakerly text', privileging the oral speech acts of Black culture that exuberate the power of fluid language to disrupt existing hierarchies which create binary relations of domination and subordination.

By the end of Mary's narrative of the brutalities of plantation life, the fact of her killing the plantation manager becomes a moot point. The interventions of her two auditors – the Constable and the Sergeant – clearly indicate the general approval of Mary's action as an act of just retribution. As Sergeant assures Mary, 'There isn't one blasted soul in this whole village, who won't want to pelt a few stones, or one big rock-stone at Mr Bellfeels...', and adds, 'anybody who dwells within the precincts of the Plantation, any Sam-cow-or-the-duppy, man, woman, child, girl or boy, would regard it as a honour to drive a deadly lash in Mr Bellfeels arse' (372). Thus the purpose of Mary's narrative is more than served; the history of Bimshire is set right and the course of its destiny redirected as the fall of Bellfeels symbolises the end of White man's domination and the breaking of a new dawn, dawn of freedom in Bimshire.

R.E.: The novel has a continuous prologue which returns in each section. It is meant to be a detective story of sorts. Mona finds out what objects mean as part of the mystery of her past. My favourite objects are the shop books. These books were used by families with enough standing in the community to obtain credit on a continuous basis. Its usage would be most pronounced around the time of my grandmother's generation. A list of groceries would go into the book and a child or a servant would go to the shop and do the errand. The dry goods storekeeper would add and subtract and confirm the amount in the book.

E.S.: Why didn't the women go and do their own shopping then?

R.E.: It was a class thing, not an ethnic prohibition. This was the era before supermarkets. Middle class Indian women go to the supermarket now. But at that time there were very few of those and often they were far away from the home, in towns. Even if the family had a car, it was not going to be available for errands. I myself did errands for my grandmother with the shop book. They were little black covered notebooks.

E.S.: So your own memories were important in constructing this story.

R.E.: The story is constructed out of a combination of research, memory and fictional interpolation. The memory is not necessarily family history. I took great liberties. For example, some characters walked out of my head onto the page. They were not consciously formulated characters. Like Ma Toussaint - she made herself up. When that happens, I think it is one of the most gratifying moments of a writer's life. She came fully voiced. She appeared. It was thrilling.

E.S.: Her name is after Toussaint L'Ouverture?

R.E.: Yes, but I only knew that afterwards. Her name of course reinforces the Haitian connection within the novel but that was not a conscious thing.

E.S.: I found the appearance of the island of St Helena very interesting. That it was a stopping point for the indenture ships as well as the place where Napoleon died.

R.E.: There is a village in Trinidad called St Helena, in the north-central part of the island, near Centeno. Centeno is a place where an experimental farm was set up, attached to the ICTA (Imperial College of Tropical Agriculture) which later became the University of the West Indies- in the same place as the present St Augustine campus. I was well-acquainted with the area because I had relatives involved in the research into tropical flora that was being conducted there. This experience got me interested in the incredible array of plant life that we had in Trinidad and also, on the compound, in strange plants from other tropical zones, like the ylang-ylang tree, originally Malayan, its flowers a vital source for perfume at the time. In the novel this tree is called the 'lang-a-lang' tree which seemed to me onomatopoeically feasible both as a signifier of gossip and as an erotic signifier of the budding and secret sexuality of Mona and the other young girls in her world. I mention this because St. Helena is near to Centeno and the resonances of these two places are intertwined – at least to me. But at that time in my life I had no idea that the St Helena village had any connection to indenture. In my later research I encountered texts about the actual voyages of indenture (Ron Ramdin's work, for example) and realised that St. Helena was a necessary stop for the ships after the battering off the Cape of Good Hope. And so St Helena, the island, got into the story of the *Kala Pani*.

E.S.: Flowers are important at times in the novel. You use a number of motifs to connect the story, which evolves by slowly providing information about Mona and her family. I found myself sketching her family tree before I read the novel the second time. Did you work that out beforehand? It comes gradually into focus as the book progresses. I find that much more helpful than giving the reader an explicit family tree in the front of the book.

R.E.: I did several family trees but decided not to put one in, in spite of the large number of characters, because my instincts ran against it. Not for any other reason. I just did not like the idea of the book beginning with this kind

References

Clarke, Austin. *The Polished Hoe.* New York: Harper Collins, 2003.

———. Qtd in. Donna Bailey Nurse. "A Barbadian Abroad". *Publisher's Weekly.* http://www.publishers weekly.com.

Gates, Henry Louis. Jr. "The Blackness of Blackness: A Critique of the Sign and Signifying Monkey." *Black Literature and Literary Theory.* Ed. Henry Louis Gates. New York: Methuen, 1984. 285-321.

Rich, Adrienne. "Notes Towards a Politics of Location," *Blood, Bread and Poetry: Selected Prose, 1979-85.* New York: Norton, 1986: 210-231.

Ricouer, Paul. *Time and Narrative.* Chicago: U of Chicago P, 1985.

Shohat, Ella. "The Struggle Over Representation, Casting, Coalitions and the Politics of Identification." *Late Imperial Culture.* Eds. Roman De La Campa, E. Ann Kaplan and Michael Sprinker. New York: Verso, 1995: 166-78.

Spivak, Gayatri Chakraborty. "Questions of Multiculturalism." *The Postcolonial Critic: Interviews, Strategies, Dialogues.* New York: Routledge, 1990: 59-67.

20

An Interview with Ramabai Espinet*

ELAINE SAVORY

Introduction

Ramabai Espinet's first novel *The Swinging Bridge* (2003), which fictionalises the "double diaspora" of Indo-Caribbean-Canadian experience, was shortlisted for the 2004 Commonwealth Writers Prize in the category of Best First Book (Caribbean and Canada region), longlisted for the IMPAC Dublin 2005 Prize for fiction and selected for mention by Robert Adams in the 2005 pick of modern "classics" lecture series (held annually in Montreal and Toronto). *Coming Home* (2005), a documentary film focused on Espinet's work and especially *The Swinging Bridge* has also generated a great deal of interest in Canada, where it has been shown on television numerous times.

She was born in Trinidad and Tobago and emigrated to Canada more than twenty-five years ago, though she returned to Trinidad in the 1980s for a period of time. She stays close

---
* First Published in *Wadabagei*, and included here with permission of the author and the publishers (Rowman & Littlefield, Lanham, Maryland).

to Trinidadian culture in Canada, playing mas' every year in the Toronto Carnival. Her willingness to break through conventions is demonstrated in the fact that she drove a cab whilst attending university, one of the first women to go to train as a cabby, and lived in a commune on Vancouver Island. Her first visit to India, in 2001, took her to a number of places (Mumbai, Mysore, Bangalore, Kerala, Gujarat), and she reported feeling absolutely at home there, something she is still examining. Her scholarly mind will not accept conventional representations or simple impressions without examination. Her creative imagination refashions scholarship into story and so takes it out to a mass audience. Her creative and critical work has collectively challenged the stereotypes around Indian women in the Caribbean and elsewhere and brought the 'double diaspora' to be better understood.

She wrote in a number of genres before attempting her first novel. Her story "Indian Cuisine", is referenced in Brinda Mehta's *Diasporic (Dis)locations: Indo-Caribbean Women Writers Negotiate the Kala Pani* (2004). In the story, an Indo-Caribbean woman tries to communicate with her presumably white lover about the meaning of foods, so often the most visible sign of cultural shifts in diaspora. Espinet has published a collection of poetry, *Nuclear Seasons* (1991) and "Shay's Robber Talk" (1999) and poems in a number of anthologies and journals, and two children's books, *The Princess of Spadina* (1992), and *Ninja's Carnival* (1993). She edited *Creation Fire*, an anthology of Caribbean women's writing (1990). She is also a performance artist and dramatist who writes her own material which explores the Indo-Caribbean experience (*Beyond the Kala Pani*, a play about Indian women and indentureship in the Caribbean, and *Indian Robber Talk*, a performance piece). She has a Ph.D. in Literature from the University of the West Indies, St. Augustine, Trinidad, (her dissertation was on a writer she much admires, Jean Rhys). She has written essays and criticism, and teaches literature and Caribbean Studies at the University of Toronto and at Seneca College, Toronto.

She experienced a desire to write from childhood, and as she puts it, both was victim and beneficiary of a colonial education heavy in world literature. Her list of influences is eclectic, including Edna Vincent Millay and James Baldwin, T.S.Eliot and Jean Rhys, Tacitus and Derek Walcott. But she is also very much in the world, as an activist, a searcher after lost histories, an explorer of Indo-Caribbean experience which she has described (to Pooja Pande, in an interview in *First City* [Mumbai, 2004]), as giving 'rise to a complicated and contentious discourse, marked by conflicted points of view, denial and irresolution'.

Her concern about such issues was the source of *The Swinging Bridge*, which was built up by fictionalizing historical research, personal memory of childhood, family and community, and political concerns (such as gender roles in Indo-Caribbean culture, and the marked silence about AIDS in the Caribbean). It is a not only absorbing as a novel, but is an education in a history far too little understood even within the community it portrays, written in a way which is accessible by all readers.

What follows is a conversation with Espinet which explores the depth and range of her work as both a novelist and an educator about the Indo-Caribbean community and the Indian diaspora. She is also very much a cosmopolitan woman who lives between worlds and reflects on the complex syncretisms of Trinidad and Tobago. Her replies extend and complicate our sense of the terms diaspora, transnational, Indo-Caribbean, reminding us that what is lived is often far more complex that what is theorised, and so of the crucial purpose of fiction and story-telling which is well grounded in history and culture but represents the infinite cultural interactions and negotiations which characterise specifically Creole experience in the Caribbean and the lives of people who migrate everywhere.

E.S.: Your recent novel, *The Swinging Bridge* (2003) has aroused much interest and response from readers. I myself found it impossible to put down.

R.E.: I'm pleased at that response which I've had from so many people – academics as well as regular readers.

E.S.: It is a historical novel, about migration and transnational identity in the Indian diaspora, but also centrally about Trinidad and Tobago, where you were born and grew up. We travel along with Mona as she works back in time in Trinidad following clues to her history but at the same time we are occupied through her concern for her dying brother, Kello, with her life in the present in Canada. It is a wonderful journey for the reader because you've paced it really well. What I am interested in is how much was part and parcel of growing up, how much part of the wonderful intellectual history of Caribbean scholarship going on all the time (we sometimes forget what a world of knowledge has been rediscovered over the past thirty–forty years or so), and how much you really had to dig for yourself...

R.E.: I work as an educator/knowledge worker and this means that I am actively involved in the large human project of 'understanding' at all levels all the time. I don't know how this fits with the desire to convey the history of Indo-Caribbean settlement except that this area is still so underdeveloped, untold, ill-understood. And maybe this novel is a small step in pushing this understanding forward.

It was my good fortune to be somewhat self-aware when I was growing up because I was surrounded by people who dealt in ideas, particularly societal ideas of place and belonging and identity and then, as I grew older, I realised that this was tied deeply into the politics of Trinidad at that time. The adults around me had an acute sense of being 'othered' and even though they were reasonably well-integrated into T&T mainstream culture, the various small everyday ways in which their otherness came to the fore became part of the conversation around me and I had to pay attention to it. I don't at all mean that the present high-flown language of Poco theory was a part of my environment, of course. But neither the 'relative' security of a Hindu or Muslim enclave nor a Garveyite understanding of 'blackness' and the politics of Pan-Africanism informed my early understanding of where I or my family (a very large extended family) fitted into the mix. The Christian/ Presbyterian aspects of life that they took for granted formed part of the Indian community's understanding of itself, but was largely invisible to those who were the thinkers, opinion-makers and achievers in the Creole world of Port of Spain and its environs.

The deep structure of the world I have focused upon in *The Swinging Bridge* depends upon an understanding I have acquired experientially and intuitively by living in that environment. But – you are right, the enormous volume of scholarship and literature on the Caribbean that has been produced since the 30s has played a great part in helping me to make sense of the knowledge that I acquired almost by osmosis, as it were. For example, I studied the poetry of Yeats at A-levels in the sixties and this took me into research on the Irish Renaissance and the efforts made by Yeats, Synge, Lady Gregory and others to actually create a literature where one hardly existed. The use of folklore, oral tales, the embedded literature of the people through which they acted out their own lives – this was endlessly fascinating to me; I saw a parallel between this and the young Caribbean writers who were attempting to carve out a similar literary space – the young Naipaul, Walcott and Selvon, for example. At the time Walcott had published his small book, *Twenty Poems* which I found in the San Fernando library, and *In a Green Night*, as well. Quite a few people whom I knew and who were also trying to write knew whole stretches of these poems by heart. They were ours, talking about us, rendering our everyday landscape into a form both strange and familiar: 'the marl white road' for example. Or that early poem about "The Orange Tree." I wanted to be a part of this effort – I did then and do now have no ambitions but the literary. Why? I think the answer is pretty simple – I read early and experienced a larger world through books. Books had answers and they enabled understanding. I loved reading and then loved writing. Nothing more to be said.

E.S.: The structure of the text is most effective. The many stories you tell are carefully interwoven. You deliver history as a generation remembers it, for example, Enoch Powell and his violent response to immigration in the UK as that reverberated in Canada and also the Indian Presbyterian community in Trinidad. At every turn your story defeats easy cultural assumptions and the history is right there to underpin it. It is a historical novel, in a very real sense. The main story has many side alleys with stories which prove to be all part of Mona's history, and so the structure serves the idea that we are all walking compendiums of stories from the past. The opening passage anchors the novel in actual history. Whereas the *Kala Pani* is I think well known, I guess few readers would know that Brahmin widows were a disproportionate number among women who migrated from India to Trinidad. The three parts are each prefaced by a section on the *Kala Pani*, which you define in the novel as 'the black waters which lie between India and the Caribbean'. How did you arrive at the structure?

R.E.: The idea of the *Kala Pani* as a wrap for the story came close to the third draft, when the novel was practically finished. The *kala pani* piece was already written but where to put it was not clear. Originally I had a cinematic opening, Mona at the opening night of a film. Then the story was meant to go back and find Mona's history. But suddenly I began to see a different kind of historical piece. The novel at one time had four parts. I struggled with the shape. As you know, I have studied Jean Rhys very thoroughly. Rhys's technique was to cut and paste and stitch the pieces together in a physical way – like a jigsaw. I discovered that for me too, there was a huge physical component in pulling this work into the structure that I wanted. Not that I knew what that was either, but I thought if I put all the pieces on the floor and rolled around in them, something would come of it. The shape. It seemed like a physical process, not driven by any familiar internal logic.

E.S.: The reader keeps discovering more as the novel proceeds.

of explicit genealogical geometry. As if ties of kinship can be explained so easily...

E.S.: There are tantalising details of histories not usually well understood. The connections between Trinidad and Tobago and Venezuela, for example. Trinidadian workers in the Venezuelan oil fields. Marriages between Venezuelan women and Trinidadian men.

R.E.: Trinidad is such a crossroads of the Caribbean. At any given moment there are several cross-currents intersecting in that small island place – downwards from the north through the archipelago, southwards to Venezuela and beyond, outwards to North America and Europe, and then returning home to bring all of this to the Trini scene. An exciting place – full of failed effort, it is true, but also, so full of beauty and of possibility.

I did want the time lines in the novel to be perfect – I did not want to play around with them, nor with the geography, for that matter. In an early piece, I had Muddie and Dada holding hands at the edges of the cane fields - what date would that be, I asked myself? Over the years, I've realised that many Indo-Caribbean people still don't know major dates in their history. I'm not laying blame here – I myself had to dig out these historical facts well into my adulthood because it was simply not part of a West Indian education – not under a colonial nor a post-colonial administration.

E.S.: Which brings us back to the purpose of fiction, as you see it?

R.E.: The purpose – I'm wary of the notion of purposeful things, projects etc. In my daily work as an educator I am haunted by the spectre of pragmatism and its immense distance from actual learning. But I'll attempt to discuss this vexed question because why would I write if there were no purpose to my writing? I think my main interests are to enlarge the horizon of the reader, but also to delight, to entertain and to educate. I would be thrilled if my language moves the reader into becoming one with the rhythm of my text. Each text has its own particular rhythm. A disrhythmic text is infinitely more difficult to read than one that has discovered its internal harmonies. This is not the same thing as a writer finding her voice. You have to find the rhythm of the piece. If the rhythm is right, you forget everything else. It doesn't matter if it takes a lifetime if it is right in the end. That's my purpose, to make the rhythm right and to have the reader taken up into the rhythm.

E.S.: How long was your process for this novel?

R.E.: This is puzzling to answer. I worked two summers on it intensely reworking earlier pieces. At one point it was a collection of fragments, then it became clear it was a novel. But putting it together – finding its real shape – was like starting from scratch. It took two highly disciplined summers.

E.S.: Since this novel is so richly about diaspora, a term around which so much theory swirls these days, would you explain your sense of it?

R.E.: For me, diaspora is both local and global. The local becomes generalised into a practice belonging to a specific community but in the small geographical space of Trinidad, there is a permeability that is evident. The crossovers between Indian and African rhythms over time have produced chutney and soca, two forms of music where distinctiveness as well as syncretic elements are present. Then there is the custom of matikor, still secret, still practised only within the Hindu community, still restricted to women only. This ritual occurs on the night before a Hindu wedding when experienced village women instruct the bride-to-be in the sexual arts needed for her marriage. The practice involves lewd dancing, simulated sex, bawdy songs and jokes. Only women are allowed at this ritual. Then there is the form of Hindi spoken in Trinidad and Guyana – a somewhat archaic form of Bhojpuri, a rural dialect from Uttar Pradesh. This became the *lingua franca* among indentureds recruited from many different parts of India and speaking many different dialects and languages. The Indo-Caribbean diaspora has evolved in the Caribbean over a period of 166 years.

In North America, where there has been a 'second migration,' different Indo-Caribbean communities are evolving depending on whether they live in Queens, NY or Toronto, Ontario or other habitats. There are the ever-present choices of assimilation or accommodation and the complex negotiations necessary to survive. It's complex, interesting uncharted terrain and great for students in anthropology and social science disciplines. Great for literature too.

E.S.: Clearly you thought about these issues in creating *The Swinging Bridge* but were wise not to put too much anthropological material into it which would halt the story. Yet the process by which people hold onto or adapt their identity over time is clear.

R.E.: The issues around language and the utilisation of Bhojpuri as the common tongue is not part of the novel.

E.S.: The novel opens with Mona, in Canada, remembering words from her and her people's past, 'ashes, cocoyea brooms, sem, chataigne, roti, chunkaying, lepaying, washing wares...(and more)...' Did you think of putting a glossary at the end of the novel for readers not familiar with Trinidad and Tobago? The novel is presently being translated into French to be published in Paris by Editions du Rocher. Will there be a glossary in the French edition?

R.E.: I made a decision to exclude it but my publisher, Harper-Collins asked for a glossary which I did, and quite thoroughly too. They've since put it on their website. They've also included a family tree and a "Reading Guide." One of the reasons why these reading tools are useful is because the current book club popularity in North America means readers are spending more time on the act of reading, on critically assessing their 'reads' against peer assessments, and wanting to be informed about the text they have engaged with. This is absolutely different from a decade or two ago when reading was more escapist and close reading a practice engaged in largely by the intelligentsia. Popular wisdom credits Oprah with this sea-change and if she is, may Jah-Jah continue to make her strong. About the French translation – I'm not sure about a glossary yet. I'm still thinking about it.

E.S.: A number of your characters are composites of people you know, such as the experience of one of your siblings as an ER nurse which is a key aspect of Babs, Mona's sister in the novel.

R.E.: I modeled Babs on about three people in the family. The nursing role has a function in the plot in relation to the theme of AIDS but that came after my idea for the character who is a nurse/a healer. I didn't start with the plot in strict terms. It kind of evolved. For example, Bess, the outside child of Mona's beloved uncle, Sweetie-Boy, was there before her parents were. The issue of 'family land' was there, very much part of my imagery about Trinidad because of the numerous tales of owning and losing land in my own family history. Kello, Mona's brother, who is HIV-positive and who dies of 'lymphoma,' a euphemism used to conceal the fact that he is dying of AIDS, is entirely fictional. Where did his character come from? Many different emanations of maleness, I think, and I have to say that I fell in love with this character and had to make major efforts to distance myself from him.

E.S.: Clearly the theme of shame and denial over AIDS is a political one. Politics is a strong theme in the novel. Muddie, Mona's mother, is clearly political, which plays against the stereotype of Indian women being silent and quiescent about affairs outside the home. The role of Presbyterianism in Indian life in Trinidad is very key in the novel.

R.E.: This is very important in understanding the manner in which Indo-Caribbean society has been constructed. It is, however, a little understood part of the history. In 1981 I was back at the time of elections, when the ONR (a racially-mixed party) was canvassing in Woodford Square in Port of Spain. Candidates were being introduced and one after another, the Indian candidates turned out to have been educated at Naparima College, a prestigious high school and one of the large family of Canadian Presbyterian

An Interview with Ramabai Espinet 269

schools, where the vast majority of Indians were educated. I listened to this and realised the error of assuming that Indians were a homogenous group in terms of Trinidad politics. No attention was paid to issues of class and the history of Presbyterianism within that. This explains why so many Indians voted for the PNM, the African party, in the early days after the island became an independent state. The first Indian middle-class in Trinidad was Presbyterian and despised those they regarded as peasants. Of course later once oil wealth arrived in Trinidad in the late 1970s and 1980s, Presbyterians fell from prominence and a new merchant class of orthodox Hindus replaced them. There was a lot of interest in the early PNM among educated Indians who shared their agenda for independence and self-government.

I grew up in the south, in San Fernando, in the Presbyterian community, which I took entirely for granted. But in the east-west corridor, the seat of intellectual life in Trinidad, no one was aware of this other middle class – it was as if it were a big secret.

E.S.: Which brings me to ask, why didn't you name Eric Williams in the novel? The character "De Doctah", Dr Hector James, is clearly based on him.

R.E.: People have asked me that over and over. I did not want to paint a portrait of Eric Williams and be confined to the historical facts. I wanted to have a generic African leader, or African-identified, which is more to the point in Williams' case. The details of "De Doctah" mostly fit Williams but I took liberties and wanted to be free to do that.

E.S.: The same thing seems to be happening with La Rosette, the dancer and folklorist character in the novel?

R.E.: She is partly based on Beryl McBurnie who was known as La Belle Creole. Beryl influenced everybody. Her aesthetic sensibilities about dance, but also about art as a whole, were astonishing, prescient, and infused with a deep response to the undertow of Caribbeanness as it was/is being invented in Trinidad. I was enormously informed by her insights into everything. I did dance classes with her for a short period when I was a teenager. Later I got to know her well and I loved her. I listened to her incredible timing of the unique beat of Trinidad, its personal idiolect moving through all of its art, any of its art – Beryl understood this. She was moved to signify this intangible – or at least try to. Again, this was not a portrait of Beryl. In the novel, La Rosette sees, hears and feels the beat of the Indo-Caribbean experience and tries to represent it in a marvellously inventive dance but she fails. With all of her supreme gifts, her openness to all experience, all movement, she fails. Why does she fail?

E.S.: It is one of the details which conveys the ways in which even well meaning and educated people can miss the subtleties of a culture which at that time had not yet begun to fully explore itself. Your novel has much to say about gender, working against stereotypes of Indo-Caribbean culture. Scholars are just beginning to explore this in depth. Curdella Forbes (2005) remarks that the Indian community in the Caribbean brought its own 'liminal gender codification' in both Hindu and Moslem culture.

R.E.: In terms of gender and sexuality, I am interested in the role of the hijira or transvestite in indenture. It is believed that some prostitutes and hijiras became indentures in the hope of starting a new life. Certainly this seems to have been the case with widows. There is a strong element of transgendered culture in the Caribbean - men partying and performing dances which simulate sex with each other, wearing skirts, using fruit or objects to create makeshift breasts. This is done in less ritualised settings than the women's matikor dances and the spontaneity of this kind of transgendered performance activity is notable. I suppose this is fertile ground for the kind of analysis that queer theory offers. Sean Meighoo's article in *Small Axe* suggests a reading of this activity as homosocial.

E.S.: Have you had any response to the portrayal of an AIDS victim, namely Kello, and since he is gay, has this drawn comment given the homophobia of much of Caribbean culture?

R.E.: I haven't had any comment from the Caribbean. But it has come to my attention that it is regarded as an AIDS text in certain quarters in Canada. Also, I believe it is being used in a university course description on religious attitudes to death. But I haven't had any feedback on these uses, really.

E.S.: The 'bamboo marriage' of Mona's grandfather is a moving story. This is also clearly based on your understanding of the role of traditions in Trinidad. Curdella Forbes recently argues that Indian women entered Western style marriages in the Caribbean because these would not count back in India, and they were hoping to return.

R.E.: I don't know if that was true in Jamaica, but my understanding is that it was the other way around. Traditional or 'bamboo' marriages had no real status in Trinidad because they were not legal and so property could not be inherited through them. Therefore men often entered into these marriages and simply left them if they wanted to for whatever reason. Often the reason was a more socially advantageous or more lucrative union. Women were no doubt able to do the same thing, but most of the oral accounts I know have to do with male abandonment. In Trinidad, the period when indentured people thought they would return home was very brief. Indentures arrived in Trinidad in 1845. By 1868 the conversion to Christianity and its promise of education and permanence had already begun.

E.S.: Race is subtly present in the novel, partly through Mona's relationship with Roddy, who is Scottish Canadian, and partly through her youthful love for Bree, himself of mixed race. What is your vision of race in the period in which the novel is set?

R.E.: In the late 1950s (1958-62) Federation crashed and the thinkers and idealists and dreamers in the Caribbean (Sam Selvon among them) wept that we could not make something new out of the inherited falsehoods and hypocrisies of race and class. In that period, there was a real articulation of the possibility of creating a world that was free and just and raceless. There were debates at my school about this new world. We thought that our parents' attitudes to race was more essentialist and backward. The word dougla was used to describe the offspring of an African/Indian union; it is an old term one of whose meanings in Hindi is 'bastard.' It is still the only descriptor used for a person of such racial admixture. The literary critic, Shalini Puri, who shared her research into the etymology of the word from Persian into Hindu culture, notes that all of its several meanings are involved with notions of contamination - spotted, mongrel, etc. The African community was more accepting of the dougla but, tellingly, the only word used to describe such a racially mixed person was the Hindi word dougla, possibly meaning bastard. Eventually, the pejorative aspect of the word became more neutral, although, even in such a small territory, there are marked inconsistencies in usage.

I was concerned to show in Bree's and Mona's relationship that they are both afflicted with pretending that race does not exist. Her awareness that they never discussed it then comes much later after she moves to Canada. When he says he is black she is shocked because in their youth they did not identify themselves as racially different.

I was involved as a young woman with a group of people of all races, all trying to write. We talked a lot. We wanted to know how we could create a literature which was not simply about defining racial difference.

E.S.: There has been a documentary film made about you called "Going Home", (directed by Frances Ann Solomon), which has been very successful in Canada. Is this about San Fernando and this dream of racial unity your generation had?

R.E.: The film complicates the issue of race in many arresting episodes. One of these shows me buying fish from a group of African fishermen on the San Fernando wharf against the backdrop of the words of the passage in the novel about San Fernando: 'African and Indian, each lacerating the other with blows, each tolerating the other's crossovers, the strayaways...' My San Fernando friends call this section: "Ode to San Fernando".

E.S.: Is Gainder, Mona's Indian ancestor who makes the journey across the *Kala Pani*, based on your own sense of a particular ancestor from India?

R.E.: No, Gainder is entirely fictional. There is a kind of genealogical research which is becoming very popular in the Indo-Caribbean community right now. I find this research is highly suspect. Consulting the rolls of indenture and finding a name there and then tracing it back to claim a direct ancestor and place of origin is so fraught with error that I have been wondering about its appeal. But I met a man recently, a highly educated and skeptical lawyer, who said simply and directly that he didn't care about the veracity of the claim or not. I only want to belong somewhere, to have roots, he said. India is too big, too meaningless, he explained. A piece of paper giving him a name, a date, a place, is preferable to saying that he does not know who his ancestors are. I know I'm here because they came as indentured labourers, he said. So why not have something like proof?

I've thought about this often. Why not? My problem with this pop genealogical approach is that it ignores the fact that the Indian kinship system, using the father's first name as the son's surname, was the practice in Trinidad well into the early years of the twentieth century. So names are almost meaningless in this genealogical quest.

E.S.: Gainder's songs are important in the novel. Music is one of your key linking devices, isn't it?

R.E.: There is a great deal of music in *The Swinging Bridge*. I listened to a lot of music growing up. Caribbean music but lots of other kinds too... Music which marked times and moods, like "Moon River." Then too it was the era of Pat Boone and Elvis Presley. In the novel, Muddie and Da-Da respond to each other through a variety of Hollywood scenarios. The society that I grew up in was not insular though it was so small. It was very rich in its associations. Gainder's songs I made up completely. I did do some research, though, on the hypnotic nagara beats which were commonly used on the ships of indenture.

E.S.: This is a very filmic novel for me, for it moves through vivid scenes, connected by the characters, and has very effective visual details. Clearly the film that Mona is working on as the novel opens is an important motif. Did you think of the novel in visual terms, in each of its locations, by which I mean did you think of the story as being partly told by what you make us see, such as the shop books, or Mona's family house and garden in Trinidad, or Indian women with trays of food to sell at a railway junction in Trinidad?

R.E.: Visual details are very important to me. I saw the scenes as I was writing them. Then there are those aspects of a scene that also work on several levels – metaphor, symbol, signifier, mnemonic device.

E.S.: What is your conception of 'home'? As a migrant myself, I know it is complicated for me. You've defined it as infinitely complicated in the text. The novel ends with Gainder thinking of her lost love, but also Mona recognising that her first sense of home, as a child, understood the Caroni Dub- the process by which home is built out of disparate and colliding identities which come together...

R.E.: Disparate and colliding identities are intrinsic to any home I have ever known. One cannot afford to be complacent. But there is too a very real sense of belonging and wherever I am, I recognise that belongingness instantly. Place does not matter to me because I know that things change constantly. For me, 'home' is a moveable shack on a beach, a moveable feast.

APPENDICES*

Appendix I

Indenture or Slavery?[1]

M. K. GANDHI

Girmit[2] is a corrupt form of the English word agreement. The term cannot be dispensed with. What it suggests, 'agreement' does not. There is no alternative word in the language. The document under which thousands of labourers used to emigrate and still emigrate to Natal and other countries on contract for five years is known by the labourers and the employers as *girmit*. A labourer so emigrating under *girmit* is a *girmitio*.[3] About 12,000 such indentured labourers emigrate annually from India, mostly to the Fiji Islands near Australia, Jamaica near South America, British Guiana, Dutch Guiana and Trinidad.

The late Mr Gokhale, a brave soul, held indenture to be a state bordering on slavery; it was described in the same terms by the famous historian, the late Sir William Wilson Hunter; the same analogy was used by Mr Harry Escombe, a well-known former Minister of Natal.

---

* From *Collected Works of Mahatma Gandhi*. Vol. XIII. New Delhi : Publication Division Ministry of Information and Broadcasting, 1964.

Indenture is indeed a state of semi-slavery. Like the slave before him, the indentured labourer cannot buy his freedom. A slave was punished for not working; so also is an indentured labourer. If he is negligent, does not attend work for a day, if he answers back, - he will suffer imprisonment for any one of these lapses. A slave could be sold and handed over by one owner to another, so too the indentured labourer can be transferred from one employer to another. The children of a slave inherited the taint of slavery; much in the same way, the children of an indentured labourer are subject to laws specially passed for them. The only difference between the two states is that while slavery ended only with life, an indentured labourer can be free after a certain number of years. It should be noted, moreover, that indenture came after the abolition of slavery and that indentured labourers were recruited to take the place of slaves.

The following facts concerning indentured labourers have been established. In the countries to which they emigrate, they receive no moral or religious education. Most of them are unmarried. On every ship carrying indentured labourers, there is provision for taking women to the extent of 40 per cent. Some of these are women of ill fame. They do not, as a rule, enter into a marriage alliance. In this state of affairs, even if 20 per cent of the men wish to marry, they cannot. Going to lands so far away, they get into the habit of drinking. Women, who in India would never touch wine, are sometimes found lying dead-drunk on the roads.

After all this degradation, the profit which they point to is that the economic condition of these people improves. Everyone will admit that even though we may stand to gain economically by selling our souls, we ought not to do so.

How is it that this thing has been allowed to go on for fifty years now? None of us will be prepared to submit himself to a condition such as this. How then did we tolerate it for our own brethren? In raising this question, I have not the least desire to make people feel sorry for the past, but the question helps us to realise our duty in the present. The late Mr Gokhale introduced, in March 1912, a resolution in the Imperial Legislative Council, asking for the repeal of the law governing indenture and demanding that the emigration of indentured labourers from India be stopped. At that time, 22 members took a pledge that 'they would bring forward the resolution every year till indenture was abolished'. It is for us, the survivors, to fulfil that pledge. Mr Andrews and Mr Pearson have gone to Fiji for this very purpose. It is not too much to say, therefore, that every educated Indian is in duty bound to apply his mind to this question and join in discussing it so as to help in getting it finally settled.

This is not the place to go into details; for those, however, who wish to study the subject, there is literature in plenty and easily accessible: in particular, the debates in the Imperial Legislative Council on the resolution mentioned above, the Lord Sanderson Committee Report and the report of Messrs MacNeill and Chimanlal on the condition of indentured labourers. If any paper gets a special note prepared on this literature, it is bound to prove useful.

(From Gujarati)
Satyagrapha Ashram, Ahmedabad.
Samalochak, December 1915

Endnotes

[1] This appeared as an article in *Samalochak*
[2] Indenture
[3] Indentured labourer

Appendix II

Indentured Labour
M. K. GANDHI

The question of indentured labour is a seasonable subject for more reasons than one. Messrs Andrews and Pearson have just returned from Fiji after finishing their self-imposed labours for the sake of India which they have learnt to love as they love their motherland. Their report is about to be issued. There Mr Malaviya has given notice for leave to move a resolution[1] in the Imperial Council which will, if adopted, commit the Government to a repeal of the system of indentured labour. Mr Malaviya's resolution will be, it may be recalled, a continuation of the late Mr Gokhale's work in 1912, when in a speech full of favour and weighted with facts and figures, he moved his resolution demanding repeal of this form of labour. The deceased statesman's resolution was thrown out only by the force of official majority. The moral victory lay with Mr Gokhale. The death-knell of the system was rung when that resolution was moved. The Government, as in could not then abolish the system, outvoted Mr Gokhale but did not fail to note that they must hurry forward to do so at an early date. Mr Malaviya's proposed resolution and the report of Messrs Andrews and Pearson, which latter, it is known, is to suggest total abolition of the system, will enable Lord Hardinge fittingly to close his most eventful viceroyalty removing this long-standing and acknowledged grievance.

These lines will be merely an attempt to give personal observations and to indulge in a few reflections upon the question. For facts and figures, the readers and the public workers must look up Mr Gokhale's speech referred to above and Messrs Andrews and Pearson's forthcoming report.

Indentured labour is admittedly a remnant of slavery. The late Sir William Wilson Hunter, when his attention was drawn to it in 1895, was the first to call it a state 'perilously' near to slavery. Most legislation only partly reflects the public opinion of its time, Legislation abolishing slavery was really a bit in advance of public opinion, and that was a big bit. And its effect, like that of all and legislation, was largely neutralised by the dissatisfied slave-owner resorting to the dodge of indentured labour. The yoke, if it fell from the Negro's black neck, was transferred to the brown neck of the Indian. In the process of transfer, it had to be somewhere polished, it had to be lightened in weight and even disguised. Nevertheless, in all its essentials, it retained its original quality. The hideousness of the system was forcefully demonstrated when the cure descended upon South Africa in the shape of indentured labourers from China for working the gold mines. It was no mere election cry that the late Sir Henry Campbell-Bannerman[2] had taken up when he made the British Isles from end to end ring with denunciation of the system. No cost was counted as too great for ridding South Africa of the evil. The great multi-millionaires of Johannesburg spread nothing to be enabled to hold on to the indentured Chinaman. They asked for breathing time. The House of Commons remained unmoved. Mine-owners had to shift for themselves. The interests of humanity overrode all other consideration. The mines were threatened to be closed. The House did not care. The millions promised to Mr Chamberlain[3] would not be forthcoming. The House laughed. Within six months of the passage of the measure for the abolition of Chinese indentured labour, every Chinese labourer had been repatriated bag and baggage. The mines survived the shock. They discovered other methods of life. And now be it said to the credit of the mine-owners as well as of the conservatives who opposed the measure, that both these classes imagine the abolition was a great deliverance.

Indian indentured labour is not less demoralising. It has persisted because its bitterness like that of a sugared pill has been clearly though unconsciously concealed. The one great distinction between the two classes was that the Chinese were brought in without a single woman with them, whereas every hundred Indian labourers must include forty women among them. Had the Chinese remained, they would have sapped the very foundations of society. The Indian labourers confine the evil to themselves. This may be important to non-Indians. But for us, the wonder is that we have allowed the sin to continue so long. This business about the women is the weakest and the irremediable part of the evil. It therefore needs a somewhat closer inspection. These women are not necessarily wives. Men and women are huddled together during the voyage. The marriage is a farce. A mere declaration by man and woman made upon landing before the Protector of Immigrants that they are husband and wife constitutes a valid marriage. Naturally enough, divorce is common. The rest must be left to the imagination of the reader. This is certain – that the system does not will to the moral well-being of India. And it is suggested that no amount of figures adduced to show that the labourer is far richer at the end of his contract of labour than when he entered upon it can be allowed to be any set off against the moral degradation it involves.

There is another most powerful consideration to be urged against the continuance of this system. The relations between Englishmen and Indians in India are not of the happiest. The average Englishman considers himself to be superior to the average Indian and the latter is generally content to be so considered. Such a state of things is demoralising to both and a menace to the stability of the British Empire. There is no reason why every Englishman should not learn to consider every Indian as his brother, and why every Indian should not cease to think that he is born to fear every Englishman. Be that as it may, this unnatural relationship is reflected in an exaggerated form outside India when the artificial state of indentured service under the white employer is set up. Unless, therefore, the relation between the English and ourselves is put on a correct footing in India, any transference of Indian labourers to far-off lands, whether parts of the Empire or otherwise, even under a free contract must harm both employer and employed. I happen to have the privilege of knowing most humane employers of Indian labourers in Natal. They were their men. But they do not, they cannot, give them more than the most favoured treatment that their cattle receive. I use this language in no uncharitable spirit. The humanest of employers cannot escape the limitations of his class. He instinctively feels that the Indian labourer is inferior to him and can never be equal to him. Surely no indentured Indian, no matter how clever and faithful he may be, has ever inherited his master's state. But I know English servants who have risen to their master's state even as Indian servants have risen to their Indian master's state. It is not the Englishman's fault that the relationship with his Indian employees has not been progressive. It is beyond the scope of these lines to distribute the blame, if there is any, on either side, or to examine the causes for the existence of such a state of things. I have been obliged to advert to it to show that apart from all other considerations, the system of indentured labour is demonstrably so degrading to us as a nation that it must be stopped at any cost and that now.

The Leader, 25-2-1916

Endnotes

[1] In March, 1916, Madan Mohan Malaviya moved a resolution in the imperial Legislative Council for the abolition of the indenture system.

[2] Prime Minister of England, 1905-8.

[3] Joseph Chamberlain (1836-1914), British statesman; Secretary of State in the Colonies, 1895.

Appendix III

Indian Colonial Emigration

M. K. GANDHI

I have carefully read the resolution issued at Simla by the government of India on the 1st instant, embodying the report of the Inter-Departmental Conference recently held in London.[1] It will be remembered that this was the Conference referred to in the Viceregal speech of last year at the opening of the session of the Viceregal Legislative Council. It will be remembered, too, that this was the conference which Sir James Meston and Sir S. P. Sinha were to have attended but were unable to attend owing to their having returned to India before the date of the meeting of the conference.[2] It is stated in the report under discussion that these gentlemen were to discuss the question of emigration to certain English colonies informally with the two Secretaries of State, i.e., the Secretary of State for India and the Secretary of State for the Colonies. Lord Islington[3], Sir A. Steel Maitland[4] and Messrs Seton[5], Crindle[6], Green[7] and Macnaughton[8] constituted the Conference. To take the wording of the Resolution, this Conference sat 'to consider the proposals for a new assisted system of Emigration to British Guiana, Trinidad, Jamaica and Fiji'. The public should therefore note that this assisted emigration is to the self-governing Colonies of South Africa,

Canada or Australia, or the Crown Colony of Mauritius.[9] What follows will show the importance of this distinction. It is something to be thankful for, that 'the Government of India have not yet considered the report and reserved judgment on all the points raised in'. This is as it should be on a matter so serious as this and one which only last year fairly convulsed the whole of India and which has in one shape or another agitated the country since 1895.

The declaration too that 'His Majesty's Government in agreement with the Government of India have decided that indentured emigration shall not be reopened' is welcome as is also the one that 'no free emigrants[10] can be introduced into any colony until all Indian emigrants already there have been released from existing indentures'.

In spite, however, of so much in the report that fills one with gladness, the substantive part of it which sets forth the scheme which is to replace indentured emigration is so far as one can judge, to say the least of it, disappointing. Stripped of all the phraseology under which the scheme has been veiled, it is nothing less than a system of indentured emigration no doubt on a more humane basis and safeguarded with some conditions beneficial to the emigrants taking advantage of it.

The main point that should be borne in mind is that the conference sat designedly to consider a scheme of emigration not in interests of the Indian labourer but in those of the Colonial employer. The new system therefore is devised to help the colonies concerned. India needs no outlet at any rate for the present moment for emigration outside the country. It is debatable whether in any event the four colonies will be the most suitable for Indian standpoint is that there should be no assisted emigration from India of any type whatsoever. In the absence of any such assistance, emigration will have to be entirely free and at the risk and expense of the emigrant himself. Past experience shows that, in that event, there will be very little voluntary emigration to distant colonies. In the report, assisted emigration means, to use a mild expression, stimulated emigration; and surely with the industries of India crying out for labour and with her legitimate resources yet undeveloped, it is madness to think of providing a stimulus for the stay-at-home Indian to go out of India. Neither the Government nor any voluntary agency has been found capable of protecting from ill-usage the Indian who emigrates either to Burma or Ceylon, much less can any such protection avail in far-off Fiji or the three other colonies.

I hope that leaders of public opinion in India will therefore take their stand on the one impregnable rock of not wanting any emigration whatsoever to the colonies. It might be argued that we, as a component part of the Empire, are bound to consider the wants of our partners, but this would not be a fair plea to advance so long as India stands in need of all the labour she can produce. If, therefore, India does not assist the colonies, it is not because of want of will, but it is due to want of ability. An additional reason a politician would be justified in using is that, so long as India does not in reality occupy the position of an equal partner with the colonies and so long as her sons continue to be regarded by Englishmen in the colonies and English employers even nearer home to be fit only as hewers of wood and drawers of water, no scheme of emigration to the colonies can be morally advantageous to Indian emigrants. If the badge of inferiority is always to be worn by them, they can never rise to their full status and any material advantage they will gain by emigrating can therefore be of no consideration.

But let us for the moment consider the new system.

> The system to be followed in future will be one of aided emigration and its object will be to encourage the settlement of Indians in certain colonies after a probationary period of employment in those colonies to train and fit them for life and work there and at the same time to acquire a supply of the labour essential to the well-being of the colonists themselves.

So the resettlement is to be conditional on previous employment under contract and it will be seen in the course of our examination that this contract is to be just as binding as the contracts used to be under indenture. The report has the following humorous passage in it:

> He will be in no way restricted to service under any particular employer except that for his own protection a selected employer will be chosen for him for the first six months.

This has a flavour of the old indentured system. One of the evils complained of about that system was that the labourer was assigned to an employer. He was not free to choose one himself. Under the new system, the employer is to be selected for the protection of the labourer. It is hardly necessary for me to point out that the would-be labourer will never be able to feel the protection devised for him.

> The labourer is further to be encouraged to work for his first three years in agricultural industries by the offer, should he do so, of numerous and important benefits subsequently as a colonist.

This is another inducement to indenture and I know enough of such schemes to be able to assure both the Government and the public that these so-called inducements in the hands of clever manipulators become nothing short of methods of compulsion in respect of innocent and ignorant Indian labourers. It is due to the framers of the scheme that I should draw attention to the fact that they have avoided all criminal penalties for breach of contract. In India itself if the scheme is adopted, we are promised a revival of the much-dreaded depots and emigration agents, all no doubt on a more respectable basis, but still of the same type and capable of untold mischief.

The rest of the report is not likely to interest the public, but those who wish to study it will, I doubt not, come to the conclusion to which I have been driven, that the framers have done their best to strip the old system of many of the abuses which had crept into it, but they have not succeeded in placing before the Indian public an acceptable scheme. I hold that it was an impossible task. The system of indenture was one of temporary slavery; it was incapable of being amended, it should only be ended and it is to be hoped that India will never consent to its revival in any shape or form.

The Indian Review, September 1917

Endnotes

[1] In May 1917 to discuss a new system of emigration

[2] Sir James Meston and S.P. Sinha represented India at the Imperial War Conference held in April, 1917. They were also nominated by the Government of India as its representatives to the Inter-Departmental Conference, but both of them had to return to India before the Conference could meet formally.

[3] Chairman

[4, 5, 6, 7 & 8] Members of the respective Secretaries of State's establishment

[9] *Vide* also "Statement on Abolition of Indentured Labour", after 7-2-1917

[10] "Emigration" in the report published in *The Indian Review*, September 1917.

Notes on Contributors

Asma Shamail worked on Caribbean-American Women writers for her doctoral work. Her teaching interests include American, African-American and Women's Writing. She is located in Vishakhapatnam, Andhra Pradesh.

C. Vijayshree is Professor of English at Osmania University, Hyderabad. Her many publications include *Mulk Raj Anand* (1998), *Suniti Namjoshi* (2001), an anthology of critical essays titled *Writing the West* (2004), translated short stories and poems from Telugu *Kanysulkans* (2002, co-translated with T. Vijay Kumar) and *Gold Nuggets* (2004, co-edited with Bh. Krishnamurti.)

Charu Mathur teaches English in the University of Rajasthan, Jaipur. She has worked for her doctoral dissertation on "Perspectives on Women in the Selected Plays of Eugene O'Neill and Tennessee Williams". Her areas of interest are American and Indian drama, Postcolonial literature and Women's Writing.

Cyril Dabydeen is of Guyanese birth and migrated to Canada in 1970. He has several volumes of poetry and fiction to his credit. Frank Birbalsingh refers to him as the most prolific Caribbean writer in Canada today. *Jogging in Havana, A Shapely Fire, Coastland* are only some of his works. His latest novel *Drums of My Flesh* (2006) has been nominated for the International Dublin Literary Award.

David Dabydeen, a poet and a novelist, is Professor at the University of Warwick. His two early books *Hogarth's Blacks* (1985) and *Hogarth, Walpole and Commercial Britain* traced the history of racist ideas. His first collection of poems *Slave Song* (1984) won him the Commonwealth Prize. Other volumes of poetry and works of fiction have followed these successes.

Elaine Savory, a poet and writer, is Associate Professor and Chair of Literature at New School University. She co-edited the first feminist collection of criticism on Caribbean Literatures and has published expensively in this area, especially on poetry, drama and women's writing. She is presently editing the MLA Teaching Approaches to the Work of Kamau Brathwaite and writing the Cambridge Introduction to Jean Rhys.

Indira Babbellapati is Associate Professor in English, Andhra University College of Engineering, Vishakhapatnam. She has published on African, Indian postcolonial writers and diasporic writers. She has also translated and published translation on Telugu poetry and short stories.

Jasbir Jain is an independent scholar, currently engaged in research on Feminist Thought in India. Jain has published extensively. Her most recent publications include *Beyond Postcolonialism : Dreams and Realities of a Nation (2006)* and *Gendered Realities, Human Spaces* (2004).

288 Notes on Contributors

Jayita Sengupta teaches English in South Calcutta Girls College, Calcutta University. A British Council Fellow (2000) she has a wide range of interests, which include feminist and postcolonial studies and has published extensively in these areas. She also translates from Bengali into English and vice versa.

M. Rosary Royar teaches English at Fatima College, Madurai and has worked on Caribbean writers. She has participated in several conferences and is a serious scholar of West Indian writing.

Madhuri Chatterjee teaches English at Subodh PG College, Jaipur. She worked on John Updike for her doctoral work. Since then she has extended her work to women writers, more specifically their autobiographies. Her current research work is on travelogues.

Manveen Brar is in the Rajasthan Education Service, currently working for her doctoral degree on women short story writers across cultures.

Mini Nanda is Associate Professor at the University of Rajasthan. Her doctoral work was on Graham Greene. Since then she has diversified her interests and is now working on Muslim Women Writers in the Mid-Twentieth Century Novel.

Nidhi Singh is on the faculty of English, University of Rajasthan, Jaipur. She has worked on her doctoral dissertation on "The Mythic Reconstitution of Character and Place in the Novels of Rudolph Stow". Her areas of interest are Australian and Postcolonial Literatures and Indian Writing.

Punam Gupta worked for her doctoral thesis on Afro-American women writers and is engaged in post-doctoral research in the same area. She teaches in Dev Samaj College for Women, Chandigarh.

Purabi Panwar teaches English in Delhi. Her work *India in the Writing of Kipling, Forster and Naipaul* has been well received. Dr. Panwar has published extensively and is a well-known Naipaul scholar. She is also a translator and is deeply interested in Indian writing across languages.

Sudha Rai, Professor of English in the University of Rajasthan, worked for her doctoral work on *The Expatriate Sensibility*. She has a published a monograph on Naipaul and has written extensively on postcolonial writers including women poets. Co-editor of *Films and Feminism* with Jasbir Jain, Rai is currently working on Chitra Divakaruni.

Supriya Agarwal worked for her thesis on nineteenth century British fiction but has extended her interest to American and Canadian writers. Co-editor of *Gender and Narrative*, she is currently working on the concept of Canadianness.

Vishnupriya Sengupta worked on V.S. Naipaul for her doctoral thesis from Jadavpur University and is Guest Editor of a special number of the *Journal of Caribbean Literatures* (University of Arkansas US). By profession a journalist, she works for *The Telegraph* in Kolkata.